PIVOTAL DECISIONS
SELECTED CASES IN
TWENTIETH CENTURY
INTERNATIONAL POLITICS

CAROLYN RHODES
Utah State University

THOMSON
━━━✶━━━
WADSWORTH

Australia • Canada • Mexico • Singapore • Spain • United Kingdom • United States

Publisher	Earl McPeek
Executive Editor	David Tatom
Market Strategist	Steve Drummond
Project Editor	Katherine Dennis
Art Director	Vicki Whistler
Production Manager	Diane Gray

ISBN: 0-15-503517-7
Library of Congress Catalog Card Number: 99-60753

Wadsworth/Thomson Learning
10 Davis Drive
Belmont CA 94002-3098
USA

For information about our products, contact us:
Thomson Learning Academic Resource Center
1-800-423-0563
http://www.wadsworth.com

For permission to use material from this text, contact us by
Web: http://www.thomsonrights.com
Fax: 1-800-730-2215
Phone: 1-800-730-2214

Printed in the United States of America
10 9 8 7 6 5 4 3

For Brett and Matthew

PREFACE

....

RATIONALE FOR THIS CASE STUDY READER

Professors who are contemplating the use of this case study reader as a supplementary text have probably already considered the value of case study approaches for teaching and generating classroom discussion about international politics. Having the ability through a brief and accessible narrative to place one's students—even for only a class period—in a particular situation in the arena of international politics can be a very effective teaching method. However, for those of us who utilize and believe in the effectiveness of case method teaching, the most frustrating aspect of course preparation has been the spotty availability of appropriate cases, especially at the introductory level.

In an effort to address this gap in published case studies for introductory international politics courses, this volume focuses on some of the most important and interesting decisions made in this century. This set of case studies includes a chronological range of "pivotal decisions"—decisions which have directly affected the course of international politics at the global level and which have come to be regarded as crucial to our collective historical understanding of international relations since World War I.

The collection consists of ten explanatory narratives about particular influential responses to key events, or dramatic new initiatives, which have shaped the evolution of recent global history. Starting with the aftermath of World War I—and the diplomatic conundrum regarding relations with Germany prior to 1939—and ending with the disintegration of Yugoslavia in 1991, these cases represent the good and bad of international diplomacy, the temptations of power and the temperance of humanitarianism, self-interest versus common interests, and the evolutionary role of the state in international political and economic competition, conflict, and cooperation.

I have chosen the end of World War I as my starting point because in so many ways the international political, military, and economic world our students encounter today emerged with the end of the Great War. It was also during the inter war years that statesmen and analysts alike became more self conscious about the potential for international cooperation (for purposes other than survival and conquest) in the face of ongoing international suspicion and conflict. Forces of democracy and of international interdependence contributed to new ways of looking at relations between states and between states and their people. Even though those forces remained (and continue to remain) unable to overcome all sources of international conflict, they have often affected how nations interact with each other, restraining or propelling action.

While attitudes and sources of influence have evolved during the past eighty years, the era since World War I has been characterized by nations choosing between national preoccupation and international influence, between differing views about self-preservation and self-interest in the global arena, and between apathy and confrontation (whether that has meant confronting one's responsibility in the global community or confronting an enemy in a showdown over perceived unacceptable differences). Moreover, many of the international structures, attitudes, and debates which emerged during this period have continued to characterize the global environment up to the present day. Of course, historians will remind us that the Concert of Europe or the German Zollverein, for example, reflected aspects of this consciousness about the ability of statesmen to alter international relationships and to make cooperative as well as adversarial arrangements. Yet, in so many respects, World War I marked a turning point between nineteenth- and twentieth-century-style political structures and politics, and although the line cannot be so neatly drawn as my categorization might imply, my goal of achieving coherency and relevancy for contemporary students influenced me to begin the collection after 1918.

All of the decisions which have been chosen for inclusion in this volume have left indelible marks on the pages of history, and it is my hope that even if students read only this one set of historical cases they will be better educated about international politics in this century. Professors will be able to utilize the case reader to supplement students' knowledge of the world around them as well as their analytical understanding of how and why decisions are made. This volume is based upon the premise that an educated citizenry should have a rudimentary understanding of the circumstances that produced these decisions and of the consequences that emerged from them. Thus, as focal points for classroom discussion, teachers of international politics can utilize these cases to help achieve better historical understanding, as well as to generate better analytical comprehension of the fundamental principles of international relations theory and practice.

Consequently, students in introductory international relations courses should, by reading and discussing the cases which follow, gain a basic historical appreciation for pivotal decisions that have affected—and are continuing to affect—international relationships, along with a deeper understanding of our ways of thinking about them. While twenty-page explanations are clearly inadequate to fully represent the complexities of the individual decisions included, I have made a concerted effort to "get to the heart of the matter" under discussion and to present to the reader the essential features of the historical case. Of course any interpretation of these pivotal decisions will have competing views, and instructors should help their students understand that whenever an author attempts to generalize she or he risks oversimplification and the omission of important information. I do try to provide readable narratives that include a number of pertinent causal factors, rather than attempt to offer one theoretical explanation for each decision. However, I fully recognize that I still interpret these historical events in my own way and that other authors might well take very different approaches. It is my hope that instructors will utilize these cases to generate useful discussions about the different ways one might explain these events, and I encourage them to pursue issues beyond the narrow interpretation at hand.

Also, I realize that any effort to encapsulate the essence of twentieth century international politics in a handful of representative cases faces the reality that not everyone will agree with my particular choices. Depending upon the author's purpose in choosing one case over another, a very different set of examples could legitimately represent international political decisions in this century. Therefore, I do not pretend that this case reader is in any way exhaustive, and I am well aware of the wealth of cases not chosen for inclusion in this volume. However, I think this set of cases does offer professors of international politics a unique and very useful resource for teaching about key world events that have shaped international politics over the past seventy-five years.

....

CHOICE OF CASES FOR THIS VOLUME

The choice of cases for this volume is based on criteria which consider the value of the case for purposes of historical knowledge, as well as its value for illustrating key concepts in international relations analysis. There is a definite bias in favor of cases involving "big power politics," or of cases which represent, or have had a significant impact on, the structure of power and economic relationships in the global arena. Consequently, instructors of a course which examines such global issues as the environment, migration, economic underdevelopment, and women's rights, etc., will not find this collection particularly useful. *Rather, it is designed to complement more orthodox courses which focus on issues of power and influence and conflict and cooperation in both political-military and political-economic circumstances.* Because it has also been designed to inform students about the reality of the world they have inherited, this collection contains cases that either have had a significant impact on their world or represent compelling illustrations of the origins and function of far-reaching international arrangements and of the limitations of others.

In selecting these cases I have been guided by five interrelated questions: 1) How have nations responded to the political and economic challenges which confront them? 2) Why are certain initiatives taken or certain responses generated? 3) How do statesmen react to the world around them? 4) What forces prompt them to assume internationalist roles versus nationalist roles? 5) What prompts military reactions versus other kinds of responses? and 6) How do international structures, as well as domestic forces, influence decisions? In general, then, the cases examine international actors involved in pivotal decisions regarding their roles in the world of international politics. The case studies assume that leaders make conscious choices which have profound effects, and these decision points provide rich cases for analysis and discussion.

I selected decisions that I believe have been crucial to shaping the character of international politics since World War I or which illustrate especially well fundamental concepts in the analysis of international politics. For example, the United States' decision to reconstruct West Germany after World War II had a profound effect on European and global history. It contributed to forty-five years of Cold War with the Soviet Union. It was crucial to the emergence of an integrated Western Europe, and it made possible the revival of an economic powerhouse with substantial influence in global financial and commercial affairs. This one decision affected so much of the history that followed that it is difficult to explain the Cold War division of Europe, the creation of a European Union, the precarious position of West Berlin for over four decades, or the eventual end of the Cold War without understanding it. Whenever practical I have also consciously selected cases that are interrelated, so that, for example, the reunification of Germany is purposely included in order to help complete the story about the Cold War that was begun in 1945.

On the other hand, we don't know yet the far reaching implications of the decision not to intervene to prevent the devastating Yugoslavian war which began in 1991. However, this recent case represents an example of the inability of the international community, despite being freed from Cold War preoccupations, to take decisive action to prevent horrendous human tragedy. In fact, it is in bitter irony that this collection of essays begins with the World War I settlement and ends with an examination of the breakup of the Balkan country that was created in that peace settlement seventy years earlier. The questions that arise from this case are key to a deeper consideration of the current state of U.S. leadership, European statesmanship and the European Union's avowed commitment to a common foreign policy, the role of the United Nations, and underlying humanitarian versus national interest concerns.

Both cases illustrate well how national self-interests can alter the course of international politics and also how different institutional arrangements can affect political outcomes. Each case also offers the student a glimpse at the structures of international politics at a given point in time and an introduction to the forces that influence countries to become involved in the affairs of others and the forces that tend to dissuade countries from direct intervention. These two examples illustrate the juxtaposition of historical and analytical rationales for guiding case selection for this book. Cases in part one represent major decisions that have shaped the global security and political economic environment within which nations have interacted since World War I, including post-World War II efforts to shape economic relations to encourage growth and cooperation as well as conflict and competition in the Cold War. Part two includes cases which illustrate new directions in international politics—initiatives not predicted by the post-World War II structures, and whose impact is contemporary. The four cases included historic decisions in the economic realm as well as in political-military affairs, and help to focus attention on recent important developments in international relations.

THEORY AND CASE UTILIZATION

Finally, it is important to note that the cases selected for examination allow teachers of international politics to apply a variety of explanatory models to explain the situations represented. Those who want their students to have an understanding and appreciation of the value of *levels of analysis* for explaining international events and decisions will find this set of cases to be rich with illustrative examples. No specific theoretical perspective has been predetermined for the individual cases which follow. Some of the narratives contain enough detail about the personalities involved to allow students to utilize the individual level of analysis to examine the impact of key players, while other cases take a more general view, pointing students toward the identification of systemic factors such as geopolitical considerations or resource competition that may have influenced key decisions. Still other cases allow the student to make use of state level analysis, taking into account the institutional structures and domestic politics that shaped particular decisions.

Thus, a diverse range of theories can be made more meaningful to the students by applying them to the particular case at hand. For example, the creation of the GATT case can be utilized to illustrate "hegemonic stability theory," or "interdependence theory," while the Vietnam case can be used to illustrate "the security dilemma" and balance of power politics during the Cold War. It is not my purpose to offer an interpretation of each case within a specific theoretical perspective; however, instructors who want to demonstrate the relative usefulness of competing analytical frameworks will find these cases useful for grounding various theories in actual historical situations.

CONCLUSION

Placing students "at the scene" of pivotal decisions has meant that I have tried to avoid providing information that would not have been available at the time, except as an orientation to the student and in the conclusions that remind the students of the place the various cases hold in twentieth century history. Instead, I focus on the issues, trade-offs, and pressures faced by the key players involved during that period in history. It is my goal in the cases that follow to introduce students to the realm of international politics as they have inherited it and at the same time expose them to the complex systemic, institutional, and personal forces that shaped those decisions in the first place.

ACKNOWLEDGMENT

My interest in case study teaching began with my first assignment as a new faculty member to teach international law, but my understanding of, and appreciation for, the case method was developed through a Pew Fellowship in International Relations at Harvard University during the summer of 1991. John Boehrer, the director of the program, and my Pew colleagues made me a firm believer in the effectiveness of case discussion for developing student understanding and analytical skills. What an honor it was to be in the company of such wonderful teachers!

This particular book project grew out of that experience, and was further encouraged by the Stanford Cazier University Professorship I was awarded at Utah State University in 1994 for developing cases for use in my courses. The professorship provided me with much needed time for launching this effort. Furthermore, it is important that I acknowledge the support of the Department of Political Science, and particularly my Department Head, Randy Simmons, who takes great pleasure in the success and productivity of his faculty and who does whatever he can to see that we have the resources to achieve our goals. Finally, I want to thank the many students who read and discussed these cases during the past few years in my courses in International politics, U. S. foreign policy, International trade policy, and European politics. Their input regarding the readability and effectiveness of the cases was instrumental in their development.

CONTENTS

PART I

UNDERSTANDING THE HISTORICAL FORCES THAT HAVE SHAPED OUR WORLD

Causes and Consequences of World War II and the Cold War

CHAPTER I

THE FUTILE ATTEMPT TO AVOID A SECOND WORLD WAR

1920s Revisionism and 1930s Appeasement in Europe

....

INTRODUCTION

Most historians agree that the Second World War between 1939 and 1945 was not a new war but was still part of the ongoing conflict in Europe that had never been settled with the First World War (1914–1919). In retrospect this is fairly obvious, but at the end of World War I few would have predicted that the continent of Europe would be plunged so soon into another devastating conflict. In order to understand why the peace settlement after World War I failed, to understand the linkages between this failure and the rise of Nazi aggression, and to comprehend the willingness displayed by most of Germany's neighbors to allow that aggression, one must review the events of the 1920s and '30s in the international politics of European relations. Crucial decisions were made that set Europe on a course to tragedy. Had you been a policy maker at the time, would you have acted differently?

....

THE IMPACT OF WORLD WAR I AND
THE VERSAILLES PEACE SETTLEMENT

Even today one is struck by the sheer numbers of World War I dead immortalized on etched stone monuments in villages—no matter how small—across Europe. It was known as "The Great War" or "The War to End All Wars," its horror and destruction was so traumatic. There were 37.5 million total casualties (including those who were killed, wounded, or missing), and these became known as "the lost generation," the young men who never returned home to live productive lives, who, with very few exceptions, never survived to succeed their fathers as statesmen, teachers, merchants, or laborers.[1]

Yet the peace settlement in 1919 that concluded the war left many animosities and discontented people. The map of Europe was radically altered, and new governments arose to take up the challenge of self-determination, while vestiges of empire and authoritarianism hung on them like chains. Mortally wounded by the heavy casualties of war and economically disrupted by reparations, war debts, and the protectionist nationalism of their neighbors, the nations of Europe entered an era of political and economic uncertainty.

Nowhere was this more evident than in Germany, which had not only lost the war but suffered the ignominy of defeat in the vindictive settlement that followed. Historians now generally agree that World War I resulted from the combined animosities, misadventures, and miscalculations of all the major players. However, the Versailles Treaty pointedly blamed Germany for the war, and as the victors forced Germany to accept its position, they also decided how best to benefit from their victory. Kept outside the conference halls where the peace treaty provisions were being considered, the German delegation was faced with "an ultimatum" by the Allies "in which they declared that they would resume hostilities if the Germans had not agreed to sign the treaty within a week."[2] With their armies in full retreat and their people unable and unwilling to further support war, Germany had little choice but to accept the blame for the war and the terms of the peace:

> The Allied and Associated Governments affirm and Germany accepts, the responsibility of Germany and her allies for causing all the loss and damage to which the Allied and Associated Governments and their nationals have been subjected as a consequence of the war imposed upon them by the aggression of Germany and her allies.[3]

France, in particular, wanted territory returned that it had lost in 1871 in the Franco-Prussian War and wanted to ensure that Germany could never again rise as a military threat to its interests. And despite objections from the American president, Woodrow Wilson, who hoped for a peace settlement that would depart from the traditional European pattern of "spoils to the victor," the French perspective dominated. Not only were severe reparations exacted on Germany, the very character of its boundaries and the nature of its national defense were dictated by outside powers. The German army was to be pared to a force of 100,000 men (from the prewar force of 750,000), and in both western and central Europe borders were altered at the expense of Germany. Counting the return of the Alsace-Lorraine region to France, Germany lost 13.1 percent of its prewar territory and 10 percent of its 1910 population.[4]

In addition, a new set of states was formed from the demise of the Austro-Hungarian Empire and the abdication of territorial control by the Soviet Union in the Treaty of Brest Litovsk.[5] The map of Europe was vastly different in 1919 than it had been on the eve of World War I, bringing with it the political and economic challenges of such massive change. Thus, as new states like Czechoslovakia attempted to create identities for themselves during the 1920s, Germany sought to recover from the traumas of the war and cope with the humiliation and difficulties created by the external constraints imposed at Versailles.

Most crippling for Germany were the provisions that forced it to forfeit its merchant marine, part of its fishing fleet, and control over the coal- and iron-rich Saar basin.[6] These, combined with a requirement to export coal and timber and build new ships as reparations in kind, made it extremely difficult for Germany to recover from the war, let alone advance economically enough to provide the reparations in gold and hard currency that the victors also demanded.

Ironically, these demands were exacted on an entirely different government from the one that had entered the war. Prior to the end of the war in 1918 a new form of government was adopted in Germany, for the first time based upon universal suffrage and organized as a parliamentary democracy. Given the incredibly weak position of the exhausted German army at that time, the new government had contacted the United States with its desire to enter peace negotiations, and the German public finally began to appreciate that Germany's ability to continue the war was nonexistent. When the German kaiser Willhelm II refused at first to abdicate, mutinies, demonstrations, and strikes followed demanding both his abdication and an end to the war. On November 9, 1918, a new German republic was proclaimed, and two days later the armistice was signed.[7]

Despite this revolutionary change within Germany, the Allies pursued their demands for a harsh settlement. And unfortunately for the architects of the Weimar Republic (as the new government was called), the Versailles Treaty with its perceived unfairness and vengeful provisions became associated in Germany with those public figures who were truly committed to representative democracy and civil rights.

Throughout the 1920s German public resentment against the Versailles provisions festered and at times erupted into open resistance. Moreover, the war's devastation, four years of reparations, high import costs, efforts to meet government pension commitments after the war, and the Reichsbank policy of printing money in a desperate effort to provide capital after the war produced disastrous inflation rates that threatened the very fabric of the German economy, and in turn the international economy as well. Between January 1919 and January 1923 the German mark fell in value from 8.9 marks to the dollar to an incredible 18,000 marks to the dollar![8] This hyper-inflation, which continued throughout 1923, overwhelmed Germany, creating an economic crisis that deeply affected Germany thereafter, both in terms of public attitudes toward monetary policy and in terms of public willingness to put international commitments ahead of national interests.

During this period of economic crisis France—which had been especially damaged and traumatized by the war—maintained constant pressure on the fledgling republic, threatening to militarily occupy the Rhine region and offering no reprieve from the reparations (both in kind and in gold) that it demanded. In 1922 this pressure came to a head after Germany fell behind in its shipment of telegraph poles to France as required by the Versailles Treaty. Ostensibly in an effort to ensure that coal shipments would be met, France and Belgium intervened and assumed military control of the Ruhr region in 1923. Convinced that France actually intended to use this incident as an excuse to assume permanent control of the Rhineland, the German government encouraged a policy of passive resistance against French occupation forces, and tensions between the two nations became even more strained.[9] Paradoxically, the outcome of this policy was further disaster for the German government, which "supported the idle population of Germany's industrial heartland with federal cash grants-in-aid . . . financed by authorizing the indiscriminate printing of money."[10] A consequence of this deficit spending was more spiraling inflation, which caused the mark to fall at an even more precipitous rate. In January 1923 the mark was already valued at a disastrously low 18,000 to the dollar; however, after the policy of passive resistance was implemented against France, the mark fell to an "astronomical" 4.2 trillion![11]

Resentment against foreign intervention and economic hardship caused by hyperinflation combined to create a German polity that was increasingly attracted to those political perspectives that offered more radical approaches to governance and diplomacy. Those who preached the virtues of nationalism and the repudiation of international commitments (particularly the Versailles Treaty) appealed to a people whose nation's war guilt had been imposed because it had lost the war, not because it was the only guilty party. During the decade of the 1920s German politics became increasingly polarized between the dominant right-wing, which chaffed under the constraints of parliamentary democracy, and the vociferous left wing. Moderate democrats and liberals were constantly pressured by the extremes from right and left.

REVISIONISM AND GERMAN TREATMENT

Abroad, observers were also wondering whether the commitments imposed on Germany at Versailles were in fact too harsh, and a strong sense of sympathy was developing in many circles for the plight of the Weimar Republic. In addition, there were those who believed that the peace and prosperity sought by everyone after the Great War were threatened by the punitive treatment of Germany. In Britain this viewpoint had a number of prominent advocates. Economist John Maynard Keynes's 1919 book, *The Economic Consequences of the Peace,* charged that the settlement that was imposed on Germany was too harsh economically and would in fact destroy the ability of Europe to recover to its pre-war level of prosperity. Prime Minister Lloyd George had in 1920 "led the way" in an effort to appease German resentments, believing that an enduring peace depended upon a reduction in the enmity between France and Germany, and that this could be accomplished only if the old "enemy" and "allied" differentiation embodied in the Versailles Treaty ceased "to disturb and irritate Franco-German cooperation."[12] This revisionist perspective also carried with it a growing impatience with France, which seemed to many observers in Britain to be placing its own special interests ahead of peace and prosperity in Europe.

Lord Curzon, British foreign secretary during the Ruhr crisis, vehemently argued against French actions, especially when France declared that " 'an autonomous Government of the Palatinate' had been established in the Rhineland, which France supported."[13] Publicly denouncing this statement as a ploy by the French government to extend its control over western Germany, the foreign secretary effectively ruined French plans. His criticism added further influence to public opinion, which was becoming more anti-French and shifting away from punitive treatment of Germany, especially as German economic difficulties disrupted international financial and commercial trade flows. Increasingly, British diplomacy became occupied with the task of mediating between France and Germany, and a chorus of voices from policy-making circles was calling for a revision of Versailles Treaty demands. By 1924 both Britain and the United States sought revision of the reparations schedule but continued to be constrained by the French, who had no interest in such compromise.

Coupled with this revisionist attitude, there was by the end of the decade considerable concern developing in Britain over the increasing fragility of the Weimar Republic. Many were worried that without revision of the Versailles Treaty—from reducing reparations to allowing League of Nations membership—the republic was doomed to topple under the rising tide of radical politics. After all, what fate might befall Europe if moderate relations between France and Germany could not be developed and if republican government failed in Germany?

The fears of those who worried about the character of German politics were well founded. Within Germany—even within the establishment of the republican government—there was ongoing pressure to move away from the center of politics to more radical perspectives. Even after the German currency was stabilized in 1924 and an era of relative prosperity emerged, old affinities for authoritarian politics and hatred for France remained to thwart democratic development and international cooperation with the Western powers. Despite a number of diplomatic successes for Germany, including some revision of the reparations schedule as well as membership in the League of Nations, right-wing pressures continued to influence the character of German policy.

With an eye on the vulnerable position of the Rhineland, as well as general Reichswehr resistance to the constraints that had been imposed on it, the Reich surreptitiously sought to avoid compliance with the disarmament measures of Versailles by carrying out clandestine arms arrangements with the Soviet Union. Both having been ostracized from the international community following the war, the German government and the government of the Soviet Union found in each other an opportunity to build a sense of international legitimacy and a degree of latitude in foreign affairs. Building upon their secret military arrangements, the two nations signed the Treaty of Berlin in 1926, which pledged each to neutrality in the event that one of them was attacked by a third nation. In Germany concern over France and resentment of the West in general dwarfed any reluctance to do business with the Bolsheviks.

Right-wing counter-revolutionary forces continued to exploit German sentiments against France, adding pressure to the Weimar government to resist its international commitments as much as possible. The centrist coalition that governed the Weimar Republic went through a series of ups and downs as it attempted to maintain a semblance of moderation through economic crises and amidst strong political pressures for more authoritarian governance.

In foreign affairs the challenge was particularly great. Gustav Stressemann, Germany's foreign minister between 1923 and 1929, cautiously pursued (with British mediation) an accommodation with France that would stabilize relations on Germany's western border as well as reduce the severity of reparations. Yet this approach, even though partially successful, was considered by many as a sell-out.[14] Increasingly, political groups in Germany not only attacked the Versailles arrangements but also discredited anyone who sought revision through standard diplomatic processes. More radical repudiation was demanded.

The general appeal of this perspective became particularly strong with the advent of the Great Depression. The economic chaos of the 1920s, despite the brief hiatus between 1925 and 1929, finally brought the collapse of global markets and caused high levels of unemployment. The German public, having suffered through the years of hyper-inflation during the first part of the 1920s, in 1930 faced rapid economic contraction, falling wages, and loss of jobs.

THE RISE OF NAZISM AND GERMAN ASSERTIVENESS

It was in this context that Adolf Hitler rose to power and the brief republican experiment in Germany was rejected. The National Socialist (Nazi) Party, which had become a parliamentary party in 1924 with 12 seats in the Reichstag, had had an early uphill struggle when Hitler, its leader, was imprisoned for advocating the overthrow of the government, and its leadership was in question. However, by 1933 the Nazis had become the dominant political force in Germany and had fully revolutionized German government. What caused this rapid rise to power?

The answer lies within three different realms. First, the character of German politics and governmental structure by 1930 was highly unstable with no coalition of parties strong enough to govern but many groups of parties strong enough to obstruct governance. This created a vacuum in leadership, and increasingly political competition manifested itself in the streets instead of in the Reichstag. The centrist parties rapidly lost strength in comparison with the Communists on the far left and the conservatives and Nazis on the right. Parliamentary democracy appeared ineffectual to throngs of near-starving Germans as well as to establishment figures who were frustrated with the government's inability to govern.

Second, this "paralysis of parliament elevated the Reich president to a position as supreme arbiter of the nation."[15] This meant that the burden of leadership fell on the shoulders of an 80-year-old former general whose advisers held deep-seated suspicions about parliamentary democracy. Even before Hitler came to power, the republican character of government was being transformed. The position of the president was enhanced at the expense of the parliament, providing extraordinary powers that allowed a near dictatorship to exist. This became crucial a few years later when the Nazis cemented their partnership with the conservatives under Adolf Hitler's chancellorship.

Third, desperate for solutions to their plight, the German public found the message that the Nazis conveyed both appealing and convincing. Hitler blamed the economic distress they were suffering on the terms of the Versailles Treaty, which had stripped Germany of its economic capability as well as its prerogative in foreign affairs. He was unequivocal in his position that Germany should repudiate its international commitments and strike out in the pursuit of its own rightful place in history. The honor of the German people was at stake, he argued, and their destiny depended on a radically new direction in foreign and domestic policy, which placed Germans first and dealt ruthlessly with the enemies of the fatherland both without and within.

This part of his message coincided with what the conservatives were already saying (which made them inclined to support cooperation with the Nazis), but in addition Hitler added that only under Nazi leadership could a genuine unity of the German people be achieved. He argued that the enemies of the nation—whom he identified as democrats, republicans, Jews, and Marxists—had to be eliminated in order to achieve a true national community of Germans and to embark on a new course in German history. Their only experience with democracy and republican government having been the difficult, if not disastrous, previous 13 years, the German people seemed ready to embrace the simple solutions that this authoritarian approach offered. Long-standing anti-Semitic attitudes, distrust of foreign interference, and a deep desire to escape the chaos of recent years combined to pave the way for Hitler's popularity.

This peaked in 1932, after which there were indications in land elections that Nazism was losing some of its appeal to voters. But a true democratic test was never allowed. In 1933 Hitler had engineered his appointment as chancellor by President Hindenburg, and within the next few months he established totalitarian control over the country, ruthlessly eliminating opposition, crushing the Communist movement, and initiating his persecution of the Jews. He also launched an ambitious set of programs to revitalize German power and prosperity. Massive public-works projects combined with rearmament to create jobs and encourage recovery. Economically, Germany was becoming the envy of other nations still caught in the throes of depression. Politically and militarily, however, reactions abroad were generally less complimentary and much more confused.

Increasingly, reports coming from Germany contained accounts of Nazi thuggery reigning over human rights. Hitler's racism and brutal attitude toward the Jews created strong misgivings among liberals and social democrats. In Britain, where revision of the Versailles settlements had long been advocated by the political mainstream as a better way to deal with Germany, a new debate emerged over whether it was too late to do any good. On the one hand, advocates of revising the treatment of Germany had argued that "if treated well, [Germany] would become a peace-loving democracy."[16] However, between 1930 and 1933 it became clear to most onlookers that even if this had been true at one time, it was no longer so. Authoritarianism had won out.

Moreover, the anti-French sentiment that had influenced many in Britain to favor further revision diminished after all the Allied military forces (including French) were withdrawn from the Rhineland in 1930 and it appeared that finally the French were willing to respect the new international arrangements regarding Germany. In fact, concern began to shift away from France and toward Germany when, on the heels of this withdrawal, Germany announced that it should now be able to reclaim its right to militarize the region.[17]

When Hitler came to power in 1933 his actions "confirmed all the worst fears in British minds," and "feelings of sympathy toward Germany gave way to feelings of loathing and anxiety."[18] People were watching and waiting and hoping that the internal affairs of the German nation would remain far removed from their own national concerns. Even when it was clear that Germany had embarked on a massive rearmament program, people were generally taking a wait-and-see attitude.

Still deep in depression, the British public and British politicians were preoccupied with issues of the economy and social welfare—trade relations, the position of the currency, and mounting unemployment. While there were those who argued that Britain should assume a more assertive role with Germany, including the adoption of its own policy of rearmament, this policy option remained very unpopular.[19]

The Great War remained too vivid in people's memories—or if not in their own memories, in the stories told to them by others who had experienced this terrible episode of the recent past. The lessons inherited from that war cautioned against precipitous or confrontational military action. Arms races and mobilization had, after all, been part of the chain of events that had ignited the worst war in history. Pacifism was very strong in Britain during the 1930s. Recollection of the horrors and destruction of the war and echoes of the cries of the lost generation haunted the House of Commons, where rearmament was debated. Military preparedness seemed to many not to be a deterrent but a step along the path to yet another war. Very few had the stomach for that—at least not yet.

Among diplomatic circles, another source of hesitancy about German rearmament existed. Many during this period were very concerned about the rising power and influence of the Soviet Union, fearing the spread of communism more than any other potential threat they could foresee. For these individuals the rise of Nazism, while disturbing in its disregard for democratic values, offered a counterweight in the balance of power against communism. Especially in the midst of the Great Depression, when economic circumstances were ripe for the appeal of Bolshevism among the working classes of Europe (including Britain), the idea that Germany was clearly moving right rather than left reassured many people. Hitler, vociferously anti-communist in his statements and actions, offered a potential bulwark against the Communist threat from the East.

Thus, between 1933 and 1937 pacifism, extreme economic difficulty, and fear of communism contributed to British reluctance to be more assertive against rising German power. These factors, combined with over a decade of revisionist advocacy regarding the treatment of Germany at Versailles, made it difficult for British policy makers to adopt a firmer policy toward Germany. After all, they had recently been arguing that Hitler was in fact right about Versailles, that its terms were too harsh and that the Germans were right to be frustrated by it. As Hitler moved to fulfill his promises to repudiate the international commitments imposed at Versailles, some Britons watched in disgust, others in empathetic understanding, but all watched in trepidation as they wondered what the future would hold.

When Germany remilitarized the Rhineland in 1936, the French were particularly alarmed, but internal divisions and policy vacillations, coupled with the absence of international support, prevented them from taking any action. In Britain enough concern mounted to bring the debate over rearmament again into the forefront. However, it was not until 1938 that German actions began to dramatically draw British public attention. It was during this pivotal year that "the Nazis dropped the mask of peaceful revisionism" and embarked upon a policy of expanding German territorial control beyond the borders that had been established in 1919.[20]

The first object of this policy was Austria, one of the new states that had been created from the Austro-Hungarian Empire by the Paris peace agreements. Bordering Germany on the southeast, Austria, which was predominantly German speaking, offered a logical target for German expansionism. It was in a highly unstable political position in 1938, ruled by a fascist regime that had been in alliance with Italy's Mussolini until the Italian fascist leader decided to sacrifice his relationship with Austria to a new alliance with Berlin. Without the backing of Italy, Austria's government became vulnerable to the pressures of Nazi Germany. Hitler, wanting a sympathetic arrangement between the two countries, demanded that Austria's government invite the participation of the leaders of the Austrian Nazi party. Kurt von Schuschnigg, the leader of the government, attempted to sidestep this demand by announcing a plebiscite on the question of Austria's independence, which he hoped would force the Germans back from their interference in Austrian affairs. Hitler, however, refused to back down and instead went on the offensive, demanding that the plebiscite be canceled and that Schuschnigg resign and turn the government over to the Austrian Nazi leader Arthur Seyss-Inquart. If Schuschnigg did not cooperate, Germany would invade Austria.

On March 11, 1938, Schuschnigg resigned, and in his first act as the new head of the Austrian government Seyss-Inquart invited German troops into the country to "maintain law and order." Met with throngs of public support, the German military was then followed by a visit from Hitler, who proclaimed that he had finally returned home and that his homeland now had become a part of the Third Reich.[21] The *Anschluss,* as this union between Austria and Germany was called, was greeted by most Germans and Austrians as a triumph of German destiny, the uniting of a greater Germany.

Outside, however, this development intensified the debate over German intentions. Was Nazi Germany merely fulfilling its goals of uniting Germans under one common roof, or did it have broader designs? Again, there were many who believed that arrangements between different groups of Germans posed no serious threat and had little to do with them at home. Still others wondered whether Hitler was merely redressing the unfairness that had been enforced in the Versailles Treaty against Germany and minority Germans living outside Germany. Regardless, neither France nor Britain took any action. There simply was not a consensus that the situation was worth risking war by confronting Germany.[22]

On his side of the issue, Hitler did have the argument that "despite the existence of a German national state, there were large numbers of Germans who had been scattered in a centuries-old diaspora over Eastern Europe and who were not part of the new German polity."[23] When Germany and the Austro-Hungarian Empire were defeated in the Great War, this added to the numbers of Germans outside German governance and tended to put German minorities in more subjugated positions. Moreover, the creation of new democratic states in 1919 placed many Germans under the authority of Slavs, something that was "an affront to *volkisch* antidemocratic and racial biases" and that began to encourage separatist movements.[24] Consequently, Hitler's plan to unite Germans coincided with strong revolutionary tendencies on the part of Germans living elsewhere.

APPEASEMENT AND THE MUNICH AGREEMENT

Nowhere was this more evident than in Czechoslovakia, which was the only surviving democracy of the new states created by the Versailles Treaty. Created from a portion of the Hapsburg Empire, Czechoslovakia combined ethnic Czechs, Slavs, Hungarians, Poles, and Germans into one polity. Germans in Czechoslovakia constituted the single largest German minority outside Germany and Austria. They were concentrated in the Sudeten region (or Bohemia, as the Germans called it), where they had dominated economic and political affairs for centuries. With the defeat of the empire in 1918, however, they found themselves under the rule of the Czechs—people "they themselves had long suppressed."[25]

Under Czech rule a number of new policies were introduced that aimed at providing more equal treatment for all citizens, including education, financial policy, and language requirements. However, having long benefitted from their dominance of the region, these policies rankled the German minority, who saw the changes as intrusions on their traditional rights. Coinciding with the hardships caused by the Great Depression, the Germans in Czechoslovakia saw this interference as the reason behind their economic distress, and increasingly they agitated for greater autonomy from Prague.[26] At the same time, the Bohemian Nazi movement, in existence far longer than in Germany itself, was gaining in strength and had become a major focal point of resistance to the Czech state. In February, less than a month before the *Anschluss,* Hitler announced his promise "to protect all German minorities outside the Reich."[27] This fostered stronger resistance among the Sudeten Germans but also fueled the Czech government's resentment of foreign interference.

In May 1938 the Sudeten Nazi leader Henlein visited London to press his case for German autonomy. Basically, he argued that the national government of Czechoslovakia should provide "foreign policy, defence, finance and communications," but that the regions

> should enjoy local autonomy; that is to say, they should have their own town and country councils, and a diet in which matters of common regional concern could be debated within definitely delimited frontiers. . . . The officials . . . in the German-speaking regions, would of course be German-speaking, and a reasonable proportion of the total taxes collected should be returned to these regions for their administration.[28]

These demands appeared reasonable to the British, who worried that the Czecho-slovakian government might create a broader conflict with Germany if it did not react favorably to its German minority. Strategically, the *Anschluss* had put Germany in a strong position to pressure Czechoslovakia, and its military mobilization along the Czech border made onlookers very nervous. While the Czech government officially announced its willingness to negotiate an arrangement along these lines with the Sudeten Germans, they also were mobilizing their own army, which added to concerns abroad over how to contain the crisis.

In July the Conservative British government led by Neville Chamberlain dispatched a peace mission to Prague with the purpose of seeking a solution between the Czech government and the Sudeten German leader Henlein. Chamberlain had little confidence in the collective security approaches of the League of Nations and preferred instead high-level, one-one-one diplomatic missions. Chamberlain also held the belief that Germany's treatment after the Great War had been unjustly harsh and that he should work toward redressing those grievances in order to create strong Anglo-French-Italian-German relationships against potential Soviet meddling. This predisposed him toward a diplomatic settlement that would prevent escalation of the situation and would also avoid involving the Soviets and affronting the Germans. However, in August the negotiations broke down, and the situation became more tense.

Increasingly, British observers were worried that war would erupt over the region, and despite the recent initiation of a rearmament program, everyone knew that Britain was ill-prepared. There were those like Winston Churchill, however, who believed that Britain should take a firm stand against German interference in Czechoslovakia. In a speech to his constituents during the last part of August, Churchill warned:

> . . . the danger to peace will not be removed until the vast German armies which have been called from their homes into the ranks have been dispersed. For a country which is itself not menaced by anyone, in no fear of anyone, to place fifteen hundred thousand soldiers upon a war footing is a very grave step. . . . It seems to me, and I must tell it to you plainly, that these great forces have not been placed upon a war footing without an intention to reach a conclusion within a very limited space of time. . . . [L]arger and fiercer ambitions may prevent a settlement, and then Europe and the civilised world will have to face the demands of Nazi Germany, or perhaps be confronted with some sudden violent action on the part of the German Nazi Party, carrying with it the invasion of a small country and its subjugation. *Such an episode would not be simply an attack upon Czechoslovakia; it would be an outrage against the civilisation and freedom of the whole World* . . . .[29]

On September 12 Hitler delivered a speech at a Nuremberg party rally demanding autonomy for the Sudeten Germans and attacking the Czech government. On the next day the Czechs declared martial law in a state of emergency, negotiations with Henlein were broken off, and Henlein fled to Germany. Despite French Prime Minister Daladier's opinion that a joint mission to Berlin should be undertaken to avert war between Czechoslovakia and Germany, Prime Minister Chamberlain decided to meet unilaterally with Hitler, having received an invitation to Hitler's personal retreat at Berchtesgaden. At this meeting Hitler demanded that for their protection the German Sudeten region of Czechoslovakia be ceded to Germany, and "he told Chamberlain he would risk war if necessary to obtain these 'just' demands of self-determination."[30] Chamberlain was personally convinced that Hitler was only interested in annexing the Sudetenland, and that if he was appeased Czechoslovakian security would be assured; however, he was equally convinced that Hitler was ready to fight if he was thwarted in his demands.

In the meantime the Czech government was aghast and dismayed at Chamberlain's willingness to meet directly with Hitler without at least consulting them. In their view they had a number of reasons not to give in to Hitler's pressures. First, support for Henlein's Nazis had not increased among the local Sudeten population, despite a revolt by his adherents and Hitler's provocative speech. Moreover, when Henlein fled to Germany, his German party dropped its plan for further revolt, especially when the Czech government offered a very promising new proposal for regional autonomy.

Second, Czechoslovakia had long-standing defense pacts with France and the Soviet Union, which pledged assistance in the event of an attack on Czechoslovakia. In these arrangements France was crucial. The French guarantee had been formalized in a 1926 agreement, and the Soviet assistance pledge, made in 1935, was conditional upon whether the French acted. If France did come to the defense of Czechoslovakia, so too would the Soviet Union. With France and the Soviet Union behind them, the Czechoslovakian government was prepared to meet Nazi pressures with a show of force and with strong military resistance if an attack did come. Their forces were mobilized at the border with Germany, and they were unwavering in their commitment to defend their territorial integrity. However, the diplomacy of the great powers was quickly eroding their confidence.

Following Chamberlain's meeting with Hitler, French governmental representatives met in London with the British government, carrying with them their own proposals for dealing with Germany. They favored ceding the Sudetenland to Germany and then offered French and Russian (though they had never consulted with Russia) guarantees of the new, much reduced, Czech borders.[31] In this proposal the French not only abdicated their responsibility toward Czechoslovakia, they stripped their ally of Soviet support even after the Soviets had communicated their intention to follow through on their commitments. Soviet Foreign Minister Litvinov reported at the League of Nations a few days later that his government had unequivocally conveyed its commitment to France prior to the French government's meeting in London:

> We intend to fulfill our obligations under the Pact, and together with France to afford assistance to Czechoslovakia by the ways open to us. Our War Department is ready immediately to participate in a conference with representatives of the French and Czechoslovak War Departments, in order to discuss the measures appropriate for the moment.[32]

A similar communication was conveyed to Prague, reassuring President Benes that the Soviet Union was planning to meet its treaty obligations against Nazi adventurism. Yet, in apparent disregard for this Soviet position, Daladier chose appeasement over confrontation, and Chamberlain, already predisposed to such a plan, agreed with him.

Two days later British and French ministers met in Prague with Czech president Benes to urge him to accept their proposals "before producing a situation for which France and Britain could take no responsibility."[33] Faced with what for all intents and purposes was an ultimatum, and bereft of French (and therefore Soviet) military support, Benes reluctantly agreed.

As others became aware of what was occurring, reactions were mixed. Daladier and Chamberlain were optimistic that they had negotiated an arrangement that could appease Hitler, and they remained cautiously pleased with their accomplishment at this stage in the process. Many were hopeful that war would be averted. However, others were worried that the opposite was true. Winston Churchill, the most outspoken critic of appeasement policy, held a very pessimistic view. In a statement made on September 21 he unleashed his criticism against the proposed settlement:

The partition of Czechoslovakia under pressure from England and France amounts to the complete surrender of the Western Democracies to the Nazi threat of force. Such a collapse will bring peace or security neither to England nor to France. On the contrary, it will place these two nations in an ever-weaker and more dangerous situation. The mere neutralisation of Czechoslovakia means the liberation of twenty-five German divisions, which will threaten the Western Front; in addition to which it will open up for the triumphant Nazis the road to the Black Sea. It is not Czechoslovakia alone which is menaced, but also the freedom and the democracy of all nations. The belief that security can be obtained by throwing a small state to the wolves is a fatal delusion. The war potential of Germany will increase in a short time more rapidly than it will be possible for France and Great Britain to complete the measures necessary for their defence.[34]

In Czechoslovakia criticism of the government, which had lost control of its foreign policy, led to its resignation, and there was considerable agitation in favor of "going it alone" against Hitler if necessary. France and Britain both continued to appeal to the Czechs to restrain themselves, worrying that they "might provoke incidents" before the negotiations with the Germans were completed.[35]

Following a second meeting between Hitler and Chamberlain on September 22–23, in which Hitler threatened that if his deadline for a settlement of September 28 was not met his forces would attack Czechoslovakia, French and British leaders became increasingly worried about their ability to defuse the crisis. Tensions were running very high. The Czech army of 1.5 million men was fully mobilized, lined up behind what at the time was the strongest fortress line in Europe and facing across it the largest army in Europe. The French partially mobilized their forces, and on September 28, the day Hitler's ultimatum was to expire, the British fleet also mobilized.

In the eleventh hour, however, on September 27 Chamberlain received a letter from Hitler in which he offered assurances about respecting the boundaries of Czechoslovakia once the Sudetenland was ceded to Germany and about holding a plebiscite to verify the national preferences of the citizenry. The guarantee of boundaries was an important development, and the communication did take a more conciliatory tone, opening an opportunity for further discussion. Chamberlain, eager for such an opportunity, replied that "after reading your letter, I feel certain that you can get all essentials without war, and without delay. I am ready to come to Berlin myself at once to discuss arrangements for transfer with you and representatives of the Czech Government."[36] He followed this reply with a note to Mussolini regarding his proposal for a conference with Hitler. Mussolini in turn proposed to Hitler that the four powers of France, Britain, Italy, and Germany meet together to settle the issue. Hitler agreed to the conference, which was held in Munich on September 29–30. No one considered including the Soviet Union in the discussions, and the Czechs themselves were also excluded, "allowed" to wait across the street while the four Western powers determined their fate.

The Munich Conference was a culmination of several months of diplomatic maneuvering, and it offered no surprises. Hitler's demands were met. "The Czechs would evacuate areas designated by Hitler. An international commission would determine what areas of Czechoslovakia should be German, Polish, or Hungarian because these latter two governments had demanded 'justice' for their people. Britain and France would guarantee the new Czech frontier."[37] Moreover, Hitler proclaimed that he had no designs on the rest of Czechoslovakia and in fact would "make no more territorial claims in Europe."[38]

Prime Minister Chamberlain returned home triumphant that his diplomacy had saved Europe from war. On arrival in Britain he waived the agreement and proclaimed that his policy of appeasement had achieved "peace in our time."[39] The mobilization of the fleet was canceled; gas-mask drills in London stopped; and Chamberlain encouraged Britons to take advantage of this new era of peace and enter into commercial arrangements with Germany.

Less than six months later Hitler's promises at Munich were nothing more than mockeries of Chamberlain's good intentions. On March 15, 1939, Hitler proclaimed German control over Bohemia, Moravia, and Slovakia, moving in his forces and eradicating what was left of the independent state of Czechoslovakia. Despite their guarantees at Munich, France and Britain did nothing but protest Hitler's actions. However, the two nations then rejected further appeasement in a new pledge to Poland that if it were threatened by Germany they would go to war against the Nazis. The United States, watching from across the Atlantic, condemned Germany's aggressive behavior and refused to recognize German sovereignty over the area. The Soviet Union sent a "quietly worded response on March 18. It disputed the constitutional right of the Czech President Hacha [who had succeeded Benes when the latter resigned in September] to agree to the German measures, and refused to recognize the incorporation of Czechoslovakia into the German empire."[40]

Shortly after, however, the Soviets began to pursue their own policies of conciliation with Germany in light of the Western collapse of resolve. In August, Germany and the Soviet Union signed a non-aggression pact that contained a secret protocol partitioning Poland and the Baltic states between the two countries. Assured of Soviet cooperation, on September 1, 1939, Germany in a blitzkrieg attack invaded Poland, and Britain and France acted on their commitments. Not quite a year after the Munich Conference was to have ensured peace for the next generation, World War II began.

Discussion Questions

1. What linkages existed between international politics and domestic politics in Germany during the 1920s and '30s?
2. What role did international economic relations play in the rise of Nazism?
3. What linkages existed between World War I revisionists and appeasement advocates?
3. Did revisionism necessarily have to lead to the appeasement policy pursued by Chamberlain?
4. Using this case as an example, under what conditions may diplomacy fail to avoid war?
5. What linkages exist between international economic relations and international military conflict?

Notes

1. Felix Gilbert with David Clay Large, *The End of the European Era, 1890 to the Present* (New York: W.W. Norton, 1991), p. 151.
2. Ibid, p. 174.
3. Treaty of Versailles, Article 231, as quoted by Martin Gilbert, *The Roots of Appeasement* (New York: New American Library, 1966), pp. 22–23.
4. Gilbert, *The End of the European Era*, p. 173.
5. As a consequence of the 1917 Bolshevik Revolution, Russia, which had been an ally of France and Britain during the war, sought a separate peace with Germany. A primary aim of the Bolsheviks in opposing the tsar had been withdrawal from this disastrous war, which the monarchy had pursued despite repeated criticism that the country simply could not physically or economically sustain its involvement. The 1918 Treaty of Brest Litovsk resulted in the forfeiture of Finland, the Baltic states, and territory to create Poland and augment Rumania. When the allies met at Versailles, the regions ceded in the Brest Litovsk Treaty were granted independence or were attached to neighboring states.
6. Gilbert, *The End of the European Era*, p. 174.
7. Ibid, p. 176.
8. Dietrich Orlow, *A History of Modern Germany: 1871 to Present*, 2nd ed. (Englewood Cliffs, N.J.: Prentice Hall, 1991), pp. 142–143.
9. Orlow, *Modern Germany*, p. 144, and Gilbert, *The Roots of Appeasement*, pp. 102–103.
10. Orlow, *Modern Germany*, p. 144.
11. Ibid, p. 144.
12. Gilbert, *The Roots of Appeasement*, p. 81.
13. Gilbert, *The Roots of Appeasement*, p. 103.
14. Orlow, *Modern Germany*, p. 171.
15. Ibid, p.175.

16. Gilbert, *The Roots of Appeasement,* p. 127.

17. Ibid, pp. 127–128.

18. Ibid, p. 138.

19. Ibid, p. 151.

20. Orlow, *Modern Germany,* p. 213.

21. Ibid, pp. 213–215.

22. Thomas Brooks Jones, *Munich: A Tale of Two Myths* (Philadelphia: Dorrance and Company, 1977), p. 25.

23. Ronald M Smelser, *The Sudeten Problem 1933–1938: Volkstumspolitik and the Formulation of Nazi Foreign Policy* (Clinton, Mass.: The Colonial Press, Inc., 1975), p. 5.

24. Ibid, p. 6.

25. Ibid, p. 8.

26. Ibid, p. 9.

27. Lester H Brune, *Chronological History of United States Foreign Relations: 1776 to January 20, 1981,* Vol. II (New York: Garland Publishing, Inc., 1985), p. 742.

28. Winston S. Churchill, *The Gathering Storm* (New York: Bantam Books, 1961), p. 256.

29. Ibid, pp. 261–262.

30. Brune, *Chronological History of United States,* p. 744.

31. Churchill, *The Gathering Storm,* pp. 269–270.

32. Ibid, p. 273.

33. Ibid, p. 271.

34. Ibid, p. 272.

35. Ibid, quoting Chamberlain, p. 275.

36. Ibid, p. 282.

37. Brune, *Chronological History of the United States,* p. 744.

38. Jones, *Munich,* quoting Hitler, p. 31.

39. Ibid, p. 745.

40. Georg von Rauch, *A History of Soviet Russia* (New York: Praeger Publishers, 1972), p. 272.

CHAPTER 2

THE GREAT DEPRESSION AND THE ORIGINS OF THE WORLD TRADING SYSTEM

....

INTRODUCTION

After World War II the United States embarked on a new path of leadership in the global economy. Having traditionally been rather trade protectionist, the United States took a new direction that promised much greater openness for foreign imports as well as U.S. leadership in encouraging other nations to also liberalize their trade policies. Most economists agree that the willingness of the United States to assume this new role contributed significantly to the postwar economic miracle that created an unprecedented era of prosperity and interdependence. Today we tend to take for granted the fact that as consumers we have nearly limitless access to goods from all over the world, but in the period prior to World War II this was not at all the case. Even though trade policy continues to be manipulated for a variety of political purposes, the world trading system in historical terms is generally open and fluid. The economic and political history of the 1930s and '40s is important for understanding why the United States decided that it was in its vital interest to adopt a different trade policy and why this in turn was pivotal in creating the global trading system we know today.

When the fateful attack by Japan at Pearl Harbor in 1941 brought the United States into the Second World War, it had already been raging for years elsewhere, and the situations in Europe and Asia had become very bleak. In Asia, Japan's militarist government had extended its imperialist control beyond the puppet state in Manchuria to China's other regions. It had spread its territorial domination into Southeast Asia and Micronesia, seeking hegemony over East Asia and the Pacific region. Hitler's Nazi Germany had renounced republican government and international cooperation, becoming a repressive police state bent upon world domination. Since 1938 it had overtaken neighboring countries in an arrogant disregard for national boundaries, international law, and diplomatic goodwill. The only major European nations holding on to their independence and resisting Nazi domination were Britain, whose island location had kept the Nazi onslaught at bay, and the Soviet Union, which had become Hitler's most recent victim.

From the vantage point of U.S. leadership, Europe's predicament was particularly alarming, and as the United States prepared for war with Japan, its government also pledged its support to Britain and the Soviet Union in the larger struggle against the aggressive dictatorships. In pondering the role that the United States might take in this terrible war, foreign policy makers were convinced that American leadership would be necessary, not only to see the war to a successful conclusion but also in framing the character of the postwar diplomatic arrangements. Even as American leadership went about the business of making war against Japan and Germany, the State Department was devoting a significant portion of its energy to planning for the postwar world. To those like Secretary of State Cordell Hull, who had observed recent history and who were devoted to avoiding war in the future, much of what was going on in Europe appeared rooted in the aftermath of the last Great War. Looking back over the previous two decades, a number of Washington analysts were convinced that this particular moment in history would not have occurred had a different course been pursued at the end of World War I. Armed with this belief, key figures in the State Department set about understanding the forces that had brought the world into such turmoil and conflict during the 1930s. It was their belief that the mistakes of the past should not be repeated, and that from the lessons of history a new, more stable world order could emerge. Thus, when the United States entered the war in 1941, it did so not simply with a strategy for winning the war but also with a plan for winning the peace that would follow.

Interestingly, it was the economic analysis of the failures of the World War I peace settlements that drew the most attention. The explanation of why World War I, which was thought in 1919 to be "the war to end all wars," was in actuality merely a prelude to World War II, became grounded in an analysis of the character of post–World War I international economic policies. Focusing in particular on the failure of the international community of nations to recognize their economic interdependence and to cooperate in sharing the burden of postwar recovery, U.S. State Department officials argued that a new, more assertive and internationalist role would have to be played by the United States, the one country that had the economic potential necessary to provide leadership for long-term economic stability. In order to understand this perspective and the policies that followed, we must first turn to the period of history commonly known as the Inter-War Period, the lessons from which were considered crucial to achieving international coexistence and prosperity in the future.

PRELUDE TO DEPRESSION: EUROPE, THE UNITED STATES, AND THE ECONOMIC AFTERMATH OF WORLD WAR I

Despite an increasing awareness among Treasury officials and American financiers that the United States economy was tied interdependently to the economies and trade policies of other nations, U.S. import policy during the 1920s was decidedly restrictive. This protectionist outlook was supported by the Department of Commerce, which represented the interests of Big Business in the United States, and by Congress, which was dominated by the Republican Party (traditionally the party of Big Business). In fact, protectionism—that is, the policy of protecting domestic producers from foreign competition—had long been the dominant tradition in American economic history. Most American firms were oriented toward the domestic market, and in their view opening American doors to foreign competition spelled hardship and potential disaster. Therefore, even though there were efforts from the 1870s onward to liberalize the American tariff, a generally protectionist orientation was maintained.

This perspective was hardened during the 1920s when the post–World War I recessions caused agricultural interests to join the manufacturing sector in turning to protectionist policies in an attempt to prop up price levels. This coalescence of protectionist interests was an interesting departure from past patterns, because generally in U.S. trade history agricultural producers favored low tariff policies. They did so for three major reasons. First, they favored any policy that helped to keep the machinery they purchased at lower prices. Imported machinery parts and tools often kept manufacturing costs lower so that the finished products were also cheaper. Moreover, competition from abroad for U.S. industry helped to prevent U.S. manufacturers from garnering the windfall profits that were possible in a protected market. This, too, helped to contain prices. Second, agricultural producers and farm laborers made up the vast majority of American consumers. Since these consumers had meager incomes, any policy that created competition and lowered prices was attractive. Along with urban labor, agricultural interests tended to support the availability of cheaper imports. Third, agricultural producers were themselves interested in expanding markets for their own products. Long before U.S. manufacturers became interested in the potential of foreign markets, agricultural producers were exporting abroad. Restrictive U.S. trade policies always had the potential for engendering similar policies by other countries, so agricultural exporters tended to be more conscious about the possibility that trading partners, confronted by a high U.S. tariff, might impose retaliatory tariffs of their own.

However, the agricultural industry was not a homogenous entity, and certain sectors (sugar, for example) were more concerned about import competition than they were about losing their own export potential. When prices plummeted after the Great War, the downward plunge began with agricultural goods. This caused politicians from farming states to plea for governmental intervention, and the 1921 Emergency Tariff Act was passed in response. This measure raised tariffs on vulnerable agricultural products in an effort to support domestic prices. Incorporating the Emergency Tariff Act, the Fordney-McCumber Tariff Act was then passed in 1922 to govern U.S. trade relations through the rest of the decade. It raised tariff rates generally and included highly restrictive provisions that allowed the president to impose exclusionary tariffs on any imported good competing with a similar good manufactured in the United States.[1] This protectionist choice for dealing with decline in prices was the traditional option for American politicians. Had the world been less interdependent economically, the repercussions of American policy might not have been so far-reaching. However, in hindsight the choice was tragic. To understand why, it is necessary to examine the conditions in Europe at the time.

A coup against the German monarchy in the last months of World War I resulted in the emergence of a new government based in Weimar that was more interested in suing for a peace arrangement. After the guns of war had finally been silenced, the victorious Allies met in Versailles, France, to set the terms of the peace settlement. Despite the efforts of U.S. President Woodrow Wilson, who wanted an evenhanded peace but who was also very ill at the time, the European nations returned to their old patterns of big-power politics, where "to the victors go the spoils." France in particular was immovable in its claims against defeated Germany, regardless of the latter's change in government. Having lost the Alsace-Lorraine region to Germany in the Franco-Prussian War in 1871, France demanded its return. Given the horrible destruction of World War I, France was also adamant that Germany pay reparations that were punitive as well as compensatory. France and Great Britain (as well as most of the other countries of Europe) were themselves suffering terribly in the aftermath of war. Agricultural production in France had been extensively damaged. Manufacturing in both countries had been geared totally toward the war effort, leaving very little for civilian consumption. And both nations had become deeply indebted to U.S. interests in order to finance their respective war efforts. Reparations would help the other two nations recover economically.

Reparation demands on Germany were severe. Having also suffered terrible losses in the war, Germany was hardly in a position to pay the amounts set in the time demanded. Reparations were to be made either in gold or in goods such as coal and lumber, all of which were necessary for Germany's own recovery. Thus, as Germany attempted to resurrect its own economy from the war, it was saddled with financial burdens that made recovery nearly impossible. Ironically, the one nation that was in a position to assist Germany in meeting these obligations was the United States. Unscathed by the war and economically sound at its end, the United States was the one potential source for financial support and the most viable market for the goods Germany was able to sell. Moreover, the United States was the one great power that, if necessary for the health of the world economy, could have absorbed some of the costs of European recovery in general by offering more lenient repayment provisions on the debts owed to the Allies and by offering new loans to the beleaguered Germany.[2] It was also the one nation whose population, industrial sectors, and agricultural interests could afford to buy goods from abroad—goods that European nations would have to export in order to launch their own recoveries at home. Open markets and freer lending policies might have been all it would have taken to ease pressure on the Allies, which in turn would have eased pressure on Germany, allowing a more orderly recovery from the war. Had the United States seriously considered this role and taken this responsibility early on, the events of the 1920s, '30s, and '40s might have been very different.

As it was, however, sentiment in the United States was decidedly indifferent to the plight of Europe. Having been pulled into Europe's war reluctantly, and having disagreed with the character of Europe's peace settlement, Americans were not eager to embroil themselves financially in Europe's economic problems, let alone make more sacrifices for what they considered to be Europe's own mess. While there were individuals who argued that such isolation was short-sighted self-interest that would haunt long-term economic recovery, the dominant view was against involvement and in favor of tending to American interests. This included the unilateral efforts to maintain domestic prices by erecting tariffs and other exclusionary policies to discourage imports.

Thus, at the very time that Germany, France, and Britain desperately needed the revenue from exports, the United States was protecting its market from their goods in the form of the Fordney-McCumber tariff. By 1923 this set of circumstances produced the first major economic crisis. In an effort to meet international demands for reparations and at the same time supply its citizens with promised pensions, the German government had been printing money that had no intrinsic value. Investment in Germany from abroad had been meager, German exports beyond those necessary for reparations were very limited, and Germany was unable to amass gold or other hard currency reserves. Moreover, the German government did not have the tax revenue to support its commitments, either from imports or from domestic tax income, because recovery was so slow.

Given that there were no significant sources of credit to help Germany cope with its untenable situation, and given that France and Belgium remained rock solid in their demands that reparations continue to flow (their own recoveries partially depended upon these payments and resources), the German government had few options but to try to slow the pace of reparations and to keep the domestic economy afloat by printing money. However, the French and Belgians became increasingly agitated over what they considered to be unacceptable stalling by the German government, and in early 1923 they occupied an area of the coal-rich Ruhr region "ostensibly . . . to ensure that coal earmarked for France and Belgium was actually shipped."[3] This incensed the Germans, who were convinced that their neighbors to the west were merely using Germany's late reparations as an excuse to take over the Ruhr area (they were already unhappy with the fact that Allied troops occupied the border regions).

In reaction, the German government overtly encouraged the coal miners in the area to follow a policy of passive resistance against the foreign occupiers, and these workers complied with a general work slow-down. Aimed at punishing the occupiers for their heavy-handed presence in German territory, the coal workers' strike also had the unfortunate and unintended effect of overburdening the German economy.

In order to support the workers in the area while they were on strike, the government issued them federal grants. These grants could not be financed from governmental reserves or investment arrangements, because there were none, so they were generated by the printing of money. Already suffering inflationary pressure, the government unwittingly pushed the economy over the edge with this policy. Instead of pressuring the Allies to reconsider the reparations arrangements, the German government merely made matters worse at home.

Demands from all sides were relentless. By 1923 inflation had spun out of control, and the results were disastrous. Between January 1922 and November 1993 the German mark had fallen from 192 marks to the U.S. dollar to an "astronomical" 4.2 trillion marks to the U.S. dollar.[4] For all intents and purposes the German currency was worthless at home and abroad. This hyper-inflation wreaked havoc with the domestic economy, stripping the elderly of life-time savings, making it impossible for the German people to buy even the simplest necessities of life, and crippling the government.

Moreover, the government's policy toward the Allies failed to have the desired effect. The Allies had no interest in reconsidering the terms for reparations payments (although Britain would have renegotiated, they were not willing to do so without the concurrence of the French and Belgians), and they certainly had no intention of backing down to such ploys.

Thus, having worsened Germany's situation instead of improving it with the policy of passive resistance and printing-press finance, the government resigned in the fall of 1923. The new government moved quickly in 1924 to restabilize the currency with a scheme that offered notes of credit backed by Germany's agricultural and industrial enterprises. It also achieved the acquisition of an American loan under the so-called Dawes Plan, which offered U.S. dollars from a consortium of American banks, set up an American banker as the intermediary in future reparations payments, and removed the provision that Allied countries could occupy German territory in punishment for being late in making those payments. Although most analysts agree that this was "too little, too late," the Dawes Plan helped to stabilize the German economy and buy time for Germany's reparations effort.[5] Unfortunately, the political wounds from this tragic episode in German economic history remained unhealed and ran very deep.

Thus, as the German economy began to recover at the end of the decade, currents of resentment and mistrust coincided with ongoing misgivings about the economy. Even though foreign investment had grown steadily since 1924, by 1929 neither investment nor exports had reached pre–World War I levels. Also, despite emerging economic stability, the government's strategy of seeking piecemeal financing from abroad (since that was all that the Americans were willing to provide) occurred against a backdrop of rising public resentment against Germany's international commitments and rising pressure for more radical national leadership. In the military there was growing restlessness against the constraints imposed at Versailles, and across the political spectrum there was growing frustration with what most people considered to be an unjust peace settlement.

One of the manifestations of these sentiments was a clandestine arrangement between the German army and the army of the Soviet Union, which made it possible for Germany to circumvent the restrictions on its military by receiving Soviet arms and training. In the domestic political realm, German politics became more and more unstable, as the proportionally elected parliament had difficulty operating and governments changed frequently. Clear-cut majorities were difficult to achieve, and governing coalitions were difficult to maintain as consensus and trust were elusive. Moreover, the parties at the center of the political spectrum, which were committed to democracy and republican government, were increasingly challenged by the fringe parties, which demanded radical solutions to Germany's difficulties.

By 1928 the German government had decided to overstep the military limits set at Versailles, but it remained committed to the economic obligations, despite their unpopularity with the German public. It did, however, seek to again reschedule its reparations payments, and because it had met its international financial commitments for the previous five years, the Allies were willing to do so. In the fall of 1929 its reparations schedule was again renegotiated under the so-called Young Plan, an American-sponsored arrangement aimed at maintaining stable financial flows and setting the terms for the withdrawal of remaining French and Belgian troops from the border regions.

....

THE GREAT DEPRESSION, ECONOMIC REVISION, AND THE ORIGINS OF WORLD WAR II

Ironically, the Young Plan was barely announced when the New York stock market crashed, causing similar crises around the world and the emergence of the Great Depression. In the United States the economically constricting effects of the stock market plunge were met with panic and confusion. Banks collapsed, factories shut down, and unemployment skyrocketed. At the national political level Congress turned to the one economic policy action with which it was most familiar—raising the tariff. The orthodox political response to economic depression was to limit imports in order to save domestic producers from foreign competition. Just as had occurred in 1921 and 1922, when the nation faced recession following World War I, a new tariff was debated that was aimed at again buttressing domestic prices by keeping out foreign imports.

Every congressman and senator scrambled to put the goods produced in his district or state on the list of items protected by the new U.S. tariff or by discriminatory quotas. Thus, even when the American public might have been better served by lower tariffs on some goods, a protectionist momentum had overtaken congressional politics, resulting in nearly across-the-board protection. Once Congress awarded new or higher levels of protection for one set of producers, it had no rationale for not protecting others.[6] Worse yet, the Hawley-Smoot tariff of 1930 was "a fatal blow to any remaining hope of international economic equilibrium," because it catalyzed a spiral of trade restrictions around the globe. Not only did it restrict trade with the United States, it also engendered a series of retaliations and defensive actions by other countries.

In addition to raising tariffs and creating quotas of their own, nations turned to currency devaluation as a means of protection. These competitive currency devaluations forced Britain—the country that had previously supplied the world's major trading currency (the pound sterling)—to abandon the gold standard and devalue its own currency as well. Thus, at a time when the world most needed a strong national economy to enforce stability in exchange-rate markets, Britain was too weak to do so. It was also clear that although the United States might have had the capability to perform this role, it did not have the political motivation.[7] After all, much of what had occurred to worsen the world economy had been stimulated by American defensive and inward-looking actions. Prior to 1932 there was little political will in the United States for assuming a more internationalist role.

Retaliatory trade restrictions and competitive devaluations ripped through the world economy, and each nation sought to protect itself at the expense of its trading partners. Instead of protecting their domestic interests, however, these "beggar thy neighbor" actions worsened relations and tightened the world economy even further, deepening and widening the Great Depression.[8] In just a handful of years the value of world trade contracted to one-fifth what it had been prior to the stock market crash as nations scrambled to raise trade barriers and devalue their currencies. For the United States alone the value of its exports fell by 71 percent between 1929 and 1933!

In Germany, the economic crisis fostered political opportunities for the extremists who had been pressuring the Weimar government for some time. As the constricting effects of the market collapse and U.S. protectionism began to be felt in Germany in late 1929 and early 1930, the immediate reaction by radical critics of the government was that the Young Plan had caused a new round of economic hardship and that Germany's willingness to enter into yet another set of arrangements for reparations was folly of the worst sort. It was time, vocal opponents cried, for Germany to seize control of its own economic fate—to repudiate the international chains that kept it subjugated—and embark on a new course of German nationalism. At the forefront of these cries was the voice of Adolf Hitler, whose plans for Germany included economic recovery with special trade arrangements of its own, remilitarization, and territorial expansion. But they also included the establishment of an autocratic fascist state, the annihilation of the Jews, and the domination of all of Europe.

Between 1933 and 1941 Hitler's progress toward these awesome and troubling goals was impressive, as Germany gobbled up territory and dominated economic relations in continental Europe. Holding out against Germany's plan for total domination were Britain and the most recent victim of Hitler's megalomania, the Soviet Union. From across the Atlantic, the situation in Europe appeared extremely grim, and it was clear to the U.S. government that it would take a monumental effort to defeat Hitler's Germany. When the United States entered the war, however, it did so with the determination not only to achieve that defeat but also to lead the postwar world in a new and more positive direction. Its leadership believed that the United States could and should pursue a different course in post–World War II relationships, a course that would avoid the mistakes of the past and fashion a new set of arrangements for peace and prosperity.

This belief had been developing for some time within the foreign policy circles of the United States. Since 1933 a new way of thinking about international economic relations had emerged within the new Democratic administration under Franklin Roosevelt. Leading this perspective was Secretary of State Cordell Hull, a man keenly committed to the ideal of international economic cooperation and dedicated to reversing past patterns in U.S. economic policy. Within the first two years of the Roosevelt administration Hull had succeeded in reversing the protectionist trend of the Hawley-Smoot tariff (four years after it had been passed) and had wrested the initiative for trade policy away from Congress, placing it in the hands of the executive, who was much more internationalist in his orientation. Believing that recovery from the Depression required a willingness on the part of the United States to open its borders to foreign imports so that the United States in turn could expect other countries to open their borders to American imports, Hull led the nation in the establishment of a new trade policy.[9]

Hull believed that in order to benefit from the world market the United States must also offer its market reciprocally to foreign producers. His rationale was that "to effectively expand trade, the new program would have to incorporate lessons learned from previous policy failures. Therefore, reciprocity must be based on principles of liberalism and a negotiable tariff."[10] This is because U.S. trade policy to that point had been based upon preferences for a very protected market as determined unilaterally by the U.S. Congress. His view was that the spiral of trade retaliations following the Hawley-Smoot Tariff Act had proven the folly of protectionism and the counterproductivity of the practice of setting tariffs arbitrarily without consulting America's trading partners. Unlike the adverse effects of the 1922 Fordney-McCumber tariff, which were largely felt in the European nations recovering from World War I (without directly being revisited on the United States), the adverse effects of the Hawley-Smoot tariff had come full circle to injure U.S. exporters. Both tariffs had been set autonomously by the U.S. Congress with no regard for their effects on trading partners, and Hull was convinced that only when the United States accepted that its interests were intrinsically tied to the interests of other nations could it lead the world in recovering from the Great Depression.

Therefore, under his helmsmanship, the United States embarked upon a new course in trade policy. Based upon the complementary principles of reciprocity and most-favored-nation treatment, the 1934 Reciprocal Trade Agreements Act made it possible for the U.S. president to negotiate on a bilateral basis trade agreements to liberalize the tariff and wherever possible to eliminate discriminatory quotas. In exchange the U.S. Congress expected the executive to make agreements that benefited U.S. exporters "reciprocally." This strategy had the political value of demonstrating to domestic interests that trade negotiations were aimed at opening markets for American products, assuaging "congressional fears that the executive branch might grant unilateral concessions without bargaining for reciprocity."[11] Moreover, other nations, who in the past could not trust the United States to offer genuine access to its market, now had the same assurance that if they agreed to liberalize their markets, the United States would do so as well.

Alongside the principle of reciprocity in the new U.S. trade orientation was the principle of most-favored-nation treatment. Most-favored-nation treatment had existed previously in U.S. trade policy, but never coupled with a genuine effort to open the American market to foreign trade. Now that the Roosevelt administration was committed to liberalizing trade as a component of its foreign policy and its policy for economic recovery, this principle took on new significance. The way reciprocity and most-favored-nation treatment would work in practice is that any nation that negotiated its tariff downward in good faith with the United States would not only receive reciprocal access to the U.S. market, it would also be given the status of most favored nation. This would mean that in all other cases where the United States reduced its tariff (as the result of trade negotiations with different countries) the most favored nation would be granted the same benefits from that arrangement. This practice of multilateralizing trade agreements resulting from bilateral negotiations, Hull argued, would multiply the liberalizing effects of each and every set of negotiations. This would speed the process and widen the effect of trade liberalization, rapidly moving the world away from the tight trade policies of the early 1930s to a much more open and equal trading system. It would have the immediate effect of helping to pull participating nations out of economic depression as expanding markets would increase profitability and employment. It would have the long-term effect of creating trust between nations and laying the foundation for global prosperity.

Between 1934 and 1941 a number of bilateral trade agreements were reached under the authority of the 1934 Reciprocal Trade Agreements Act. Even Germany, now fully under the control of the Nazi dictatorship and hoping for a more favorable trade arrangement, approached the United States in 1935 about negotiating a bilateral deal. The United States responded by saying that it was U.S. policy to negotiate with any country "provided that its commercial policies do not in fact impose discriminatory or inequitable conditions upon American commerce and do not arbitrarily divert its trade from this country to other countries."[12] Because Germany's trade policy during the 1930s had become decidedly discriminatory as it sought to better its economic circumstances at the expense of other nations, it did not meet this criteria. But other countries (such as Canada and Mexico), who had previously retaliated against the 1930 U.S. tariff and had pursued discriminatory policies of their own, were convinced of the value of the new American approach to trade and accordingly shifted their policies in order to reach agreement and benefit from the most-favored-nation clause in the 1934 U.S. Trade Act.

Encouraged by the success of the 1934 act, State Department officials set about broadening their goals to include international monetary cooperation as well as international trade cooperation. Because competitive currency devaluation had wreaked as much havoc in international economic relations as had formal trade barriers, it was considered imperative that in order to achieve a more open and stable trading system, international finance and exchange rate policies must also be addressed. In 1937 Leo Pasvolsky, special assistant to the secretary of state, sent a memo to the White House that outlined State Department recommendations for this wider effort. It called for (among other things) American leadership in reaching agreement on achieving international means of "reestablishing monetary relations based on stable foreign exchanges; reexamination and, if necessary, adjustment of existing international debt obligations"; and "resumption of international lending."[13] Implicit in these recommendations was the belief that the world economic system (which had so deteriorated that virtually no systematic means of cooperation now existed) must be newly established through a "multilateral means for liberalizing trade and regulating monetary and credit policies."[14]

Events in Europe and Asia precluded much progress on this program, however. Yet, even though the U.S. trade expansion initiative and State Department goals for monetary cooperation were postponed by the emerging conflicts in Asia and Europe, planning continued for what many realized would now have to be post-war arrangements for global economic cooperation. Fundamental to these plans was the conviction within the State Department that the Second World War would not have erupted if post-1934-style U.S. trade and economic policy had been in place since World War I. Regrets about past American behavior and policy were fueling new prescriptions for behavior once World War II was over. This was especially true as Americans witnessed from afar the disintegration of international cooperation and the rise of the Nazi and Japanese military machines.

By 1938 Germany had seized territory well beyond its 1919 borders, and it was on its way toward achieving economic domination of much of the Balkan region.[15] Exploiting German resentments about the Versailles peace settlement, the failure of the Weimar government to deal forcefully with foreign powers over the reparations issue, and fears of the consequences of international cooperation, Hitler embarked upon a course of conquest and domination. In Asia, some argued, the situation was not dissimilar. Japan's quest for resources and trade had been met in the United States with restrictions and discrimination, and when thwarted, its government was emboldened to seize direct control of what it could not get through trade. In both cases, it was being argued, the beneficiaries of American policies were the dictatorships whose power and control were enhanced by their ability to blame their nation's plight on the selfish interests of foreign nations.

Increasingly, Hull, his followers in the State Department, and other economic analysts of the period were voicing their belief that the new American approach to trade cooperation must be the blueprint for the world economy once this new war was behind them. Fundamental to this view was the belief that post–World War I–type policies must be avoided because they had proved so disastrous. Albert Hirschman, a contemporary analyst of Nazi Germany and of international economic relations in general, was typical in his argument, saying that "[the spiral of] economic nationalism, more restriction, and more discrimination, [that characterized the period following World War I had proved disastrous to peace because] restrictionism and discrimination undoubtedly sharpen national antagonisms. They also provide excellent opportunities for nationalist leaders to arouse popular resentment. And if these leaders, once in power, should feel the slightest doubt concerning the best policy to adopt, they will be much encouraged in their aggressive intentions by realizing that international economic relations provide them with an excellent instrument to achieve their ends."[16]

Within U.S. foreign policy circles the sentiment was similar, where officials were increasingly committed to the idea of coordinated planning for the post-war era and a recognition that the United States was the only power in the position to take a leading role. They also "recognized that a major reason for the breakdown of the last peace settlement lay in the inadequate handling of economic problems [and] placed great emphasis on economics in drawing blue-prints for a better world."[17]

LESSONS LEARNED: THE POST–WORLD WAR II WORLD ECONOMIC ORDER

Thus, when the United States signed the Potsdam agreements in July regarding Germany's defeat and accepted Japanese surrender in August of 1945, plans for the post-war world economy had already been drawn. Discussions about trade and international finance with Britain—the foremost ally of the United States, fellow capitalist power, and former financial leader—had been carried out during the war. Resulting in general agreement on the character of post-war economic plans, these discussions culminated at Bretton Woods, New Hampshire, in 1944 and lay the foundation for later arrangements.

The Bretton Woods "regime," as it would come to be called, established the principles for future exchange rate and financial stability. First, it was agreed that the U.S. dollar would replace sterling as the world's major trading currency. The dollar would be backed by gold at a rate of $32 per ounce. Other currencies would be tied in value to the dollar, and if financial crisis at home caused balance-of-payments difficulties (that is, more money flowing out of the country than is coming in), then the country in crisis could turn to an international organization to secure loans to help it out of its distressed situation and maintain its currency's value. This International Monetary Fund (IMF) would be set up initially by the United States, which was the one nation in a financial position to extend such loans at the end of the war. Later, as other nations recovered and eventually became economically sound, they too would be expected to contribute.

The purpose of the IMF would be twofold. First, it would provide a source of loans for countries in economic distress (as Germany had been after World War I), which in turn would help that country meet its international financial obligations. Second, by stabilizing a distressed country's balance of payments, it would prevent drastic currency fluctuations that could stimulate other nations to follow suit in the "beggar thy neighbor" pattern of the 1930s. Therefore, even during times of local economic hardship, it was hoped that general depressions would not be precipitated by defensive currency policies.

In addition to the IMF, American planners also agreed to create the International Bank for Reconstruction and Development (IBRD, or World Bank, as it later was called). The purpose of this bank would be to assist nations in their effort to recover from the devastation of World War II—to help them rebuild infrastructure so that they could then begin to participate more normally in world commerce. Beyond the war, the World Bank would exist to assist lesser developed nations with development projects that would enhance their ability to enter the world of trading nations.[18]

Both projects would be long term, designed to provide the foundation for a new international cooperative economic system, and both would be financed and managed by the United States. Coupled with the Bretton Woods regime were plans for a new international organization for trade. Efforts to create a multilateral cooperative organization based upon U.S. principles of reciprocity and most-favored-nation treatment eventually resulted in an executive agreement, called the General Agreement on Tariffs and Trade (GATT). Negotiated with prospective signatories between 1946 and 1948, the GATT created at the international level the same process for negotiating trade barriers that the United States had begun to pursue in the mid-1930s. Based upon the principle of reciprocity in order to achieve "mutual and balanced" reductions in trade barriers and fairness in the settlement of disputes, GATT would periodically bring the world's nations together to deal cooperatively with trade restrictions.[19] The individual trade agreements negotiated between signatory nations would then be automatically passed on to all other signatories via the most-favored-nation clause. Thus, every GATT member had the guarantee that it would receive benefits equal to every other GATT member. Taking the lead in establishing open markets was the United States.

The 10-year period following World War II was very different from the 10-year period that had followed World War I. The United States assumed very different roles in each era, and many have argued that this was an important factor. Certainly, in the minds of American State Department planners, it had made all the difference. Except for the failures of cooperation caused by the Cold War, the 1950s and '60s were generally characterized by cooperative economic liberalization and stability. At least in the West, a new era of prosperity and economic cooperation had emerged.

Discussion Questions

1. What linkages existed between the post–World War I European economy and U.S. policies?

2. What linkages existed between the Great Depression and world trade relations during the 1930s?
3. Why did U.S. State Department officials see a link between the rise of aggressive dictatorships and the economic instability of the Great Depression?
4. Why did U.S. State Department officials think it necessary for the United States to take a leading role in stabilizing the global economy after the war?
5. Why was the institutional reform that placed international trade policy under stronger executive influence such an important development?
5. Is there a relationship between liberal trade and global peace and stability?

Notes

1. Carolyn Rhodes, *Reciprocity, US. Trade Policy, and the GATT Regime* (Ithaca: Cornell University Press, 1993), pp. 47–48.

2. Charles P. Kindleberger, *The World in Depression, 1929–1939* (Berkeley: University of California Press, 1973), pp. 296–297.

3. Dietrich Orlow, *A History of Modern Germany: 1871 to Present,* 2d ed. (Englewood Cliffs: Prentice Hall), p. 144.

4. Ibid

5. Ibid, pp. 163–164.

6. For the classic analysis of this episode, see Elmer E. Schattsneider, *Politics, Pressures, and the Tariff: A Study of Free Private Enterprise in Pressure Politics, as Shown in the 1929–1930 Revision of the Tariff* (New York: Prentice Hall, 1935).

7. Kindleberger, *The World in Depression.*

8. Quoting J. B. Condliffe, *The Reconstruction of World Trade: A Survey of International Economic Relations* (London: Allen and Unwin, 1941), p. 184 in Rhodes, *Reciprocity,* p. 49.

9. Hull's views were well documented at this time. See Cordell Hull, *International Trade and Domestic Prosperity* (Washington, D.C.: United States Government Printing Office, 1934).

10. Rhodes, *Reciprocity,* p 56.

11. Ibid, p. 57.

12. Henry J. Tasca, *The Reciprocal Trade Policy of the United States* (Philadelphia: University of Philadelphia Press, 1938), pp. 81–82.

13. Leo Pasvolsky, "Memorandum from the Special Assistant to the Secretary of State to Sumner Welles, November 10, 1937, on Possibilities of Action in International Economic Field," as quoted in Rhodes, *Reciprocity,* p 66.

14. Rhodes, *Reciprocity,* p 67.

15. Albert O. Hirschman, *National Power and the Structure of Foreign Trade* (1945; reprint, Berkeley: University of California Press, 1980).

16. Ibid., pp. 72–73.

17. Richard N. Gardner, *Sterling-Dollar Diplomacy in Current Perspective: The Origins and the Prospects of Our International Economic Order,* 2d ed. (New York: McGraw Hill, 1969), p. 4.

18. Ibid

19. GATT, Preamble, Basic Instruments and Selected Documents, vol. 3 (Geneva, 1958), p. 3.

CHAPTER 3

THE DECISION
TO DROP THE BOMB

....

INTRODUCTION

The decision to drop atomic bombs on the Japanese cities of Hiroshima and Nagasaki is one of the most hotly debated topics in the modern history of world politics. Some have argued that the bombs were simply used to bring a final end to a long, drawn-out war with Japan. Others argue that the use of the bombs was part of a diplomatic power play aimed not so much at Japan (even though it was the Japanese who suffered the reality of their explosions) but at the Soviet Union, whose rising influence preoccupied Washington in 1945. Still others argue that the use of the bombs was at least in part the result of technological imperative—that is, a desire to use the new technology because it was there. Finally, many claim that there was a racist element to the American decision, that U.S. policy makers believed the Japanese had to be cowed in such a devastating way. Keeping these perspectives in mind, it is important to put yourself in President Truman's place during this pivotal period in 20th-century international politics.

....

U.S. PLANS FOR THE DEFEAT OF JAPAN

It was the summer of 1945. The war in Europe had ended in May, and President Truman was en route to his first World War II summit with Stalin, the leader of the Soviet Union, and Churchill, Britain's prime minister. Set to begin on July 16 in the town of Potsdam on the outskirts of Berlin, the summit's purpose was to clarify the terms of occupation for defeated Germany, the arrangements for the ongoing conflict between the

Allies and Japan, and other questions that had arisen with the liberation of former Nazi territories. For Truman it was also the first summit of his presidency, presenting a number of challenges as he established his own presence with the leaders of Britain and the Soviet Union. Assuming leadership of the United States in April upon the death of Franklin Roosevelt, Truman had yet to meet personally as president with the other Allied leaders.

Meanwhile in the Pacific the war against Japan continued to occupy American policy makers and military strategists. By the spring of 1945 Japan's navy and air forces had been virtually destroyed, and the United States had begun to advance against the home islands. Once U.S. forces were within striking distance of Japanese cities, ports, and production facilities, they had begun launching almost continual bombing raids against Japanese cities. Aimed at weakening Japan's resolve to continue the war, incendiary bombing missions were flown day after day against urban centers. Between March 9 and June 15 the United States carried out nearly seven thousand raids.[1] This fire bombing had devastated Tokyo in particular. On March 9–10 alone, in the most destructive conventional air raid in history, one-quarter of the city had been destroyed and 83,000 people were killed.[2] Yet, despite suffering such devastation, as well as succumbing to territorial losses throughout the Pacific region, the Japanese government had so far resisted demands by the United States to unconditionally surrender, a demand that had been enforced against Nazi Germany but which some argued was too extreme to expect from Japan. Without being invaded and undergoing utter defeat, some argued, Japan would hold out indefinitely. All indications up through May 1945 were that the Tokyo government planned to fight to the end if necessary to avoid surrender.

In fact, even as the Allies were accepting the unconditional surrender of the German forces, the Japanese government issued a statement proclaiming its commitment to continuing the war. Premier Suzuki affirmed that "Although the present changing situation in Europe has in no respect been unexpected on our part, I want to take this opportunity to make known once again at home and abroad our faith in certain victory."[3] U.S. intelligence reports in the summer of 1945 predicted that the Japanese government would be prepared "to fight as long and as desperately as possible in the hope of avoiding complete defeat and of acquiring a better bargaining position in a negotiated peace."[4]

Not only did the government appear unwilling to consider surrender at that time, it was also entertaining the possibility of obtaining assistance from the Soviet Union, which had not yet joined the war against them. This, including Soviet oil and aircraft, it was argued, might be achieved in exchange for offering certain concessions to the Soviets, including a return to the pre–Russo-Japanese War (1904–05) boundaries in the northern Pacific.[5]

The United States was conscious of the possibility of a Japanese–Soviet rapprochement. American policy continued to emphasize the importance of securing the Soviet commitment to enter the war against Japan in order to quash any such possibility and to shock the Japanese government into realizing the futility of its war effort. However, many American policy makers had strong doubts about whether the Japanese government—even without Soviet aid—would be willing to forfeit the historically and culturally powerful imperial institution as a requisite of unconditional surrender. In fact, by the end of May "every important senior American policy maker, including the President, had decided that, if necessary, the rigid surrender formula would be substantially modified to assure the Japanese that the Emperor would retain his throne."[6] However, publicly this was not an easy possibility given American sentiment throughout the war that only unconditional surrender would be acceptable.

The formation in April of a new, relatively moderate government headed by Admiral Suzuki had created some optimism in the United States that Japanese surrender could be more easily achieved than when the militarists were in control. Yet past experience with the tremendous commitment of the Japanese to their war effort made policy makers reluctant to assume that surrender was imminent. In the aftermath of the recent bombing campaigns, which had not visibly dislodged the Japanese government from its commitment, this pessimism in Washington was reinforced. Thus, even though an acceptance of a modification of surrender terms was emerging unofficially as a possible approach, the United States continued to plan for the worst and to publicly maintain that only unconditional surrender would be accepted. Therefore, as U.S. air forces continued to pound Japanese targets, and policy makers were assessing what it would take to coerce Japan to surrender, U.S. military strategists pursued plans for a massive invasion of the Japanese home islands. Everyone hoped that the invasion would not have to take place. Given the tenacity of Japanese forces encountered throughout the Pacific campaign, U.S. military planners were convinced that an invasion would be "resisted to the last man" and that casualties would be extremely high—as many as 250,000 U.S. soldiers and potentially one million people combined.[7] The battles to secure Okinawa had graphically illustrated this potential. Over 12,000 American and 110,000 Japanese soldiers were killed, and some 150,000 Japanese civilians lost their lives in the process. As General Marshall explained, "The Japanese had demonstrated in each case they would not surrender and they fight to the death. . . . It was to be expected that resistance in Japan, with their home ties, could be even more severe."[8] The United States could not rely upon the possibility that Japan would surrender without suffering an invasion and undergoing utter defeat.

There were two and a half million regular troops on the home islands of Japan, "but every male between the ages of fifteen and sixty, every female from seventeen to forty-five, was being conscripted and armed with everything from ancient brass cannon to bamboo spears, taught to strap explosives to their bodies and throw themselves under advancing tanks. . . [and] thousands of planes were ready to serve as *kamikazes*."[9] Therefore, the terrible reality of what the invasion would involve, as well as the complexity of executing it, required extensive advance preparations. The tentative date for the invasion was set for November 1, and President Truman had authorized the deployment of one million troops for the purpose, including the transfer of thirty divisions from the European theater.

For three and a half years the United States, with some assistance from Britain, had borne the burden of the war in the Pacific. Yet it had also put its vast productive capacity into the war effort in Europe and had played an increasingly prominent role in the bombing war against Germany, the Allied invasion in 1944, and ultimately in the defeat of the Nazi regime. Fighting a two-front war had been a monumental effort, but early on President Roosevelt had agreed that the immediate peril to Britain and the Soviet Union warranted a commitment by the United States to ensure the defeat of Germany before American allies could be expected to enter the war against Japan in any meaningful way. From the beginning of the alliance Roosevelt believed that Stalin, the leader of the Soviet Union, would eventually declare war on Japan, but not until Germany's defeat had been achieved. This understanding was put into a formal agreement in January at Yalta on the Crimean Sea during the last wartime summit prior to Roosevelt's death.

....

POTSDAM SUMMIT, THE SOVIET UNION, AND THE ATOMIC BOMB

At Potsdam President Truman planned to verify this earlier arrangement for the Soviet army to join the war against Japan. A concern of the United States since 1943, when it was formally agreed among the Allies to make the defeat of Nazi Germany the first priority in the war, the burden of defeating Japan alone was something U.S. strategists had not wanted to face. General Douglas MacArthur had in fact "twice insisted that Russian help was needed," and Truman viewed securing a Russian commitment as "his main purpose" in going to Potsdam.[10]

Yet, as reports from Eastern Europe filtered to the West about the authoritarian nature of Soviet liberation policies, many in the United States were beginning to worry about long-term Soviet intentions wherever the Red Army intervened. In fact, Secretary of State Byrnes specifically stated that he hoped the war could be ended before the Soviet Union joined the U.S. effort because "I feared what would happen when the Red Army entered Manchuria."[11] Also, the circumstances by the summer of 1945 were very different than they had been prior to the series of U.S. military successes that had resulted in the defeat of the Japanese navy, a steady advance toward the Japanese home islands, and the massive destruction of Japanese population and war production centers wrought by the bombing raids. The United States was in a much stronger position regarding Japan than it had anticipated months earlier. The necessity of Soviet participation in order to defeat Japan was no longer a foregone conclusion, even though this continued to be U.S. policy.

Therefore, despite President Truman's intention at Potsdam to verify Soviet participation in the war against Japan, misgivings about Soviet intentions and its future role in the region, as well as growing confidence in the ability of the United States to convince Japan to surrender without an invasion, created a good deal of ambivalence about how to proceed. On the one hand, the United States definitely preferred to end the war in the Pacific without allowing the Soviets to "liberate" territory for their own purposes. On the other hand, if a land invasion was truly necessary to force the capitulation of the Japanese government, the United States did not want to suffer the undertaking on its own—especially given the War Department's estimates of casualties in the event of an invasion.

This ambivalence was also intensified by a yet unknown factor—the results of the American atomic bomb test, which was to take place at the testing range in Alamogordo, New Mexico, while President Truman was in Germany. The U.S. government effort to create an atomic bomb with massive destructive power had been under way for some time, with efforts intensifying during the latter months of the war. German work in this area had made American scientists and officials very worried that Hitler might gain the technology first, thereby solidifying his terrible control over Europe and preventing either the Soviet Union or the United States from resisting his domination of the continent. However, the combined Allied defeat of Germany not only ensured that the German atomic bomb effort was stopped, but it also completely refocused the attention of U.S. strategists from potential use of the bomb on Germany to its role against Japan.

The creation of the atomic bomb had become a very high priority during the war, and while scientists knew that the potential existed for a weapon of mass destruction to be created from nuclear fission, no one yet knew for certain when that moment would arrive and what the actual result would be. As U.S. bombers dropped their existing means of devastation on Japan, American scientists were rapidly pursuing their goal of testing a new form of devastation. If the device worked as expected, the U. S. government planned to use it. However, if the device was not created in time, President Truman felt compelled to maintain other options, including the Soviet promise of entering the war against Japan.

Therefore, as he sailed toward Europe, Truman was considering all of his options for Japan's defeat and for the position of the United States following the war. First, the possibility remained that Japan might surrender unconditionally to the United States as a result of the incessant bombing raids against her cities and production facilities. Second, if Japan refused to surrender, the "shock value" of a Soviet declaration of war might tip the scales and convince its government to reconsider.[12] Third, if the shock value of a Soviet war declaration did not cause Japan to surrender, early Soviet assistance in a land invasion of the home islands continued to be preferable to a U.S. unilateral invasion (or an invasion where U.S. forces bore the brunt of the effort only to be joined by the Soviets at the end in a bid for influence in the region). Thus, maintaining favorable relations with the Soviets and pressing their promise to join the war against Japan would be a prudent course of action in case this was necessary.

Fourth, even though the clear American priority was the defeat of Japan rather than other foreign policy considerations at the time, U.S. leaders were increasingly concerned about the spread of Soviet power and influence. The alliance that had seemed so important months ago was now more and more troubling to U.S. officials, who increasingly were seeing Soviet troops as potential aggressors in East Asia rather than as allies. This attitude was due largely to reports that the Soviet Union was imposing its own form of authoritarian control over the Eastern European countries it had liberated from Nazi occupation. The commitment made by the Allies at Yalta to ensure the self-determination of the liberated countries had become a mockery in the wake of the Red Army's coercive role in the formation of postwar governments. The United States was becoming increasingly alarmed about the evident intention of the Soviet Union to establish its own sphere of influence across Eastern Europe. What had always been an uneasy alliance was filled with even more suspicion and trepidation as the wartime leaders converged on Germany for their final summit of the war.

Finally, the potential of the atomic bomb served as the wild card among all of these considerations. If the United States could successfully deliver the bomb against Japan and secure its surrender before Stalin's promised date for entering the war (August 8), then the United States would not be forced into sharing the defeat of Japan with the Soviets. Moreover, scores of thousands, if not millions, of lives would be saved by avoiding the invasion, and capitulation to the United States would maintain U.S. hegemony over the postwar peace. As a War Department report indicated, "[An early] Japanese surrender would be advantageous to the U.S., both because of the enormous reduction in the cost of the war and because it would give us a better chance to settle the affairs of the Western Pacific *before too many of our allies are committed there and have made substantial contributions to the defeat of Japan. . . .*"[13]

Therefore, as President Truman prepared to participate in the diplomatic negotiations at Potsdam, he also awaited vital news regarding the atomic bomb test scheduled to occur at any time. The test itself would be the culmination of years of scientific study and technological development. Its actual use would be the culmination of months of strategic planning and policy deliberation. The technological capability to massively destroy an extensive target area with a single bomb had raised important questions about its use and role in the defeat of Japan. The scientists involved, as well as political and military leaders, considered its destructive and political potential with gravity. The weapon was truly a two-edged sword. Paradoxically, it promised delivery from the sentence of ongoing and bitter warfare, yet it also threatened a new sentence of eternal responsibility for the use of such destructive power by one nation against another.

U.S. CONCERNS ABOUT THE USE OF THE BOMB

In the formal discussions concerning the appropriate use of the atomic bomb, a number of options and associated concerns were raised. First, the possibility was raised about whether the bomb should actually be used on a Japanese target in a surprise attack or whether instead some demonstration of its potential would be adequate to convince the Japanese to surrender. Some people favored the demonstration because it might impress the government of Japan to reconsider its position without the United States having to shoulder the responsibility of being the first nation in history to use such a terrible weapon.

However, a number of practical considerations regarding a demonstration convinced policy makers to reject this option. The most fundamental concern about the demonstration concept was whether the device would actually work as expected, especially when dropped from an aircraft. If it did not work, it was argued, the U.S. position would actually be weakened.

Secondly, it was feared, if the Japanese government was notified about a forthcoming demonstration, it could prepare to shoot down the U.S. aircraft delivering the bomb or it could move U.S. prisoners of war into the area of the proposed blast. Both of these possibilities posed unacceptable risks as far as U.S. planners were concerned.

Therefore, it was generally agreed that the bomb would have to be dropped in a surprise attack to achieve the most powerful effect on the Japanese people and government. Given this conclusion, the next question was what target to choose. Both President Truman and Secretary of War Stimson thought that to target an exclusively civilian area was not a good idea and that the bomb should be dropped on a war-production center.

However, it was also agreed that in order for the bombing to have as much psychological value as possible, the war-plant target should also be surrounded by a significant population area so that the dramatic effect of the nuclear bomb could be graphically and indisputably demonstrated. Some of the individuals involved in planning the use of the bomb also believed that its deadly potential must be revealed to the world, because "if the bomb were not used in the present war *the world would have no adequate warning as to what was to be expected if war should break out again.*"[14] Thus, the conclusion of the Target Committee was that the psychological factor of the use of the atomic bomb was the most important consideration. Its report states, "Two aspects of this are (1) obtaining the greatest psychological effect against Japan and (2) making the initial use sufficiently spectacular *for the importance of the weapon to be internationally recognized* when it is released."[15]

Early on one of the most popular potential targets was Kyoto, the cultural and historical capital of Japan as well as a major war-production area. However, Secretary Stimson (backed by President Truman) quickly vetoed this option, citing the important historical and cultural value of this city and urging the consideration of other sites. He was particularly concerned about the future practical problems associated with reaching a working relationship with a postwar Japan whose people were not only utterly defeated but who were bitter about such a "wanton act."[16] Stimson's view prevailed, and the committee charged with making these recommendations settled on the following cities as potential targets for a succession of atomic bombs, to be dropped as they were produced until the Japanese government surrendered: Hiroshima, Kokura, Niigata, and Nagasaki.

If the atomic bomb was successfully tested at the military testing site in New Mexico, the components for another bomb would be flown immediately to the Pacific for use as soon as possible against its Japanese target. Everyone involved, from the President of the United States on down, was prepared to carry out this plan. Thus, as President Truman readied himself to meet with Stalin and Churchill in Potsdam on July 16, scientists and military personnel in the United States prepared to observe the first atomic bomb test in the history of the world, launching the final phase of World War II and initiating a new era in mankind's relationship to technology.

....

THE SUCCESSFUL TEST AND THE DECISION TO DROP THE BOMB

At 5:30 A.M. the bomb was detonated at the test site at Alamogordo. The specter that confronted the observers was more awesome and impressive than even the experts had conceived. First, the blast of brilliant orange and blue lights lit the early-morning sky— a fire ball "as bright as several midday suns,"; then a blossoming mushroom-shaped cloud billowed hugely above the horizon, and a blast and shock wave broke windows 145 miles away. It would be reported later that, at the explosion site, a crater 1,200 feet in diameter was formed, and the desert sand had turned to glass in the intense heat of the atomic blast. In the wake of this incredible display, military personnel attempted to limit any unauthorized knowledge of its occurrence and downplayed the event to local papers and eyewitnesses, including "*a blind woman who saw the light.*"[17] In the official secret report the scientists estimated that the destructive power of the bomb was equivalent to 15,000 to 20,000 tons of TNT.

On that evening in Potsdam President Truman received a cryptic message referring to the test: "operated on this morning. Diagnosis not yet complete but results seem satisfactory and already exceed expectations. . . ."[18] For the President of the United States this was a very important message. Not only was he now assured that a nuclear bomb was a practicality and could be delivered against Japan, he was armed with information that provided a stronger hand in his deliberations with the Soviet Union. No longer so dependent on Soviet cooperation in the Far East to force a Japanese surrender, he could take a firmer, more confident stand with Stalin in the negotiations for a postwar peace.

In particular, he was critical of the fact that the goals set out in the Yalta agreements for Eastern Europe were not being pursued in good faith by the Soviets, and he was adamant that the United States expected full cooperation. He also was more and more convinced that the war in the Pacific must end as soon as possible. Delay would merely provide the Soviets with further territorial acquisitions and give them greater leverage in the subsequent peace settlement with Japan and influence with China. Diplomacy regarding the situation was becoming as important to Truman as the plans to proceed with delivery of the bomb against Japan.

Emboldened by the news that the United States now possessed the power of atomic weapons, Truman became more forceful and assertive in the meetings that followed. His displeasure with Soviet action in Eastern Europe was evident, and his expectations for better compliance with the Yalta arrangements were set forth clearly and unequivocally. Yet at the same time that Truman worried about Soviet practices in Eastern Europe, he continued to pursue the plan to encourage a Soviet war declaration against Japan in case the bomb failed to secure Japan's surrender.

During the next few days Truman (via Prime Minister Churchill) was informed by Stalin about several Japanese approaches to the Soviet Union indicating that Japan "wished to bring hostilities to an end but was determined to fight on to the death so long as Unconditional Surrender was demanded."[19] This did not come as a surprise to the President, whose own officials had received a number of overtures from Japanese officials regarding a willingness to discuss the terms of a peace settlement.. These overtures were not interpreted by the United States as "offers to capitulate." Rather, the view taken, as represented by Acting Secretary of State Grew's statement on July 10, was that, "Conversations relating to peace have been reported to the Department from various parts of the world, but in no case has an approach been made to this Government, directly or indirectly, by a person who could establish his authority to speak for the Japanese Government, and in no case has an offer to surrender been made."[20] Consequently, the U.S. government assumed that any feelers reported were mere propagandistic manipulations, and as long as the Japanese government refused to follow up formally on the gestures of some of its individual officials, this view prevailed.

In addition to U.S. skepticism regarding Japanese intentions to surrender, U.S. military intelligence had been intercepting messages from Japan regarding the use of the Soviet Union as a mediator and had forwarded them to the President on July 15. Thus, within two days of his arrival in Europe President Truman knew of Japan's wavering resolve for continuing the war and its interest in approaching the Soviets for assistance in ending the war. He also know about the successful test of the atomic bomb, a factor that strengthened his commitment to demanding unconditional surrender.

Starting in June several Japanese officials had begun to contact Soviet officials about the possibility of a Japan–Soviet Union rapprochement. Several feelers were extended, including visits with Soviet Ambassador Malik in Japan. Yet the Soviets continued to rebuff them. Japan's second-best option then was to seek the assistance of the Soviet Union in securing the most favorable surrender terms possible. Even as Stalin and his entourage prepared to depart for Potsdam, a special mission by Prince Konoye had been authorized to seek a meeting with the Soviet leader in Moscow to ask for assistance in the mediation of the war's termination. While at Potsdam the Soviet delegation continued to receive appeals from Prince Konoye for an audience with Stalin. In consultation with President Truman, the Soviets "decided to give a definite negative answer to the request that Prince Konoye be received.[21] This served as reassurance to the United States that the Soviet Union would follow through on its promise to enter the war, and it was yet another signal to Tokyo that peace terms could not be negotiated.

Truman's own news for Stalin on July 24—that "we had a new weapon of unusual destructive force"—was met with understated congratulations from Stalin. As Truman reported, "He was glad to hear it and hoped we would make 'good use of it against the Japanese.'"[22] Observers at the time (particularly Secretary of State Byrnes, who witnessed the exchange) interpreted Stalin's nearly casual response as ignorance about what Truman could have been referring to. However, since then it has been convincingly argued that Stalin clearly knew that Truman was talking about an atomic bomb because Soviet espionage and scientific efforts had been focusing on this technology for some time.[23] In fact, "according to Marshall Georgy Zhukov, Stalin instructed Molotov to "tell Kurchatov [of the Soviet atomic project] to hurry up the work."[24] Despite these new developments, which could have easily broken the fragile United States–Soviet Union relationship, the wartime alliance remained intact through the last days of the war. Truman shared this vital information, and Stalin kept his promise of not seeking a separate arrangement with Japan.

On that same day the President had authorized his scientists and military officials to proceed with the final development and necessary transport of the bomb. In his diary on July 25 he wrote, "This weapon is to be used against Japan between now and August 10th. I have told the Sec of War, Mr. Stimson, to use it so that military objectives and soldiers and sailors are the target and not women and children . . . and we will issue a warning statement asking the Japs to surrender and save lives. I'm sure they will not do that, but we will have given them a chance."

Consequently, on July 26 the Allies issued the Potsdam Declaration, which contained their combined expectations for the unconditional surrender of Japan. Beginning with a statement about the readiness of the United States, Britain, and China to launch "the final blows upon Japan" and a reference to how futile German resistance had been, the declaration outlined the terms for surrender. Included in those terms were the following: (1) the complete elimination of existing authority and the influence of those who "have deceived and misled the people of Japan into embarking on world conquest;" and (2) occupation of Japanese territory until "Japan's war-making power is destroyed" and "freedom of speech, of religion, and of thought as well as respect for fundamental human rights [is] established." In addition, the declaration reassured the Japanese people that the Allies had no intention of enslaving them or of destroying their nation. It appealed to the government of Japan to "proclaim now the unconditional surrender of all the Japanese armed forces, and to provide proper and adequate assurance of their good faith in such action. The alternative for Japan is complete and utter destruction."[25]

At a press conference on July 28 the prime minister of Japan, Admiral Suzuki, issued a statement regarding the Potsdam Declaration, but translations of his reaction vary. One historian recorded that Suzuki's statement was, "The Potsdam Proclemation, in my opinion, is just a rehash of the Cairo Declaration, and the government therefore does not consider it of great importance. We must *mokusatsu* it." The hisorian goes on to explain that the word *mokusatsu* literally means "kill with silence," but that Suzuki later claimed that what he meant was "no comment" for which there was no real Japanese equivalent.[26] This more benign interpretation of Japan's reaction would have left some room for further negotiation had the United States chosen to pursue it. However, U.S. officials at the time applied the more negative meaning, which was that Suzuki's intention was to "ignore" the declaration. Thus, the historical account reflecting this latter translation reads quite differently, claiming that Suzuki said, "The Government does not find any important value in it and there is no other recourse but to ignore it entirely and resolutely fight for the successful conclusion of this war."[27] This reply was not unexpected, and both Secretary of War Stimson and President Truman remained resolved to use whatever force at their disposal to force Japan to finally surrender.

Meanwhile, one million Soviet troops were amassing on the Manchurian border in preparation for Stalin's order to enter the war against Japan, and U.S. air forces had just received the U-235 portion of the weapon now being prepared for delivery against the first Japanese target. Nicknamed "Little Boy," this uranium bomb would be dropped from a special B-29 flight as soon as final authorization was received from the President and weather conditions permitted. On July 31 Truman authorized the actual use of the bomb: "Release when ready but not sooner than August 2."[28] On August 6 (Japan time) the first atomic bomb ever used in wartime against an actual target was dropped on the city of Hiroshima.

Even as the first reports of the attack were being received by Japan's Army General Staff that "the whole city of Hiroshima was destroyed instantly by a single bomb," the Japanese government was hearing over the radio President Truman's official statement: "We are now prepared to obliterate rapidly and completely every productive enterprise the Japanese have above the ground in any city. We shall destroy their docks, their factories and their communications. Let there be no mistake; we shall completely destroy Japan's power to make war. If they do not now accept our terms they may expect a rain of ruin from the air, the like of which has never been seen on this earth. . . ."[29]

THE SECOND BOMB

Japanese leaders promptly rejected that ultimatum. Confused and divided about the veracity of the President's statement, many assumed that the claim to have more atomic weapons was nothing more than typical bellicose propaganda. Some, however, including Foreign Minister Tojo, considered the situation to be perilous. On August 8 he delivered a report to Emperor Hirohito, urging him to become involved in influencing the government to accept the terms of the Potsdam Declaration. U.S. planes had also dropped millions of leaflets urging capitulation, while conventional B-29 air raids pounded Japanese targets between August 6 and August 8.[30] Meanwhile, in Moscow Japanese Ambassador Sato was finally granted a meeting on August 9 with Soviet Foreign Minister Molotov, only to be confronted with the announcement that the Soviet Union was joining the Allies in declaring war against Japan. Two hours later the Soviet army struck Japanese forces in Manchuria. The situation for Japan's government was bleak. An end to the war was now inevitable, but heated debate raged over whether the terms of the Potsdam Declaration should be accepted or whether Japan should press for negotiations. While Japanese officials remained deadlocked about what course to take, the second U.S. bomb, a plutonium bomb nicknamed "Fat Boy," was dropped on the city of Nagasaki, transforming it within minutes from a bustling industrial center to "a graveyard without a tombstone standing."[31] Confronted with the grim evidence that the Manchurian army was suffering clear defeat and that the United States truly did have more than one atomic weapon and had shown its resolve to use them, Premier Suzuki and Foreign Minister Tojo obtained the Emperor's approval for a special imperial conference with military and governmental officials. At that conference, convened hastily in the middle of the night, they presented their proposal for accepting the terms of surrender with one reservation: "*on the understanding that the Allied proclamation would not comprise any demand which would prejudice the prerogatives of His Majesty as a Sovereign Ruler.*"[32]

After hearing arguments, questions, and concerns from all sides, as well as reviewing the terms of the Potsdam Declaration, Emperor Hirohito concurred with Suzuki and Tojo that surrender was in the best interests of Japan. Visibly emotional, the Emperor explained, "I have given serious thought to the situation prevailing at home and abroad and have concluded that continuing the war can only mean destruction for the nation and a prolongation of bloodshed and cruelty in the world. I cannot bear to see my innocent people suffer any longer. Ending the war is the only way to restore world peace and to relieve the nation from the terrible distress with which it is burdened. . . . I swallow my own tears and give my sanction to the proposal to accept the Allied proclamation on the basis outlined by the Foreign Minister."[33]

This appeal to the convened members of the imperial conference had the effect Suzuki and Tojo hoped for. Following the conference a cabinet meeting was convened, which unanimously approved the Emperor's decision. By dawn on August 10 cables were dispatched to diplomatic representatives in Bern and Stockholm to then be forwarded to Washington, London, Moscow, and Chunking. In Washington, considerable attention was given to the Japanese reservation, with many advisers arguing for acceptance and others crying appeasement if the United States accepted such terms. Finally, Secretary of State Byrnes drafted an acceptable reply that rejected the Japanese condition but that offered an Allied condition in its place: "the authority of the Emperor and the Japanese Government to rule the state shall be subject to the Supreme Commander of the Allied powers. . . ."[34]

While Japanese officials considered with dismay this new clarification, the United States stepped up its propaganda efforts with the people of Japan, dropping new leaflets revealing the verbatim text of the Japanese government's proposal for accepting the terms of surrender as well as the U.S. reply. This broke the secrecy behind which the Japanese government had been deliberating and intensified pressure for a final decision. Once again the Emperor intervened to break the deadlock. "It is my desire that you, my Ministers of State, accede to my wishes and forthwith accept the Allied reply. In order that the people may know of my decision, I request you to prepare at once an imperial rescript so that I may broadcast to the nation."[35] On August 14, 1945, the war in the Pacific came to an end. Japan had surrendered.

Discussion Questions

1. What circumstances made an invasion of the Japanese home islands so daunting?
2. What was the debate among U. S. policy makers regarding a "demonstration" of the bomb?
3. What role did the atomic bombs play in the defeat of Japan?
4. What role did the atomic bombs play in U.S. relations with the Soviet Union?
5. Should the United States have used its atomic weapons (the only nation in the world to ever do so)?
6. Should the United States have used both weapons?

Notes

1. Gar Alperovitz, *Atomic Diplomacy: Hiroshima and Potsdam* (New York: Simon and Schuster, 1965), p. 106.
2. Martin J. Sherwin, *A World Destroyed: The Atomic Bomb and the Grand Alliance* (New York: Alfred A. Knopf, 1975), p. 208.
3. Robert J. C. Butow, *Japan's Decision to Surrender* (Stanford: Stanford University Press, 1954), p. 79.
4. David McCullough, *Truman* (New York: Simon and Schuster, 1992), p. 438.
5. Butow, *Japan's Decision,* pp. 83–85.
6. Ibid, p. 110.
7. McCullough, *Truman,* p. 438.
8. Ibid, p. 395.
9. Ibid, p. 438.
10. Ibid, p. 409.
11. Ibid, quoting Byrnes, p. 112.
12. Alperovitz, *Atomic Diplomacy,* pp. 107–108.
13. Ibid, p. 112. (My italics.)
14. Sherwin, *A World Destroyed,* p. 213, quoting Arthur H. Compton.

15. Ibid, p. 229.

16. Ibid, pp. 230–231.

17. Ibid, p. 223.

18. Ibid, p. 147.

19. John W. Wheeler-Bennett and Anthony Nicholls, *The Semblance of Peace: The Political Settlement After the Second World War* (London: Norton, 1974), p. 375.

20. Butow, *Japan's Decision,* p. 111.

21. Alperovitz, *Atomic Diplomacy,* pp. 184–185.

22. Sherwin, *A World Destroyed,* p. 227.

23. Wheeler-Bennett and Nicholls, *The Semblance of Peace,* pp. 372–373.

24. McCullough, *Truman,* p. 443.

25. The Potsdam Declaration quoted in Wheeler-Bennett and Nicholls, *The Semblance of Peace,* pp. 376–378.

26. John Toland, *The Rising Sun: The Decline and Fall of the Japanese Empire* (New York: Bantam Books, 1971), p. 872.

27. Ibid, p. 379.

28. McCullough, *Truman,* p. 448.

29. Butow, *Japan's Decision,* p. 151.

30. Wheeler-Bennett and Nicholls, *The Semblance of Peace,* p. 385.

31. Butow, *Japan's Decision,* p. 159.

32. Ibid, p. 173.

33. Ibid, pp. 175–176.

34. Ibid, p. 191.

35. Ibid, p. 208.

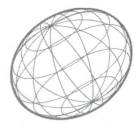

CHAPTER 4

FROM PUNISHMENT TO REHABILITATION

The Decision to Reconstruct Germany, 1943–1947

....

INTRODUCTION

The treatment of Germany at the end of the Second World War was one of the most controversial topics in the history of this century, not only because of Germany's recent past but because of Germany's vital geopolitical position in Europe at the end of the war. Moreover, the divided status of Germany from 1945 to 1990 represented the larger division of Europe between the allies of the United States in the West and the Soviet bloc in the East. To understand the origins of the Cold War between the Soviet Union and the United States and to fully appreciate the importance of Germany in the history of the past 50 years, one must understand the circumstances that surrounded the American decision to shift from its plan for Germany's punishment to a plan for embracing and reconstructing Germany.

....

WARTIME PLANS FOR DEFEATED GERMANY

Nearly two years before the United States and its allies defeated Germany in the Second World War, plans for Germany's postwar treatment were already being debated. Sentiment throughout the war had been decidedly hostile and unforgiving toward Hitler's Germany. President Roosevelt, convinced of the militaristic and authoritarian character of the German people, was particularly adamant that unconditional surrender of the German government be demanded, that no vestiges of German authority should be left to negotiate the terms of peace, and that German institutions must be dismantled so that a new society could be reared under the tutelage of Anglo-American-style liberal-democracy. His own formative experiences as a child attending school in Germany, and again in 1919 as assistant secretary to the Navy visiting the Rhineland, where U.S. troops were still stationed, influenced Roosevelt's attitude toward the Germans. He had found them to be chauvinistic and authoritarian in nature, despising all that was not German and assuming their own greatness in comparison to others.[1] The subsequent rise of the Nazi dictatorship and the ethnocentrism and brutality that followed confirmed his worst suspicions about German character and intentions. In fact, he is later quoted as saying, "Too many people here and in England hold to the view that the German people as a whole are not responsible for what has taken place—that only a few Nazi leaders are responsible. That unfortunately is not based on fact. The German people as a whole must have it driven home to them that the whole nation has been engaged in a lawless conspiracy against the decencies of modern civilization."[2]

Beyond Roosevelt himself, the lessons of the recent past were emblazoned in the minds of all the Allied statesmen. Hitler's duplicity regarding Czechoslovakia and later with the Soviet Union and the ruthlessness with which the Nazi military machine overran Europe created a strong sense of resolve toward the eradication of Nazism and German militarism and against any notion of allowing the Nazi regime to sue for peace. Ranging in terminology from exacting justice, to inflicting punishment, to preventing World War III, the combined intention of the Big Three (Roosevelt, Churchill, and Stalin) was to utterly defeat Germany and then to jointly occupy that country until all vestiges of Nazism were destroyed.

Great Britain and the Soviet Union had up to 1943 borne the direct brunt of the war in Europe. The bombing raids against British cities had come close to crippling Great Britain before the United States joined the war against Germany following the Japanese attack on Pearl Harbor in December 1941. The Soviets had an even more intimate knowledge of the ruthlessness and devastation of the German military as it swept eastward with its scorched-earth policy, killing millions of Soviet civilians in its wake. However, by 1943 the situation in Europe was looking up for the adversaries of Nazi Germany. The most important battle of the war—the Battle of Stalingrad, which raged during the cruel winter months of 1942–43—had resulted in a major defeat for German forces on the eastern front, effectively forcing them to pull back to pre-1942 lines. By May of 1943 British and American forces had eliminated the Nazis from northern Africa, giving the Allies control over the Mediterranean and allowing them to launch an offensive against Italy in July. After the overthrow of Mussolini and the assault by Allied forces up the Italian "boot," an armistice with Italy was signed. This greatly facilitated the Allied effort, because German forces had to be redirected from the eastern front to serve in Italy and in areas of the Balkans where Italian soldiers had previously been fighting, and because it allowed Allied forces to more effectively support resistance efforts against German forces in Yugoslavia.[3] Thus, when the Allied leaders met at Teheran in November 1943 the tide of the war had already turned, and many people were beginning to think about retribution, punishment, and how to keep Germany from wreaking such havoc again.

After all, many witnesses of the previous thirty years (including Roosevelt) had become convinced that Germany would rise yet again to threaten the peace of the world if it were given another chance, and public sentiment ran high in all three Allied nations (though most pronounced, as would be expected, in Britain, which had suffered from Hitler's bombing raids and especially in the Soviet Union, which had been ravaged by Hitler's armies). Reports of massive devastation and cruelty at the hands of the German military, atrocities, and concentration camps (though the full knowledge of Hitler's hideous plot to exterminate the Jews did not yet exist) fueled this sentiment, and it went without saying that the public expected its leaders to ensure not only that Germany's war-making power would be destroyed but that its war-making potential would also be kept under control.

WARTIME PLANS FOR GERMANY'S OCCUPATION

Despite a good deal of speculation about the treatment of Germany after the war, the exact character of occupation and of Germany's political-economic future was never fully specified and agreed to. When the Big Three met in Teheran in November 1943 to discuss the progress of the war in Europe and to consider postwar issues, agreement about the treatment of Germany was limited to a general commitment to unconditional surrender and what many have dubbed the four Ds: demilitarization, denazification, decartelization, and democratization.[4] In addition, the three heads of government agreed to the combined occupation of Berlin, the capital of the German Reich, along with sharing the occupation of Germany overall. While all three parties agreed in principle to the four Ds, history would demonstrate that their respective understanding of what constituted each goal varied considerably.

The Soviet understanding of democracy was radically different from that of the United States and Great Britain. Soviet expectations included socialization of the economy, including the nationalization of property and the eradication of capitalism, which they associated with German fascism. On the other hand, the United States and Great Britain expected that democratization would mean liberal democracy, with protection for individual freedoms, including property ownership and capitalism. All had considered the big German business cartels to have contributed to fascist-style economic policies and concentration of economic power in the hands of a few, and so decartelization was commonly considered an important goal, but the Soviets planned to achieve this through blanket nationalization, while the Western allies intended to use anti-trust policies to achieve a wider and more accessible means of property ownership.

Denazification also proved to be somewhat ambiguous. The Soviets consistently held a harsher and clearly Marxist view, again associating Nazism with capitalist extremism, and, therefore, planning from the beginning to strip Germany of its association with capitalist institutions as well as destroying the Nazi superstructure. On the other hand, Churchill and Roosevelt shared the view that capitalist institutions could be reformed within a liberal democratic framework. Stalin also took a broad view regarding which Nazis were to be severely punished——not just Nazi leadership and those involved in war crimes— but to include, for example, the execution of "100,000 members of the German officers corps."[5] Roosevelt and Churchill were also committed to the eradication of the vestiges of Nazism, including the punishment of Nazis throughout Germany and the reeducation of the German people, and Roosevelt tended to share Stalin's more extreme view in this regard. However, Churchill held the position that punishment should fit the crime, and he recognized that many people who were technically Nazis were not necessarily criminals. While Stalin and Roosevelt tended to indict the entire German population, Churchill did not.

The most evident divisions that appeared between the wartime allies at Teheran concerned the issues of dismemberment and reparations. Roosevelt and Stalin both preferred the indefinite dismemberment of Germany into several administrative units, their rationale being that so divided Germany would never have the potential strength to rise again as a threat to world peace. Churchill, who all along seemed wary of the power vacuum that the disappearance of Germany would create in central Europe, opposed this plan. Roosevelt was not naive regarding the potential for the extension of Soviet power. In fact, he was convinced that Stalin wanted domination of Eastern Europe in order to provide the Soviet Union with security against some potential future attack from Germany, but his view was that "if German disarmament could be guaranteed, Soviet interest in Eastern Europe would wane." Therefore, the best policy against Soviet aggression in the area would be the harsh occupation of Germany, which would reassure the Soviets about U.S. intentions and about the future security of the Soviet Union.[6] In the end, because Roosevelt was uncomfortable with becoming too involved in making postwar plans while Germany's defeat was still not completed, Germany's ultimate status under occupation was put off for further study, and this was assigned to the European Advisory Commission (EAC), which consisted of delegates from the governments of the Big Three charged with examining a number of issues regarding postwar global cooperation.

On the issue of reparations the Soviets found themselves alone (although later, once France had been liberated and Germany's defeat was imminent, France would also demand reparations). At Teheran Stalin made clear his expectation that the Soviet Union deserved at the very least German machinery to replace the industry that Germany had destroyed in its invasion of Soviet territory.[7] He wanted Roosevelt and Churchill to agree to this right to reparations, but this too was put off for later consideration, because both Churchill and Roosevelt were reluctant to force Germany to pay reparations. Their reluctance, however, was not due to strong humanitarian objections. Both Churchill and Roosevelt were concerned about the impact of reparations on their respective countries' ability to finance postwar occupation. If Germany were forced, like it had been after World War I, to pay extensive reparations—in kind or in hard currency—it would mean that the occupying powers would in all probability have the added burden of financing those reparations while also maintaining German subsistence. Neither leader wanted to saddle his nation with such a heavy responsibility. Britain simply could not afford it, and this would leave the United States as the only nation with an economy strong enough to finance Germany's debts. This prospect was not in the least attractive to Roosevelt, who knew that the American public would have little patience for supporting such an albatross. On Roosevelt's part, there was also his commitment to the American public that U.S. soldiers would not remain in Europe once demilitarization and denazification were completed.[8]

Yet, despite the differences that were emerging by the end of 1943 over the postwar treatment of Germany, the commitment to unconditional surrender and demilitarization remained firm on all sides. And while Roosevelt continued to be reluctant to spend his time considering the particulars of occupation policy, it was becoming clear among his advisers that some plan of action should be formulated. In Eastern Europe Stalin's forces had already turned the tide of the war by defeating the German army in the pivotal Battle of Stalingrad (winter 1942–43) , and Soviet forces had begun to make serious advances toward the west. Consideration of occupation policy became even more pressing after the Western Allies launched a second-front offensive on the beaches of Normandy in June 1944, effectively pressing the German military between the vices of advancing Allied troops. Finally, Germany's defeat was within sight, and it became time to consider postwar policies.

Thus, by the summer of 1944 there were basically three different U.S. policy sources for postwar planning regarding German occupation: the U.S. State Department, which had long been considering the shape of the world after the war; the European Advisory Council (EAC), which had drawn up a draft document concerning Germany's surrender at the instruction of the Allies; and General Eisenhower's Supreme Headquarters, Allied Expeditionary Forces (SHAEF), which had also completed a guide to occupation known as the "Handbook for Military Government in Germany." The U.S. State Department's proposals for the treatment of Germany after the war were predicated upon the belief that a prosperous global economy, fully recovered from the disruptions and devastations of World War II, depended in part upon the emergence of a prosperous postwar Germany. While it also noted the importance of demilitarization, the State Department proposal was mostly concerned with rehabilitation of the German economy as a requisite for European and then global recovery. The EAC's draft document, based in part on British proposals for the physical occupation of Germany, specified that there be three zones of occupation and that the Soviets occupy the eastern zone, the British the northwest zone, and the Americans the southwest zone. Berlin, as had been agreed by the Big Three at Teheran, would also be divided among the three allies for purposes of occupation. In addition the EAC document "provided for the disarming of Germany but left unsettled the question of the disposition of prisoners of war. It proclaimed the Allies as supreme political authorities in Germany and announced that they would impose 'political, administrative, economic, financial, military and other requirements,'" though details of occupation beyond the terms of surrender were not explored.[9] The "Handbook for Military Government in Germany" dealt most directly, as one would expect, with the day-to-day policies for military occupation. It stated that the "armies were to preserve the centralized German administrative system, and to retain and rehabilitate enough light and heavy industry to make Germany self-supporting and also to keep the whole European economy on 'a reasonably even keel.' The Germans, moreover, were to have a relatively high standard of living, including an average food supply of 2000 calories per person per day. . . ."[10]

Apparently, then, there was no single coordinated effort in U.S. policy-making circles to plan systematically for Germany's occupation, but despite Roosevelt's own preference for the harsh treatment of Germany, as well as the general tenor of Roosevelt's and Stalin's discussions about denazification at Teheran, none of the policies that were being formulated were particularly strict. In fact, their one common feature seemed to be the absence of any plan to dismantle the German economy. This caught the attention of Secretary of the Treasury Henry Morgenthau, who, more than any other ranking cabinet member, shared Roosevelt's prejudice toward the German people and felt compelled to devise a plan more in keeping with what he believed Roosevelt wanted and what he personally believed was necessary to preserve peace in the future. He "considered the elimination of Nazism the first requisite for a peaceful and democratic world, [and] that belief hardened in 1943 with his intimate involvement, for the first time in the fate of the European Jews."[11] Himself a Jew, he was horrified and angered by the atrocities that were revealed in his investigation of Nazi actions, and like Roosevelt, he had come to believe that there was inherent within Germany a tendency toward aggression and a lack of contrition for the crimes it had committed against others. He had become convinced that Germany's evil and militaristic aggressiveness could only be thwarted by the use of vigilant counter-measures aimed at preventing German resurgence.

This view was amplified during his visit to England in the late summer of 1944, when he saw first hand the deadly devastation rained upon London by the German air force and (while he was there) by the V-1 bombs . He was touched deeply by what he saw of British suffering, and very impressed with British resilience in the face of such terror and disruption. As he recalled in his diary:

> Going into these shelters in England, I just can't tell you. . . . There was one family there that had no home and they had been there for six weeks, living there. . . . I saw one mother with five children. I saw another mother with an eight-month-old baby. . . . But the spirit of those people!

The costs in human life at the hands of Nazi aggression and the necessary effort underway to defeat this horrible enemy were abhorrent to Morgenthau, who now felt compelled to devise his own plan for postwar Germany, a plan that would ensure that the German military machine would never again be set in motion. Consequently, on his return from London he set about informing the President about what he had learned and formulating, with the assistance of his Treasury staff, the prescription for the punitive treatment of Germany that came to be known as the "Morgenthau Plan."

Upon his arrival back in Washington, Morgenthau met with Roosevelt to inform him about the State Department study (also known as the Acheson-Pasvolsky memorandum) and to verify the President's commitment to a harsh treatment of Germany upon defeat. According to Morgenthau's recollection of that conversation, he told the President that nobody "has been studying how to treat Germany roughly along the lines you wanted," and Roosevelt replied, "We have got to be tough with Germany and I mean the German people not just the Nazis. We either have to castrate the German people or you have got to treat them in such manner so they can't just go on reproducing people who want to continue the way they have in the past."[12] Armed with the President's intention to be "tough with the Germans," Morgenthau personally oversaw the formulation of the Treasury report on the treatment of Germany. This report focused primarily on Germany's industrial capability as the essential ingredient that had allowed a militaristic people to rise from defeat in World War I and create the aggressive military capability that had caused World War II. Drawing from a number of well-known proponents of punitive treatment of Germany, Treasury officials justified their plan (even though at times staff members did not fully agree) with the premise that the German menace could be thwarted only if it were stripped of its underlying capability to make war. The future peace of the world depended on such a plan.

Morgenthau wanted a plan that called for the removal of "all industry from Germany and simply reducing them to an agricultural population of small land-owners." His view was that a pastoralized Germany would never have the means to wage war, and it would also provide a kind of Jeffersonian-style fertile ground for the eventual emergence of democracy in Germany. When Secretary of War Stimson, the most vocal opponent of the Morgenthau Plan within the administration, protested this as not being realistic for such a large population, and that to return Germany to an 1860-type existence would require taking "a lot of people out of Germany," Morgenthau countered, "Well, that is not nearly as bad as sending them to gas chambers."[13] At the heart of his plan was the destruction of the industrial and mining capacity of the Ruhr region. And when Harry Hopkins, Roosevelt's chief adviser, suggested an alternative possibility of "making the Ruhr an industrial area under international control which will produce reparations for twenty years," Morgenthau rejected the idea completely, arguing that "you have it [the international region] there only so many years and you have an Anschluss and the Germans go in and take it. The only thing you can sell me, or I will have any part of, is the complete shut-down of the Ruhr. . . . Just strip it. I don't care what happens to the population. . . . I would take every mine, every mill and factory and wreck it. . . . Steel, coal, everything."[14] To achieve this, he maintained, the Army engineers should go "into every steel mill, in every coal mine, every chemical plan, every synthetic gas business . . . and put dynamite in and open the water valves and flood and dynamite."[15]

When the plan, which was officially called the "Program to Prevent Germany from Starting World War III," was fully formulated in September 1944, it called for just that, the total removal or destruction of "all war material, the total destruction of the whole Germany armament industry, and the removal or destruction of other key industries which are basic to military strength." Moreover, the plan proposed that France should be given outright the "Saar and adjacent territories bounded by the Rhine and Moselle rivers, and an international zone was to contain the Ruhr and its surrounding territory." Poland would receive parts of eastern Germany and Silesia, and the Soviet Union would receive territory it claimed in Eastern Prussia. The rest of Germany would be divided into two states, north and south, and this would be achieved through "the military occupation as a step toward an eventual partitioning of the country." To enforce these arrangements, "for a period of at least twenty years after the surrender of Germany, the United Nations were to maintain controls over foreign trade and capital imports. Those controls were to prevent the establishment or expansion of key industries 'basic to the German military potential.'" [16]

Finally, the plan continued to reject the idea of reparations, recognizing that to force reparations upon a deindustrialized Germany would be unrealistic and would merely add to the burden of the occupying nations. In Morgenthau's view this plan directly coincided with what he believed President Roosevelt wanted, and it is true that when concerns about the realities of feeding the German people during occupation were raised, Roosevelt wrote that "if they need food to keep body and soul together beyond what they have, they should be fed three times a day with soup from Army soup kitchens. That will keep them perfectly healthy and they will remember the experience all their lives. The fact that they are a defeated nation, collectively and individually, must be so impressed upon them that they will hesitate to start any new war. . . ."[17] Thus, when Roosevelt met with Churchill in Quebec in mid-September 1944 to discuss Lend-Lease arrangements and other plans regarding the alliance, he asked Morgenthau to accompany him to present his plan to the prime minister.

However, Churchill's reaction was not at all what Morgenthau and the President expected. According to Morgenthau's account,

> I had barely got under way before low mutters and baleful looks indicated that the Prime Minister was not the most enthusiastic member of my audience. . . . I have never seen him more irascible and vitriolic than he was that night. . . . After I finished my piece he turned loose on me the full flood of his rhetoric, sarcasm and violence. He looked on the Treasury Plan, he said, as he would on chaining himself to a dead German. He was slumped in his chair, his language biting, his flow incessant, his manner merciless. I have never had such a verbal lashing in my life.[18]

After Morgenthau left the dinner for his room, Roosevelt, who was very good at cajoling agreement when agreement seemed unlikely, spent part of the evening convincing Churchill that he should consider the plan for the sake of future peace in Europe and for Britain's own sake as an industrial nation whose exports of coal and steel could directly benefit from the removal of German competition.

The next day the prime minister asked that a text of Morgenthau's plan be prepared so he could clarify a number of points and so that a memorandum on the subject could be drafted and signed by the two heads of government. According to Churchill's own account, which also noted his initial reaction,

> . . . I was glad to see Morgenthau, as we were anxious to discuss financial arrangements between our two countries. . . . The President and his Secretary of the Treasury were, however, much more concerned about the treatment of

Germany after the war. They felt very strongly that military strength rested on industrial strength. We had seen during the nineteen thirties how easy it was for a highly industrialized Germany to arm herself and threaten her neighbours, and they asserted that there was no need for so much manufacturing in a country as large as Germany, which could to all intents and purposes feed herself. The United Kingdom had lost so many overseas investments that she could only pay her way when peace came by greatly increasing her exports, so that for economic as well as military reasons we ought to restrict German industry and encourage German agriculture. At first I violently opposed this idea. But the President, with Mr. Morgenthau—from whom we had much to ask—were so insistent that in the end we agreed to consider it.

Churchill went on to clarify, however, that

> The so-called Morgenthau Plan, which I had not time to examine in detail, seems to have carried these ideas to an ultra-logical conclusion. Even if it had been practicable I do not think it would have been right to depress Germany's standard of life in such a way; but at that time, when German militarism based on German industry had done such appalling damage to Europe, it did not seem unfair to agree that her manufacturing capacity need not be revived beyond what was needed to give her the same standards of life as her neighbors.[19]

Still, Churchill was willing to sign with President Roosevelt on September 15, 1944, the "Quebec Memorandum" on postwar treatment of Germany in which they jointly expressed their view that,

> The ease with which the metallurgical, chemical and electrical industries in Germany can be converted from peace to war has already been impressed upon us by bitter experience. It must also be remembered that the Germans have devastated a large portion of the industries of Russia and of other neighboring Allies, and it is only accordance with justice that these injured countries should be entitled to remove the machinery they require in order to repair the losses they have suffered. The industries referred to in the Ruhr and in the Saar would therefore be necessarily put out of action and closed down. It was felt that the two districts should be put under somebody under the world organization which would supervise the dismantling of these industries and make sure that they were not started up again by some subterfuge. The program for eliminating the war-making industries in the Ruhr and in the Saar is looking forward to converting Germany into *a country primarily agricultural and pastoral in its character.*[20]

Many analysts assumed that Churchill was persuaded more by his country's dependency on the United States for Lend-Lease aid than he was by the logic of the Morgenthau Plan, which his own account above seems to support. Moreover, the reaction of his own cabinet was yet to be seen. Nevertheless, as the two leaders left Quebec, and as the United States and Great Britain moved into the last eight months of the war in Europe, it appeared that, despite Churchill's misgivings, the most likely U.S. plan for Germany's occupation would be the one drafted by the Treasury Department under Henry Morgenthau's direction.

DEBATE OVER THE MORGENTHAU PLAN

The matter was not so easily settled, however, because the Morgenthau Plan received considerable criticism, particularly from Secretary of War Henry Stimson, who had always opposed such punitive treatment, and also from other sources within and outside the government. Most problematic for the Roosevelt administration was the criticism leveled by New York Governor Thomas E. Dewey, Roosevelt's Republican opponent in the upcoming presidential election in November. Almost immediately upon his return from Quebec Roosevelt was met with an onslaught of vocal repudiation of the Morgenthau Plan. Opponents were charging that its harsh provisions were costing American lives in the assault on German forces because Germans had redoubled their resistance to Allied forces in the face of the plan's threats. While most historians agree that the battlefield situation had temporarily turned in the favor of Germany before the Morgenthau Plan was leaked, it was true that in Germany the radio was broadcasting that "Morgenthau wants to see 43,000,000 Germans exterminated."[21] Much was made of this by the press and by candidate Dewey, but under political fire Roosevelt remained publicly mute on the subject.

In the meantime at the White House, Stimson was demanding from the President why such a memorandum regarding the postwar treatment of Germany had been released, and Roosevelt blamed it on Morgenthau, saying that "he had no idea how he could have initialed this; that he had evidently done it without much thought."[22] It is unclear whether Roosevelt genuinely did not recall or if he was sidestepping responsibility. By the fall of 1944 he was becoming quite frail and tired, and despite his rather energetic campaign against Dewey, it was clear to all those around him that he was not well. Regardless, if Roosevelt was anything he was politically astute, and in the wake of such strong opposition he turned away from the Morgenthau Plan. It appears from many of his subsequent conversations that he still intended to have a stern occupation policy, but by October 1944 it was clear that the plan to indefinitely pastoralize Germany had become a dead letter. Yet, as had been Roosevelt's preference before Quebec, the particulars of postwar occupation policy were again shelved by the White House, and the only specific policy that existed to take the place of the Morgenthau Plan was directive 1067, issued by the Joint Chiefs of Staff in September for Eisenhower's military command. Influenced significantly by Morgenthau in the planning process during the summer of 1944, JCS 1067 "emphasized treating Germany as a defeated, not a liberated, nation. American military authorities would do nothing to rehabilitate the German economy except to avoid disease or disorder that might threaten occupation forces." In addition there was to be extensive "denazification" efforts, "including the arrest of all Nazis and Nazi sympathizers, down to and including local party and government authorities."[23] General Lucius Clay, who was later put in charge of U.S. military occupation in Germany, and who was required to administer policy as prescribed by JCS 1067, explained the directive as follows:

By the provisions of JCS/1067 Germany was to be occupied as a defeated nation under a just, firm, and aloof administration which would discourage any fraternization. The German economy was to be controlled only to the extent necessary to meet the needs of the occupation forces or to produce the goods which would prevent disease and unrest, which might endanger the occupying forces.[24]

Thus while there was no established Allied plan for occupation and no official White House and Downing Street policy, there was a general blueprint for the U.S. military in its own zone of occupation—a blueprint that emphasized stern treatment and a bare minimum economy. At the diplomatic level, however, the U.S. Department of State continued to assert its view that Germany's economy should not be destroyed, and in preparing President Roosevelt for his upcoming meeting with Stalin and Churchill in January 1945 the State Department stressed the need for centralized administration of Germany to "ensure that the industrialized parts of Germany under Anglo-American control would receive badly needed food shipments from the predominantly agricultural Soviet Zone." The State Department also "called for reducing, but not destroying, the German industrial plan in order to prevent rearmament and provide reparations."[25]

Within two months of winning his fourth term as president of the United States, Roosevelt attended his last summit meeting with Churchill and Stalin at the Crimean resort of Yalta in the Soviet Union. Besides achieving Stalin's commitment to enter the war against Japan once Hitler was defeated, Roosevelt also sought some commitment on the status of those countries that had been liberated by the Allied armies. In principle, the three agreed to self-determination and democracy for these nations, yet disagreements over Poland (as well as Soviet army actions in the liberation of Poland) made the Western Allies increasingly nervous about Soviet designs in Eastern Europe. The Big Three also discussed again how Germany was to be treated, and while they remained in agreement on dismemberment, the exact boundaries were left for further study with proposals to be made by their foreign ministers. It was also agreed that France would have a zone of occupation to be carved out of the British and American zones. Finally, the Soviets again raised the issue of reparations. It was agreed that the Soviets would be allowed to remove industrial plants as reparations in kind for a period of not more than ten years, but the Soviet demand for $20 million as well was met with resistance, and again the three leaders agreed to postpone a final decision pending an examination by a special commission assigned to ascertain the feasibility of forcing Germany to pay reparations.[26] However, Roosevelt did agree that $20 million in reparations was a figure that could be negotiated, signaling his general willingness to cooperate with the Soviets on this issue, and demonstrating his final rejection of the Morgenthau Plan.

THE REALITIES OF OCCUPATION

Just over two months later, on April 12, 1945, President Roosevelt died, leaving to his successor, Harry S. Truman, and to the military commanders in Europe the final defeat and full occupation of Germany. Not included in Roosevelt's inner circle of advisers, Truman worked diligently to become informed about America's policy toward defeated Germany, and he was increasingly troubled by the occupation plan. After Germany's unconditional surrender on May 8, 1945, Truman began to openly disagree with Morgenthau's view regarding a number of the harsher points of JCS 1067, and in July he made it clear that he "had always opposed the Morgenthau Plan."[27] He thought punitive treatment of Germany was counterproductive, committing the same errors that had made the Versailles Treaty such a disaster 26 years earlier, and he began to encourage a less austere program instead.

The experience of the U.S. military in Germany was also influencing a change in this direction. U.S. commanders were becoming more and more convinced that policy makers had underestimated the amount of damage that had been inflicted on Germany, and this was putting pressure on the U. S. government to reconsider its plans. The realities of occupying Germany and feeding and housing its people were far grimmer than Washington had expected, and at a minimum it was realized that the American military would have to import vast amounts of food just to maintain the German diet at the subsistence level of 1,500 calories per day set by JCS 1067. For example, "in the summer of 1945 the total amount of foodstuffs obtainable on rations coupons for each inhabitant of Hamburg (which was part of the British zone) amounted to a little more than a thousand calories per day."[28]

Like the State Department advisers who had argued for a centralized administration, the U.S. military complained that in the absence of a centralized administration of postwar Germany, the American and British zones could not possibly feed the populations for which they were responsible, and in order to import the food that would be required they would have to "prime Germany industry—something they were not permitted by policy to do—so that it could eventually produce exports to offset import payments." [29] Increasingly, the Americans in Germany were becoming convinced that to strip Germany of its industrial capability would be to commit the German people to starvation and themselves to an impossible task. At the same time Truman's advisers were worried that if the Western Allies did not agree to Soviet demands for reparations, the Soviets would deny food shipments from their more agriculturally based zones to the Western zones of occupation. The Reparations Commission that had been assigned the task at Yalta of resolving the reparations issue had failed to do so, and in the meantime the Soviets were already removing industrial plant and other materials from their zone of occupation.[30] In fact, they were very systematic in their extraction of reparations. "Working from lists prepared in Moscow, Russian reparation teams roamed over the Soviet zone dismantling (and shipping to the Soviet Union) everything from scores of factories (such as the Zeiss optical works and Opel car assembly plants) to thousands of bathtubs."[31] France, too, was moved by the attitude that what it had suffered at the hands of the Germans warranted compensation in the form of industrial plant from the zone it was given, and it moved immediately to extract that compensation.

For his part Truman was very concerned about repeating the mistakes made at Versailles, where harsh reparations had not only crippled Germany but had put the entire capitalist world into severe economic difficulties. Moreover, he did not want to put the United States in the position of having to guarantee Germany's reparations to the Soviet Union when Germany did not have the capacity to meet her obligations.[32] Thus, by the time the new President met with Stalin and Churchill (who was replaced by Clement

Atlee by an election at home in mid-conference) to discuss the final arrangements for Germany in late July 1945, he had already decided to alter the U.S. position on the German economy. Eventual reconstruction rather than indefinite repression would be the goal of the United States, and this cast U.S. occupation policy (and its position at Potsdam) in an entirely new light. The welfare of the German people under American responsibility now became a priority, and this was reflected most obviously in the debate at Potsdam with the Soviets regarding reparations. The United States and Britain insisted that reparations from their zones to the Soviet Union would be allowed only after "imports essential to maintain the German economy had been paid for."[33] This was also important to the American and British taxpayers, who would be the ones who would have to pay if Germany could not. After much discussion Secretary of State Byrnes offered a compromise that retained the British and American insistence on zonal self-sufficiency before reparations would be paid, but did recognize the right of the Soviets and Poles to transfer capital equipment from the Soviet zone and to receive "25 percent of the capital equipment declared [after study] to be surplus in the other three zones."[34]

At Potsdam the wartime Allies also established the legal and economic status of Germany and of Berlin, whose sovereignty and economic administration would be held indefinitely in the hands of the Four Allied Powers. (France being included at the behest of the British and Americans even though it was not present at the negotiations.) The Allies affirmed the Yalta intention that administrative policy for Germany as a whole would be made by the Allied Control Council sitting in Berlin. This, the Americans hoped, would make it easier for interzonal trade to occur, especially for freer movement of food from the Soviet zone into the Western zones. Article 14 of the Potsdam Agreement stated that "During the period of occupation Germany shall be treated as a single economic unit. To this end common policies shall be established in regard to . . . (d) import and export programs for Germany as a whole; (e) currency and banking, central taxation, and customs; (f) reparations and removal of industrial war potential. . . ."[35] However, each zone's decision-making autonomy over the denazification and demilitarization process as well as eventual reconstruction was preserved, thereby creating a somewhat ambiguous document regarding cooperative decision making. Disagreements over centralized economic policy versus decentralized decision making plagued relations between the United States and Britain on the one hand, who favored a higher degree of cooperation, and the Soviet Union and France on the other hand, who continued to insist on full autonomy within their own zones.

The American and British position on this point was further buttressed by two influential studies that were launched after the Potsdam conference to determine Germany's actual economic situation and its needs in the post surrender situation. The first produced a report that was completed in September 1945 by the German Standard of Living Board, a board under American military administration in Berlin. Dubbed the Hoover Report after its chairman Calvin Hoover, it estimated the German standard of living under the terms of Potsdam, projecting it at "about 74 percent of the 1930–38 average, or 'roughly equivalent to that which actually existed in Germany in 1932,' the worst year of the economic depression."[36] With losses of food-production areas to Poland and Russia, it was determined that Germany would have to import extensively and that this would cause a serious trade deficit. Its pessimistic conclusion was that,

. . . the conflict between an extreme degree of industrial disarmament spread over a number of key industries and the goal of maintaining a minimum German standard of living according to the assumed formula while providing for the costs of occupying forces seems insoluble under conditions such as those brought about by losses of territory.[37]

The second study, commissioned by President Truman directly, was even more compelling for revision of U.S. occupation policies as well as for central administration. Submitted in November to the President by a trusted associate, Byron Price, this study emphasized the need for German exports from the Western zones to finance "indispensable food imports," saying that "the United States . . . had to decide whether it wanted to withdraw from Germany or whether it wanted to supply the tools and funds needed to do a thorough job there. It had to decide whether it would permit starvation, epidemics, and disorders or whether it would ship in the food to prevent them." It also recommended that the daily caloric ration be increased from 1,550 to "at least 2,000 calories" to prevent disease and disorder and that basically the United States "had to decide how far denazification and industrial destruction would go."[38] These reports had the effect of further convincing military headquarters in Berlin and the White House that the principle of centralized administration established at Potsdam had to be pressed, and that better cooperation among the zonal authorities had to be achieved in order to avert the worst of economic chaos and physical deprivation.

However, the Soviet and French positions continued to obstruct a more effective Allied Control Council administration, and the United States and Britain were growing more and more pessimistic about their ability to maintain even the most meager standard of living in their respective zones. By the first of the year in 1946, the United States and Britain had begun to directly import foodstuffs into their zones from outside Germany, even though this still did not provide an adequate supply. In fact, General Lucius Clay, U.S. commander in charge of German occupation, announced in March that the U.S. military was forced to reduce the daily calorie ration to 1,275 because the food supply was so short despite U.S. imports.[39] This was clearly also pressuring administrators in the Western zones to seek some way of paying for the imports. American intentions regarding this problem were foreshadowed in a U.S. State Department policy statement issued in January, which notified the world that the United States did not intend to keep the German economy limited permanently. While this did not depart from the principles of the Potsdam Agreement, it did signal the possibility that reconstruction might begin to occur more quickly than had been envisioned months before, and it meant that the ongoing industrial dismantling process would have to be reconciled with the new policy orientation.

REVISION AND RECONSTRUCTION

This was a very important factor, because both JCS 1067 and the Potsdam Agreement pledged the occupying powers to reduce Germany's industrial capacity (and to transfer industrial plant to the Soviet Union to fulfill reparations arrangements), and the United States had a list of over 1,200 factories that were to be dismantled as the first major step toward this goal. However, even as the Allied military was working its way slowly down the list, General Clay decided in May to halt all dismantling operations. Prompted, some argue, by Clay's disgust with the Soviets for dismantling a much needed food-processing plant and removing it from the American zone, the halt was clearly aimed at preventing further transfers of industry to the Soviets when people in the Western zones were on the brink of starvation. Clay "objected," he says, "to financing reparations to the Soviet zone and to stripping the American zone of its already insufficient capacity 'without getting the benefits which would come from amalgamation of all zones.'"[40] Moreover, the Soviets had refused to provide the other Allies with an accounting of the in-kind reparations they were taking, and according to Clay, this was the final straw.[41] This resulted in a major rift with the Soviet Union, which vehemently protested that the United States had reneged on its agreement at Potsdam.

Soviet protests did not sway the United States, however, and it proceeded to take a more and more sympathetic view toward western Germany and to turn its back on further attempts at cooperation with the Soviets. Somewhat unhappy with administrative inefficiencies in the British zone, but also convinced that more central administration was necessary to enable Germany's recovery, U.S. leaders proposed the creation of a single British-American administrative zone of occupation, and this was established in January 1947. Bizonia, as it came to be called, allowed better economic coordination, but it also heightened tensions with the Soviets, who saw capitalist Britain and America joining together against their interests.

Suspicions were not one-sided. Within the American State Department a great deal of thought during the previous year had been devoted to relations with the Soviet Union. Postwar difficulties over Poland, the character of Soviet liberation in Eastern Europe, and the general lack of cooperation in Germany, all combined to make American policy makers distrustful of Soviet intentions. In particular, an interpretation by George Kennan, a senior State Department official and chargé d'affaires in Moscow in 1946, was gaining ascendancy. His view, which was shared with the State Department (just days after Stalin made his infamous speech regarding the incompatibility between capitalism and communism), was that the Soviet Union considered itself engaged in a relentless struggle with the capitalist world, a struggle in which it would press its advantages whenever and wherever it could. Accordingly, no opportunity would "be missed to reduce strength and influence, collectively as well as individually, of capitalist powers. Soviet efforts, and those of Russia's friends abroad, must be directed toward deepening and exploiting of differences and conflicts between capitalist powers. If these eventually deepen into an 'imperialist' war, this war must be turned into revolutionary upheavals within the various capitalist countries."[42] The implication of this assessment was fundamentally that the United States and its allies must resolutely resist the tentacles of communism by first understanding that the threat lay wherever there was division and unrest. The real question was what this interpretation implied for U.S. policy in Germany.

The answer was not hard to deduce from a capitalist point of view. In October 1946, speaking before an audience in Stuttgart, Germany, Secretary of State Byrnes had announced that the United States was beginning the process of reconstructing its zone of occupation (soon to be joined with Britain's), and in making that decision it was setting aside its wartime plans for decartelization and moving toward the resurrection of a market economy.[43] If the risk in Europe was Soviet exploitation of economic weaknesses and unrest, the quickest way to stabilize Germany would be through the revitalization of its economy. From the Soviet point of view this announcement confirmed their deepest suspicions about capitalist bedfellows and the ultimate unwillingness of the Americans to restructure the German economy, even though the cartels had clearly played a role in the Nazi dictatorship. German-wide cooperation between the Soviet Union and its Western Allies, never very strong, had weakened beyond the point of resuscitation.

Following the harshest winter in Europe in 50 years (1946–47), the situation in Germany and elsewhere in Western Europe remained bleak, and policy makers were increasingly concerned about the stability of democratic governments. The growing influence of Communist Party members in France and Italy, as well as Communist insurrections in Greece and Turkey, convinced the State Department that a major foreign-policy initiative was required to prevent Communist insurgency and expansion. In March 1947 President Truman announced the "Truman Doctrine," a military-oriented policy aimed at preventing the spread of communism. Prompted by Great Britain's request for the United States to replace it in its efforts to prevent Communist take-overs in Greece and Turkey, Truman's policy assured pro-Western governments that the United States would intervene militarily if necessary to thwart communism.

Then, at the beginning of June Truman's new secretary of state, George Marshall, announced an ambitious new policy aimed at strengthening the economies of the United States' Western European allies. In his speech before a Harvard commencement audience, Marshall not only emphasized the serious economic plight of the Western European nations, but also stressed the importance of helping these nations achieve "the return of normal economic health . . . without which there could be no political stability."[44] This new policy, which came to be known as the "Marshall Plan," consisted of an extensive aid package ($4 million) aimed at assisting the recovery of Europe, a set of cooperative arrangements with the recipient nations involving the guarantee of market structures, and an agreement with France and Britain to include West Germany in the full recovery effort. This was a price that France was reluctant to pay but one that it agreed to in exchange for American aid and for the future prospect of benefiting from the integration of portions of its economy with West Germany.

....

CONCLUSION

Thus, within two years of Germany's defeat, the United States had not only reconsidered its original plans to cripple Germany's economy, it had placed Germany's reconstruction at the center of its policy to contain Soviet influence and to rebuild Western Europe. Instead of pastoralizing Germany and neutralizing its industrial potential, the United States encouraged West Germany's revitalization and enjoined Germany's neighbors to embrace it in an integrated European community. By 1949 the Western zones of occupation were combined in the emergence of a semi-sovereign state, the Federal

Republic of Germany, whose international status remained constrained by the Potsdam Agreements until it was reunified with East Germany in 1990. The very symbol of cold war divisions, West Germany's separation from East Germany was solidified in 1955 when it was allowed to rearm within the framework of the North Atlantic Treaty Organization (NATO), the United States' foremost defensive alliance. This pivotal decision to embrace West Germany and make it the keystone of postwar European recovery is one of the most pivotal policy occurrences in 20th-century history, because it set the global, as well as European, geopolitical stage for the next four and a half decades.

Discussion Questions

1. What prompted the American decision to revise its policy toward dismantling German industry, and how did this affect U.S.-Soviet cooperation?
2. How were events in Germany and elsewhere in Europe affecting the American view toward Germany, and what does this tell us about how foreign policy plans are altered?
3. What was the essence of George Kennan's analysis of Soviet intentions after the war, and how might Kennan's views have affected U.S. foreign policy?
4. How did Truman differ from Roosevelt with regard to the treatment of Germany, and what does this example tell us about the role of personalities in the direction of foreign policy?
5. How did the decisions on Germany's postwar treatment affect the emergence of the Cold War?

Notes

1. John Lewis Gaddis, *The United States and the Origins of the Cold War, 1941–1947* (New York: Columbia University Press, 1972), pp. 99–100.
2. John Morton Blum, *From the Morgenthau Diaries: Years of War 1941-1945* (Boston: Houghton Mifflin, 1967), p. 349.
3. Felix Gilbert and David Clay Large, *The End of the European Era, 1980 to the Present* (New York: W. W. Norton, 1991), pp. 339–345.
4. Dietrich Orlow, *A History of Modern Germany: 1871 to Present* (Englewood Cliffs: Prentice Hall, 1991), p. 241.
5. Gaddis, *Origins of the Cold War,* p. 100.
6. Ibid, pp. 100–101.
7. Blum, *From the Morgenthau Diaries,* p. 329.
8. Churchill reported that at Yalta, a few months later, Roosevelt announced that he would not consider an occupation period longer than two years after Germany's defeat—that keeping a large American army in Europe "three thousand miles away from home" was too high a price to pay for long-term peace. Winston S. Churchill, *Triumph and Tragedy* (New York: Bantam Books, 1953), p. 303.

9. Blum, quoting the EAC proposal, *From the Morgenthau Diaries,* p 330.

10. Ibid, p. 331.

11. Ibid, p. 332.

12. Ibid, quoting Morgenthau's Diary, p. 342.

13. Ibid, p. 344.

14. Ibid, p. 354.

15. Ibid, p. 355.

16. Ibid, pp. 356–358.

17. Quoting Roosevelt, Ibid, p. 349.

18. Ibid, p. 369.

19. Churchill, *Triumph and Tragedy,* pp. 133–134.

20. Text of the Quebec Memorandum quoted by Blum, *From the Morgenthau Diaries,* pp. 371–372.

21. Frank Friedel, *Franklin D. Roosevelt: A Rendezvous with Destiny* (Boston: Little, Brown and Co., 1990), p. 560.

22. Freidel, *Franklin D Roosevelt,* p. 561.

23. Gaddis, *Origins of the Cold War,* p. 123.

24. Lucius D. Clay, *Decision in Germany* (Garden City, N.Y.: Doubleday and Co., 1950), p. 17.

25. Ibid, pp. 126–127.

26. Churchill, *Triumph and Tragedy,* pp. 302–303.

27. Gaddis, *Origins of the Cold War,* p 238.

28. Orlow, *A History of Modern Germany,* p 249.

29. John Gimbel, *The American Occupation of Germany: Politics and the Military, 1945–1949* (Stanford: Stanford University Press) p. 13.

30. Gaddis, *Origins of the Cold War,* p. 239.

31. Orlow, *A History of Modern Germany,* p. 246.

32. Harry S. Truman, *Year of Decisions* (Garden City, N.Y.: Double Day and Co., 1955), p. 323.

33. Ibid, p. 240.

34. Gimbel, *The American Occupation,* p. 15.

35. Quoted by Alfred Grosser, *The Colossus Again: Western Germany from Defeat to Rearmament* (New York: Praeger, 1955), pp. 31–32.

36. Ibid, p. 20.

37. Ibid

38. Ibid, pp. 21–21.

39. Gimbel, *The American Occupation of Germany,* p. 54.

40. Ibid, p. 59.

41. Clay, *Decision in Germany,* p. 122.

42. Kenneth M. Jensen, ed., "The Kennan 'Long Telegram,' Moscow, February 22, 1946," Kenneth M. Jensen, ed. *Origins of the Cold War: The Novikov, Kennan, and Roberts 'Long Telegrams' of 1946* (Washington, D.C.: United States Institute of Peace Press, 1993), p. 19.

43. Orlow, *A History of Modern Germany,* pp. 250–251.

44. Quoting from Marshall's Harvard speech, Lester Brune, *Chronological History of United States Foreign Relations: 1776 to January 20, 1981* (New York: Garland Publishing, 1985), p. 862.

CREATING THE
EUROPEAN UNION

....

INTRODUCTION

In 1999, a group of European nations embarked on a cooperative enterprise that fifty years before would have been unthinkable. Adopting a common currency to replace their respective national currencies, 11 member states of the European Union signaled their willingness to take the final logical step toward a true common market by integrating their monetary policies. Deutsche marks, French and Belgian francs, gilders, lira, and so forth would soon be remnants of the past, and the new "euro" would become the monetary unit for the majority of west European states. Building upon commercial integration that has taken place over the past 50 years, the decision to adopt a common currency captured the world's attention, focusing interest on the European Union, the cooperative arrangement that made such a historic event possible.

The European Union, an organization consisting of 15 European member states in 1999, is the world's largest single economic actor at the end of the 20th century. Its gross domestic product and population far surpass that of the United States, and its potential to expand to include nearly all of Europe is very high, as 10 nations line up for membership once they meet required conditions. The evolutionary creation of this union of like-minded countries, committed to the pursuit of peace and prosperity through commercial, monetary, and (to a great extent) political cooperation, is one of the great success stories of the post–World War II era. Certainly only the most visionary would have dared to predict in 1945 that decades of conflict and animosity could be replaced by a supranational union dedicated to the mutual benefit of all its members. This case study explores the origins and development of the European Union and traces some of the remarkable achievements, as well as difficult setbacks, in the evolution of economic and political cooperation.

....

THE EUROPEAN PROBLEM

The historical "problem" that existed in Western Europe following World War II was how to eliminate—or at least contain—the animosities that four wars over two centuries had engendered between France and Germany. Nationalistic competition for territories along the Rhine River had made the Alsace-Lorraine and Ruhr regions pawns in an ongoing struggle for resources and power. At the heart of this struggle was a desire to control the rich iron and coal resources on which industrial development during the previous century had been built. Most recently the French, having suffered ignominiously at the hands of the Nazi occupation during World War II, were adamant in their conviction that the German industrial capability should not be allowed to again rise as a foundation for military dominance.

Traditionally, the nationalistic rivalries between France and Germany had been fueled by restrictive import and export policies that aimed at limiting access to domestic markets as well as curtailing supplies of much needed raw materials for customers abroad. The French economy had been particularly inhibited over the years by the unwillingness of German steel and coking cartels to export coal, which was in short supply in France, or to open Germany's domestic market to steel imports from France. Because Germany had been better endowed with raw materials—particularly the coal of the Saar basin and Silesia—France considered itself at an economic disadvantage as long as Germany continued to exploit its favored position with export controls and high tariffs. Moreover, the industrial advantages that Germany enjoyed had been used against France in three wars over the previous 75 years, and the French had become convinced that only when Germany was stripped of these assets would its own security be assured.

Following liberation in 1944, France had once again assumed control of the valued Alsace-Lorraine area (having lost it in the Franco-Prussian War, regained it after World War I, and lost it again under Nazi occupation); however, the Ruhr region, the "industrial heartland" of Western Europe and the Saar basin, with its wealth of coal deposits, still remained within German territory, albeit occupied by the U.S. and British allies. With Germany's defeat in 1945 the future of this region was uncertain. Germany, under the reality of unconditional surrender, had lost its sovereignty, and the four Allied Powers (the United States, Soviet Union, Britain, and France) jointly held legal authority over the German nation. What would be done with Germany's key industrial area was yet to be determined.

Thus, when France regained its independence from German occupation it demanded from the other Allies that the Saar basin be ceded to it directly and that international control and administration of the Ruhr region be provided as a guarantee against German ascendancy. Many in France viewed international control of this vital area as necessary to a guarantee of security against future German industrial dominance and potential military aggression. Charles de Gaulle, the first postwar leader of France, argued that Germany should be dismembered into much smaller individual states that would not have the capacity to rise again as a significant military power. In addition, he maintained that the Saar basin—despite its German population—should be placed under French sovereignty, settling the future of this much coveted geographical area for the benefit of the French economy.[1]

Long before Germany was defeated in the spring of 1945 the Allied leaders had been planning for its eventual postwar treatment. President Roosevelt and Soviet Premier Stalin agreed that Germany should receive harsh treatment at the hands of the occupying powers, and plans were already under way at the end of the war for indefinite military occupation, dismemberment (dividing Germany into separate zones of occupation), denazification, and pastoralization of German society. Stripped of its sovereignty by the terms of unconditional surrender, Germany's fate was placed totally in the hands of the Allied powers. Participating in the final defeat of Germany, French officials joined their Soviet and American counterparts in supporting the plan, and although Britain also agreed to the postwar arrangements for Germany, Prime Minister Churchill was the one Allied leader who was reluctant to strip Germany of its industrial capability. Knowing that Germany was the potential economic powerhouse of Europe, Churchill was uneasy about the prospects of postwar economic recovery without the participation of Germany.

Churchill's discomfiture proved to be well founded. Almost immediately upon assuming responsibility for German occupation in the Western zones, U.S. and British officials found their task to be extremely daunting. The bombed-out conditions of Germany's cities and the harsh Soviet occupation in the East had created many homeless refugees. The winter was harsh, food was extremely scarce, and the sheer magnitude of the humanitarian effort to feed, house, and clothe the German people overwhelmed supplies. At a time when the Allied nations in Europe also desperately needed food and energy, the idea of keeping Germany in such a subjugated state that it could not supply its own basic needs seemed counterproductive. In the face of such hardship the U.S. military command in Germany began to back away from the strict occupation policy it had initiated, and with approval from the new Truman administration in Washington, it even began to allow and encourage renewed industrial activity.

At the same time, concerns in the United States about ways that the Soviet Union might exploit the economically devastated region prompted the new Truman administration to reconsider the wisdom of pursuing a punitive policy toward Germany that would result in the creation of a power vacuum at the boundary of Soviet-dominated territory. Therefore, practical and humanitarian concerns of the American and British occupation leaders joined with geopolitical concerns about Soviet intentions in the postwar environment to alter Western Allied policies toward Germany. By 1947 the United States had in fact decided to consciously reconstruct Germany as a part of the Western capitalist bulwark against communism, rather than pastoralize it and leave its impoverished citizens at the mercy of radical anti-Western elements.[2]

The story of this shift in U.S. policy is the story of the origins of the cold war between the United States and the Soviet Union. It comes of little surprise that the change in plans from stripping Germany of its industrial capability to rebuilding Germany's industry and economy seriously undermined relations between the United States and the

Soviet Union, who together had pledged themselves to the indefinite subjugation of German industrial capability. But it was not just the Soviets who were distressed and troubled by the American shift in policy. The French were equally horrified at the prospect that Germany would once again rise as an industrial (and potential military) power at its expense.

In particular, the issue of what would become of the Ruhr region and the Saar basin was of immediate concern. The French stood to lose a great deal if these areas were allowed to revert to German control. Thus, as the United States made plans for an extensive aid package for European (including German) reconstruction known as the Marshall Plan, France pressed even more desperately for ongoing international control of the all-important Ruhr region and for its continued oversight of the Saar basin. However, because France had been given a zone of occupation only at the behest of its allies Britain and the United States, and because its own zone did not include the vital Ruhr area, France found itself frustrated by the realities of changing American and British policy in their joint "Bizonia" occupation area. Faced with American and British shifts in policy that were encouraging German industrial production, France in 1947 agreed to a plan with the United States for an International Ruhr Authority, an international board consisting of representatives from the United States, Britain, France, Benelux, and Germany. In order to allay the fears of Germany's neighbors regarding access to the much needed production from the area, the board would be granted the authority to "allocate Ruhr output of coal, coke and steel between German internal consumption and exports."[3]

However, by the time France joined the British and Americans in a cooperative arrangement for all three Western zones of occupation in 1948, it found that its allies had already "loosened the Ruhr's economic shackles."[4] Therefore, even though the supervisory body envisioned in the 1947 Franco-U.S. agreement was finally created in 1949 to oversee and ostensibly constrain German industrial activity in the Ruhr, it was clear that the International Ruhr Authority had failed to have any meaningful impact.

The shift in U.S. occupation policy was due largely to the fact that the U.S. government had become convinced that rapid European recovery (just as Churchill had cautioned) could be achieved only if German economic recovery was assured as well. The next step in the U.S. plan was the creation of a West German government that could soon participate in the larger economic development of Western Europe. By 1949, as Western Allied advisers worked with German authorities to established the Federal Republic of Germany, it was clear that full West German sovereignty over the Ruhr region's rapidly rehabilitating steel mills would eventually be a reality.

For France this prospect was very troublesome. Within four short years it was again facing the prospect of German economic and political assertiveness, and while Germany's military capabilities were still being restrained by the constitutional arrangements the Allies had helped it create, no one could predict how binding those restrictions would prove to be in the future. Moreover, in the immediate term the French were very worried about the security of their supplies of coal from the Ruhr region's Saar basin for their own steel industry. Without an international authority to police them, would these supplies continue? If not, France would be put at a competitive disadvantage compared with Germany, a reality that seemed especially unfair so shortly after the

Allied defeat of the Nazis. One analyst explains this sentiment particularly well: "Not only had the Ruhr become a synonym for the evil German military-industrial complex, but its resuscitation would threaten France's own economic revival."[5]

French protests, coupled with a stronger and stronger conviction in the United States that Western Europe must be united in the goal of creating strong cooperative economies as shields against the spread of Communist influence, convinced U.S. officials that France must be brought "on board" the American plan for Western European reconstruction and economic cooperation. Having already established the Organization for European Economic Cooperation (OEEC) to serve as the European-based organization for receiving and administering Marshall Plan aid, the United States encouraged France to be a leading participant. In fact, because of the historical animosity between Germany and France and because in the most recent war France had suffered at the hands of the Nazis, the Truman administration believed that "France alone can take the decisive leadership in integrating West Germany into Western Europe."[6]

....

THE FIRST INTEGRATION EXPERIMENT: THE EUROPEAN COAL AND STEEL COMMUNITY

It was in this context that European integration was born. The United States wanted a Western Europe that was economically recovered from war, vigorous and prosperous in its capitalist development, and resolute in its resistance to communism. In setting the terms for Marshall Plan aid, it had encouraged progress toward all of these goals, including cooperation among the Western European governments, who were urged to embrace German reconstruction as pivotal to their respective economic recoveries. Within France the government plan for domestic recovery and revitalization had originally depended upon continued international control of the Ruhr and assurances of coal supplies for French industry. When it became clear that this component of French planning could not be relied on, Jean Monnet, the architect of the French "modernization plan," came up with a bold new alternative. His idea was to create a *supranational* authority for overseeing French and German coal and steel production in such a way as to guarantee French competitiveness while at the same time provide Germany with legitimacy in its return to international industrial competition. This authority would ensure that France would have free market access to the coal of the Saar basin and would also determine prices for steel to further ensure that French producers could compete with their more efficient German neighbors. The "windfall" profit that German companies might garner as a result of the authority's determined price would "buy" German producers' support for the plan. At the same time a portion of the profits would be shared with French producers so that they could use the extra funds to modernize and make more efficient their own plants. By providing a means of governing market access to resources and a means of protecting French economic interests, this plan would solve France's historical objection to German industrialization and at the same time give Germany a legitimized means of reentering the international community of trading nations. Accordingly,

Coal and steel, the two key sectors of industrial production and war-making potential, would be removed from national control and placed under a single, supranational authority. As Monnet put it, "if . . . the victors and the vanquished agreed to exercise joint sovereignty over part of their joint resources . . . then a solid link would be forged between them, the way would be wide open for further collective action, and a great example would be given to the other nations of Europe."[7]

Long an advocate of the need to subdue the nationalistic rivalries of Europe by wresting from nation-state control the key resources of war, Monnet had voiced for years his belief that only when mutual guarantees of resource and market access became tangible commitments would the repeated history of animosity and war be stopped. These guarantees, he believed, could be obtained only when the countries involved renounced national control in favor of binding supranational authority.

As early as 1941 Monnet had shared his idea with Paul-Henri Spaak of Belgium that the "pooling of Franco-German coal-steel production [was] the only way to move Europe beyond the cycle of war that reciprocating control over these resources engendered."[8] In addition, Monnet envisioned Europe based upon free trade in general, within which the cooperative effort over coal and steel would be embedded. The most revolutionary part of his idea was that it removed from French as well as German national control these crucial industries, breaking with the past European pattern of "to the victors go the spoils." His hope for creating an entirely new set of relationships within Europe rested on his deeply held conviction that there would have to be "a true yielding of sovereignty [to] some kind of central union, [and that] there should be a big European market without customs barriers, to prevent nationalism which is the curse of the modern world"[9]

In 1950 Monnet presented his idea to French foreign minister Robert Schuman, who was himself from the Lorraine, a region volleyed back and forth between Germany and France depending on who had won the previous war. Given this experience and his own political philosophy, which decidedly favored reconciliation with Germany, Schuman was particularly receptive to Monnet's idea. After all, as France faced the apparently inevitable rebirth of German industrialism and the interference of the United States in transatlantic affairs, its best choice may have been to embrace Germany in a supranational arrangement. As one historian has explained, "Fear compelled a choice. Necessity made 'Europeans' of the French."[10] Schuman immediately took the initiative to the United States and Germany to "test the waters" for their support.

Although there was some concern in the United States that the Schuman Plan had cartel-like features, the Truman administration was generally supportive of the idea because it would lock Germany into a mutually beneficial and mutually governed cooperative arrangement with France.[11] These traditional enemies together would form a partnership that would become the new force behind Western European integration, cementing and furthering the cooperative capitalist arrangements that the United States had been advocating since 1947.

In Germany, the plan was met with considerable enthusiasm. Konrad Adenauer, the first chancellor of the Federal Republic of Germany, was committed to leading Germany as a cooperative and legitimate nation into the community of democratic nations, and the Schuman Plan offered a valuable opportunity. It was Adenauer's view that if West Germany would embrace, and be embraced by, the democratic nations of Western Europe, a future of peace and prosperity would be possible. However, if West Germany remained isolated, its future would be bleak. Thus, when Monnet and Schuman approached him about an international authority for coal and steel, Adenauer considered that the economic costs of such a plan were far outweighed by the political benefits. With his eye on rehabilitating West Germany's place in Europe, Adenauer had a keen sense of purpose in pursuing integration with France.

Endorsed by the United States and welcomed by Germany, Monnet's plan was enthusiastically embraced by Foreign Minister Schuman, who authorized negotiations with other interested nations. Talks involved consideration of both the principles that would guide an arrangement and the practical aspects of its governance. The French government chose Monnet himself to lead the French negotiating team, and although Foreign Minister Schuman's name is associated with the plan, it was very much Monnet's vision that created it. The draft treaty presented by the French included "a single market in coal and steel of all the member states—in other words the basis of one Community. Customs duties, subsidies, discriminatory and restrictive practices were all to be abolished," and the common market was to be governed by a "High Authority, with powers to handle extreme shortages of supply or demand, to tax and to prepare production forecasts as guidelines for investment."[12]

The constitutional character of this coal and steel community took shape over the next few months. The "High Authority" would have the power to initiate governing proposals and would oversee the day-to-day functions of the community. However, a second institution was created that reflected the oversight of the individual member states. This "Council of Ministers" would have the decision-making power to review issues that affected the member states. Finally, a "Court of Justice," separate from the International Court of Justice in The Hague and unique to the European coal and steel community, would be formed to adjudicate disputes that would arise within the arrangement also included that was designed to prevent concentration of industry and ensure open competition.

In 1951, with the signing of the Treaty of Paris, six nations—France, Germany, Luxembourg, Belgium, the Netherlands, and Italy—reached agreement on the creation of the European Coal and Steel Community (ECSC), the first experiment in European integration. In 1952 the treaty was ratified by Italy, the last of the states that signed, and the new community came into existence with Monnet serving as first high commissioner. At the very heart of the new community lay the principles of peace and repudiation of the past that had inspired Monnet's effort. In reviewing the preamble to the Treaty of Paris, one can see his vision:

CONSIDERING that world peace can be safeguarded only by creative efforts commensurate with the dangers that threaten it,
CONVINCED that the contribution which an organized and vital Europe can make to civilization is indispensable to the maintenance of peaceful relations,

RECOGNIZING that Europe can be built only through practical achievements which will first of all create real solidarity, and through the establishment of common bases for economic development,

ANXIOUS to help, by expanding their basic production, to raise the standard of living and further the works of peace,

RESOLVED to substitute for age-old rivalries the merging of their essential interests; to create, by establishing an economic community, the basis for a broader and deeper community among peoples long divided by bloody conflicts; and to lay the foundations for institutions which will give direction to a destiny henceforward shared,

HAVE DECIDED to create a European Coal and Steel Community. . . .[13]

By the middle of the decade the change in relations this new community had created was clearly visible. In 1956 the Saar basin had been fully returned to Germany, and French worries about access to coal had been allayed by the governing arrangements of the ECSC. The ECSC was a mixed success during the next few years, the High Authority having difficulty determining price levels and at the same time encouraging market competition. However, it did prove that Franco-German cooperation was achievable and that even broader levels of cooperation were within the realm of possibility.

Monnet, Schuman, Adenauer, and Paul-Henri Spaak, the Belgian foreign minister, were all also advocates of the so-called functionalist concept of how international cooperation is achieved. The underlying premise of this concept is that cooperation in certain functional areas (like steel and coal trade) would engender cooperation in other areas, eventually obviating international conflict and war. Basically this meant that "once Europe had begun to cooperate in these areas, interdependence of policy logics would promote 'spillover' into others."[14] This dynamic seemed to be at work within Europe during the community's first decade. Not only did the existence of the ECSC help to cement the cooperative relationship of its members states, it also served as a model for further movement.

....

TWO MORE COMMUNITIES: EURATOM AND THE EEC

Even as the ECSC struggled to become a more effective example of integration, other proposals for economic cooperation were being floated. One grew out of the emerging interest in nuclear power as a source of energy for developing the European economy while also containing nuclear proliferation. The other was a more ambitious plan for creating a customs union, a free trade area with a common customs tariff, as was allowed under the American-sponsored General Agreement on Tariffs and Trade (GATT) created in 1948. Negotiations for these two new "communities" of economic cooperation ensued, and in 1957 the Treaty of Rome established Euratom, the integrative effort to develop and regulate nuclear power, and the European Economic Community (EEC) as a customs union and integrated common market.

THE EUROPEAN ECONOMIC COMMUNITY

Characterized by three major policies, the EEC sought to further encourage and manage economic relations among the six member states. First the EEC had a common external tariff, which meant that the member states could not individually raise or lower their trade barriers with third-party countries. Instead, they collaborated in setting a common external tariff that could be negotiated only collectively. Second, the EEC was to be a free trade area within which no tariffs between member states would be allowed. Third, the EEC committed itself to a policy for agriculture that was somewhat similar to the arrangements in the ECSC. The Common Agricultural Policy (CAP) would establish minimum price levels for agricultural products produced within the community. Like coal and steel, agriculture had a strategic value to the Europeans, who, having suffered embargoed food imports and blockades during the previous two wars, did not want to experience such vulnerabilities again. The CAP was designed to encourage European self-sufficiency in agricultural production and to protect member-state farmers from the vagaries of international competition and market fluctuations. The early 1960s were devoted to member-state negotiations regarding the specific workings of the CAP and regarding the removal of internal EEC tariff barriers. Institutional development also characterized the period, as the member states directed community-level organs to administer the policies they had developed. During this decade, member states accustomed themselves to, and came to rely upon, the institutions of the three communities (ECSC, Euratom, and EEC) to negotiate and regulate trade with third countries and to encourage deeper cooperation and management of intracommunity trade.

The deepening integration effort hit a major snag during this same period, however. The French government under President Charles de Gaulle had become increasingly dissatisfied with the degree of interference wielded by the European Communities in French sovereign affairs. The specific target of de Gaulle's mistrust and animosity was the European Commission, the EEC's executive institution, which was granted authority to propose policy and to implement legislative directives for the Council of Ministers (representing the respective member states). De Gaulle disliked the fact that this supranational body could propose and therefore influence policy that affected the member states, and he worried that the commission was leading European integration along federalist lines. This was becoming particularly alarming to the nationalistic French leader as January 1, 1966, rapidly approached. On this day, qualified majority voting would become the decision-making procedure for the Council of Ministers for a certain realm of issues. The timetable for this shift to qualified majority voting had been set in the Treaty of Rome. The change from a requirement of unanimity would mean that France—or any other member state—alone could not block legislation if the necessary majority was obtained. For sovereign protectionists like de Gaulle, this was not acceptable. For those (like the founders) who believed in the deepening integration of European nations toward a federal model, however, it was considered vital.

Despite agreement among the other five member states that qualified majority voting should govern certain areas of the EEC, de Gaulle eventually had his way. During heated negotiations in Luxembourg in 1966, a compromise arrangement was reached. Even though the Treaty of Rome's plan for qualified majority voting would be implemented as scheduled, any member state could invoke what came to be known as the "Luxembourg Compromise," a provision that allowed a member state to veto any measure that it deemed a threat to its vital interests. This had the effect of ensuring that only with unanimity could controversial measures pass, and for the next 20 years this intergovernmental method of decision making characterized community relations and effectively prevented significant integration in any realm not considered "safe."

Also, one of the ironic developments of the 1960s was that even as the six member countries successfully negotiated away the tariff barriers among them, nontariff barriers (technical requirements and standards, etc.) were being raised to new protectionist levels. The only realms of community[15] cooperation that appeared to be successful were the price supporting (and trade restricting) efforts in energy, coal and steel, and agriculture. Thus, as the decade of the 1960s came to an end, the community had experienced mixed success as an integrationist enterprise.

ENLARGEMENT BUT LITTLE DEEPENING

While many tend to think of the 1970s as being the period of "doldrums" for European integration, four major developments during the 1970s were very significant. First the EEC underwent its first two enlargements. In 1973 Britain, Ireland, and Denmark became members, and in 1978 Greece became a member. While these developments demonstrated that the EEC was drawing interest from its neighbors, they also demonstrated that increasing heterogeneity of membership can produce strains of its own. Britain and Denmark tended to be free-trade and "efficiency" oriented, which threatened France's traditional position of influence. In comparison, it quickly became apparent that Greece was more a net drain on community programs and budgets than a productive contributor. Some wondered if such a hodgepodge of nations could genuinely integrate.

The second significant development of the 1970s in fact put this issue to the test. In the wake of the 1971 collapse of the Bretton Woods system (the cooperative monetary arrangement established by the United States at the end of World War II),[16] the 1973 oil embargo and subsequent spiral of oil prices, and general inflation, the EEC countries attempted to collaborate to deal with the monetary crisis that ensued. In an arrangement that initially was known as "the snake" (which referred its graphical appearance in a line drawing), member states sought to stabilize their currencies' values in relation to the other member states' currencies. Hoping to keep currency values within a narrow band of fluctuation against each other, member states attempted to insulate themselves somewhat from the dollar's erratic behavior and to encourage trade and financial flows amongst themselves. While the emergence of the European Monetary System was not all that successful (the weaker currencies had difficulty maintaining their positions in the system), it did mark a major psychological breakthrough as member states turned to integrationist monetary efforts to deal with external economic challenges.[17]

Third, in 1978 one of the community's lesser known institutions rose to the forefront of the integration effort. The Treaty of Rome had created a European Court of

Justice, which was given the power to rule on issues involving compliance with treaty provisions, and by extension council directives. Disputes under this evolving body of law could be taken to the Court of Justice for an opinion. In 1978 the Court rendered such an opinion in the case *Cassis de Dijon.* In this case, a German liquor regulation was challenged by a German importer of the French liqueur Cassis de Dijon. In its complaint the importer claimed that the German regulation unfairly discriminated against the French product on the grounds that because the French product was different in recipe from the German product it did not meet German standards. Yet no genuine health or quality standard was at issue—only the difference in recipe. The European Court of Justice agreed with the German importer and ordered the German government to allow the importation of the French liqueur. However, the matter did not rest with this particular case. In its judgment, the court went on to say that regulatory standards that merely differed from state to state should not be allowed to impede commerce, and henceforth member states should adopt the principle of *mutual recognition* in their treatment of goods produced in other member states. That is, unless genuine health concerns are at stake, member states must recognize the legitimacy of the regulatory standards of other member states. No longer should different regulations constitute barriers to trade within the community. This opinion would have far-reaching implications for deepening the integration effort, because it removed the legal basis for the use by member states of standards to exclude the fair importation of products from other member states.

Finally, the 1970s witnessed the first directly elected parliament of the European Community. In 1979 direct elections for members of the European parliament were held in all the member states, replacing the governmental appointees that to that point had "represented the people." While this institutional change did not markedly affect the character of the European Community (since the power of parliament remained peripheral and strictly advisory), it did mark the beginnings of the recognition within the governing elite that European integration would one day have to include more directly democratic institutions.

"EUROSCHLEROSIS" AND THE MOVEMENT TOWARD THE SINGLE MARKET

By the early 1980s attitudes toward the European Community were mixed. On the one hand a fair amount of cooperative integration had occurred over the previous three decades. The Common Agricultural Policy had been a major success in raising levels of farm production and in moving the community from being a net importer of basic agricultural products, such as wheat, to being a net exporter.[18] There had been considerable movement toward a Common Market, as intra-EC trade benefited from the removal of tariff walls between member states. Finally, there had been impressive progress toward the institutionalization of European-level cooperative arrangements, with a high degree of collaboration occurring between member states. On the other hand, the economies of the European Community countries had slumped into a deep recession during the early 1980s, and critics of the EC were questioning its value as an instrument of economic growth and stability. Productivity was in decline, and unemployment was increasing at alarming rates, particularly in the traditional industrial sectors. Many people in Europe were referring to this economic stagnation and structural inflexibility as "Euroschlerosis." In the face of stiff competition from the rising economic powerhouses of East Asia (Japan, Taiwan, Hong Kong, South Korea, and Singapore), European nations had resorted to protectionist measures to buy time for their beleaguered industries. Also under pressure from the vagaries of U.S. monetary and import policies, member states considered their relative economic position in the world to be quite bleak, and in general the mood in Europe was pessimistic. According to one analysis, two major economic trends characterized the period of the 1970s to early 80s:

> One result . . . was the growing disparity among EC economies. Another was a rise in protectionism. Because tariffs could not be raised within the EC's customs-free zone, there was a rapid spread of non-tariff barriers, often state aids to industry to save jobs. As the use of such techniques generalized the effectiveness of the Common Market as a trade area was threatened. Growth levels fell to half what they had been in the 1960s, international trade expanded less, while intra-EC trade expansion actually stopped.[19]

At the member state level, policy responses to economic stagflation and declining competitiveness varied. In most of the member states there was a noticeable shift to the right, and governments, such as Britain's Conservative government under Margaret Thatcher, began to pry the domestic market away from past patterns of protection and subsidization. Ideologically, there was a strong sentiment across Europe that the traditional social compact between government and labor, which had attempted to maintain the status quo in industry and employment, had become obsolete and counterproductive to competitiveness and economic growth. This general shift in ideological position was reflected in official statements at the highest levels of community governance. At its summit in Luxembourg in 1981 the European Council (the heads of government of the member states meeting collectively) "expressed alarm about the state of the internal market. Trade, it argued, was increasingly being threatened by unintentional as well as intentional barriers, subsidies, and other market-distorting policies. To remedy the situation, the council endorsed a 'concerted effort . . . to strengthen and develop the free internal market.'"[20] As the third enlargement embracing Spain and Portugal was carried out, critics were wondering about the value of a community that was not expanding trade. Between 1981 and 1984 a number of statements were made by the council to encourage improved intracommunity trade conditions; however, it wasn't until the latter half of the decade that significant progress was made.

....

THE LEADERSHIP OF JACQUES DELORS

Interestingly, the failure of one member state's unilateral effort to shield its economy from global economic pressures helped to launch the community in this new direction.

The Socialist government in France under the presidency of Francois Mitterand had in 1981 attempted to cope with the economic crisis by turning toward the traditional policies of the left in an effort to insulate itself from the pressures of the external economy. Within three years, however, the French national experiment in price controls, restrictions on capital, and employment protection through governmental nationalization was abandoned, as the Socialist government reconsidered its approach and officially adopted the idea that liberalization of trade and finance was preferable to inward-oriented protectionism. One of the great ironies of recent European history is the fact that the French economic minister during this brief leftist experiment was Jacques Delors, whose name would soon become synonymous with European market liberalization and the deepening integration effort. Delors had been a veteran player in French politics. A devotee of Monnet-style integration for Europe and a stalwart moderate in French national politics, he had served in a number of positions in Gaullist center-right governments before joining Mitterand's Socialist government in 1981. Brought on board "to be a counterweight to some of Mitterand's more fervently leftist comrades in other ministries,"[21] Delors found himself uncomfortably caught up in the costly government policies that contradicted his own better judgment and policy preferences. As one analysis observes:

> The "Delorist" vision saw the market as indispensable allocator of resources, decisionmaker and source of economic dynamism. The market by itself could not, however, guarantee equity, a moralized social order, or full economic success. These things depended upon "dialogue" among different groups—employers and labor in particular-to reach clearer understandings of mutual needs about what had to be done and what could be shared.[22]

When the Mitterand experiment drove France deeper into economic difficulty and became more and more discredited, Delors was finally in a position to influence the government to move in a different direction. He called for a delay in pursuing further the leftist policies that had been introduced. He worked with the German central bank to realign and stabilize the French currency, and he began the difficult task of restructuring the domestic economy to make it less dependent on governmental aid and more competitive in the international market. Observers noted that his reforms were more "German" in character than they were "French," and market advocates throughout Europe praised him for his courageous effort to take on the entrenched interests that were stubbornly resisting change.[23]

These actions proved Delors to be a skillful economic strategist, and perhaps even more importantly for France's neighbors, they proved that Delors was an influential proponent within France of a market-oriented outlook. In 1984 this served Delors particularly well when President Mitterand nominated him to serve as EC Commission president, and he was duly elected (receiving the all-important endorsement of the German government). Taking advantage of Mitterand's desire to raise France's stature within Europe, and building upon his own personal ambitions for the community, Delors proceeded to use his new European-level position to advance the practical goals he considered so vital to European prosperity and unity. A Monnet integrationist at heart and a tireless and energetic strategist, Delors's leadership would take the European

Community from the realm of halfhearted economic cooperation into a dynamic integrationist effort that would far exceed the most optimistic expectations.

As EC Commission president Delors became the head of the executive body of the European Community located in Brussels, an institution that had been constitutionally constructed to serve as the "engine" of integration under the Treaty of Rome.[24] Following the logic of the original Schuman Plan, which named "European Federation" as the eventual goal of European functional cooperation, the commission was established as the executive body responsible for framing European Community goals and implementing policy. Members of the commission, and especially the commission president, are expressly charged with the responsibility of serving community interests and not the particular interests of their respective member states. Their task has been to work toward deeper European integration by proposing legislation to the Council of Ministers and by implementing council directives and enforcing Court of Justice decisions. The power of initiative has given the commission tremendous potential influence in shaping the character of the European Community, especially when the broad objectives of the member states coincided with commission enthusiasms. This had been true regarding the creation and development of the Common Agricultural Policy during the 1960s, and again in the 1980s there was considerable room for commission input.

Under the energetic leadership of Jacques Delors the commission took the initiative in building a momentum for deeper integration. He launched this effort with a tour of the capitals of all the member states, seeking their perspectives and finding out which issues were most troublesome to market access. He then assigned Britain's Lord Arthur Cockfield, the new commissioner for the Internal Market and a strong advocate of free trade, to the task of preparing a report on the subject. Within a few months Lord Cockfield produced a Commission White Paper, *Completing the Internal Market,* which detailed over 300 actions that needed to be taken to "eliminate physical, technical and fiscal barriers to intra-EC exchanges of 91 kinds."[25] This report was founded on the premise that Europe's economic difficulties rested with the inability of European enterprises to compete effectively, that European market integration would give these enterprises the advantages of economies of scale, and that the removal of internal border barriers would reduce transaction costs and thus alone would raise efficiencies. Basically the white paper argued that a genuinely free internal market could be achieved only with the removal of these barriers and that a plan of action would include a commitment to the principle of mutual recognition (as expressed by the Court of Justice in the *Cassis de Dijon* decision) as a means of harmonization of standards. The report also contained an ambitious timetable that set the end of 1992 as the target date for achieving the single market.

An interesting dynamic ensued. The free market principles of the white paper appealed to the British Conservative government, which, for the first time since its membership, found real merit in the initiatives emanating from Brussels. Likewise Germany, the Benelux countries, and Denmark held similar views, and because the white paper proposed a program for truly deepening integration, the German and Benelux governments (which had always been the most ardent supporters of the federalist goal of European integration) were particularly supportive. France, seeing its political strength in Europe as being tied to its leadership of European integration (in partnership with

German economic power), was also very supportive of the program and very proud of commission president Delors, who was at the helm of the effort. Moreover, as one would expect, the program for creating a single market in the European Community found considerable support in the business community.

Enthusiasm for the project was also maintained by the mechanism of an Intergovernmental Council, which brought the member states together in a round of "meganegotiations" that made the 1992 effort the center of activity and placed on the agenda yet another treaty for the deepening integration of the community. In 1986 the Single European Act, which formally pledged the member states to the 1992 single market effort, was passed by the council, and in 1987 it was ratified by all 12 member states. In appealing to the policy preferences of the major member states on economic grounds, the 1992 effort, as it came to be called, initially sidestepped some of the stickier issues dealing with political integration, and general enthusiasm for the program swept through Europe. This support was enhanced by another commission report in 1988 that emphasized (some argue greatly exaggerated) the benefits of the single market for economic growth and prosperity in Europe.[26] The appeal of a truly free internal market, with mutual recognition of standards and licensing requirements (or harmonization of standards where necessary), reached beyond business to citizens as well. The idea that the credentials of lawyers, medical doctors, and other licensed professionals from one country of the EC would be recognized in all the other countries of the EC was an attractive one. After all, even in the United States, the often cited federal model for European integrationists, such guarantees did not exist!

Finally, the Single European Act pledged the EC to the goal of monetary union. Harkening back to the historical problems associated with fluctuating currencies and trade, this initiative was based on the premise that once a single commercial market was achieved, the only remaining impediment to free trade would be exchange-rate fluctuations. In order to create a genuinely single market such fluctuations must be eliminated, and the only certain way to do this would be to eliminate the different currencies of the EC and adopt one single currency for all. The Single European Act committed member states to the first stage of cooperation toward this unprecedented goal. This would require them to cooperate in a system of managed exchange rates and pledge them to align their economies according to a common set of fiscal and monetary goals.

Despite its emphasis on economic liberalization, one of the most important commission accomplishments in the strategy for creating the single market had deep political implications. In proposing methods for achieving member-state approval for the white paper program, the commission argued that the rules of de Gaulle's Luxembourg Compromise, which since 1966 had given member states effective veto power over every issue coming before the council, would seriously impede progress toward achieving the internal market. In a major coup against member states that had previously clung firmly to their sovereign prerogative, the commission succeeded in obtaining council approval for qualified majority voting for most of the measures on the white paper's list. No longer could one country—whether it was a large country like Britain or a tiny country like Luxembourg—block progress toward the creation of a genuine common market.

As the commission expected, this institutional change significantly improved the facility with which proposals were passed as council directives (the laws of the community). Whenever a strong majority of member states supported a measure, it would pass, even if a small minority of member states opposed it. This important step toward supranational governance was pivotal to the success of the Single Market initiative, and although implementation of EC directives by the respective member states was a much slower and uncertain process, the fact that binding decisions could be made at the community level on a majority rule basis had far-reaching implications.

CONCLUSION

As member states of the European Community faced the 1990s they did so with a very different attitude than had been apparent a decade before. Even as the Single European Act began to bear fruit, plans for an even deeper integrative effort were already under way. A genuine single commercial market and monetary union were on the horizon, and a new treaty, which would include a common foreign policy and cooperation in justice affairs, was being drawn up. The eventual goal of European Union was no longer that farfetched. France and Germany, the union's original protagonists, remained bound together in a partnership dedicated to European integration. As Monnet had hoped, functional cooperation in the coal and steel industries had "spilled over" into cooperative efforts in a wide range of economic areas, and a genuine European Common Market was being realized. Perhaps most importantly, economic and territorial motives for war had disappeared, and in their place arose commercial and financial motives for peace and cooperation.

By 1994 fifteen countries of Western Europe were now members, and a slate of Mediterranean and East European countries was waiting in line to join. The Treaty on the European Union, completed in 1992, had begun to govern member state relations, creating the terms for a common currency and mechanisms for common foreign and security policy and cooperation in justice and immigration affairs. By the end of the 20th century the nations that had fought several wars and jealously guarded their own resources prior to 1945 had embarked on a commercial and political union of unprecedented proportions. As Jean Monnet's biographer comments in his assessment of Monnet's original vision:

> Every decade that passes confirms this event [the Schuman Plan of 1950] as one of the landmarks of the century. The implications go well beyond Europe. Many reforms were introduced after the war. But of all the international bodies invented to correct the weaknesses that led to war, none addressed the fragmentation of authority in the hands of numerous hands, which arguably had been one of the greatest flaws. The Schuman Plan alone . . . broke the mould by daring a federal experiment.[27]

Still far from a "United States of Europe," the commitment by the European Union's member states to peace, cooperation, and deepening integration has demonstrated that the historical problem that Jean Monnet and others had hoped to address after World War II finally may have been solved.

Discussion Questions

1. What was the "historical problem" facing Western Europe at the end of World War II?
2. Why did U.S. plans for German reconstruction so alarm and dismay the French?
3. Under what circumstances was France willing to forfeit some of its own sovereignty for market and military security?
4. How did the "functionalist" concept seem to be verified by European integration during the past 50 years?
5. How did international systemic changes influence the creation of the European Coal and Steel Community?
6. How crucial were key national leaders in the creation of the European Coal and Steel Community?

Notes

1. Francois Duchene, *Jean Monnet: The First Statesman of Interdependence* (New York: W.W. Norton, 1994), p. 183.
2. See chapter 4 for a more thorough account.
3. Ibid., p. 185.
4. Desmond Dinan, *An Ever Closer Union: An Introduction to the European Community* (Boulder: Lynne Rienner, 1994), p. 20.
5. Ibid., p. 20.
6. Quoting Secretary of State Dean Acheson, Ibid., p. 22.
7. Ibid., p. 23.
8. Ibid., p. 182.
9. Ibid., p. 183.
10. Duchene, *Jean Monnet,* p. 208.
11. Ibid., pp. 212–215.
12. Ibid., p. 210.
13. Preamble from A Treaty Establishing the European Coal and Steel Community contained within *Treaties Establishing the European Communities,* abridged ed. (Luxembourg: Office for Official Publications of the European Communities, 1987), p. 19.
14. George Ross, *Jacques Delors and European Integration* (New York: Oxford University Press, 1995), p. 20.
15. Increasingly, observers and participants alike had begun in common usage to refer to the three Communities as the European Community and often to interchange the term European Economic Community with European Community.
16. See chapter 2.
17. Madeleine Hosli, "The EMU and International Monetary Relations: What to Expect for International Actors," Carolyn Rhodes, ed., *The European Union in the World Community* (Boulder: Lynne Rienner, 1998), pp. 167–168.

18. Carolyn Rhodes, *Reciprocity, U.S. Trade Policy and the GATT Regime* (Ithaca: Cornell University Press, 1993), p. 206.

19. Ross, *Jacques Delors,* p. 24.

20. David R. Cameron, "The 1992 Initiative: Causes and Consequences," Alberta M. Sbragia, ed., *Euro-Politics: Institutions and Policymaking in the "New" European Community* (Washington, D.C.: Brookings, 1992), p. 32.

21. Ross, *Jacques Delors,* p. 19.

22. Ibid., p. 18.

23. Ibid., p. 29.

24. Ibid., p. 6.

25. Ibid., p. 30. For the text of the paper see EC Commission, *Completing the Internal Market: White Paper from the Commission to the European Council.* (Luxembourg: EC, 1985).

26. The Cecchini Report (named for its author, Paolo Cecchini, a retired commission official) was published in 1988. It claimed a tremendous cost savings from eliminating border controls and removing barriers among the member states. Dinan, *An Ever Closer Union,* p. 151.

27. Duchene, *Jean Monnet,* p. 181.

CHAPTER 6

A REVERSAL OF INTERESTS

U.S. Containment Policy and the Origins of the Vietnam Tragedy

INTRODUCTION

In 1973, after nearly 20 years of involvement in Vietnam, the United States military withdrew its forces without having achieved the goal it had set in the 1950s of preserving the existence of the noncommunist Republic of South Vietnam. Still, American leadership refused to admit failure—the Nixon administration dubbing U.S. withdrawal as the culmination of a policy aimed at "Vietnamizing" a war that had been progressively "Americanized" since 1954. Having been unable to achieve a negotiated peace settlement that would perpetuate and stabilize the boundary between North and South Vietnam, the U.S. government had finally decided it was time to pull out. In less than two years after the removal of U.S. troops in 1973, the South Vietnamese army was routed and its capital, Saigon, overtaken. All of Vietnam was united under the government of the Democratic Republic of Vietnam, the regime that had proclaimed Vietnamese independence from its North Vietnamese capital of Hanoi shortly after the end of World War II but that had battled French colonialism and American hegemony for 30 years before it achieved its goal.

The horror that was the Vietnam war was especially tragic because it could have been avoided, and its costs in human suffering were extremely high. It produced millions of casualties and refugees.[1] It wreaked ecological disaster in the region and caused global economic dislocation. Southern Vietnam, which had been the largest source of rice exports in Asia, became a rice importer, its economy becoming totally dependent on U.S. military and economic aid, and its countryside laid to waste by bombings, napalm, defoliants, and endless warfare. Globally, the economic impact of this war was also serious, causing the United States to squander vast amounts of oil and to overextend itself financially to meet this and other international and domestic commitments. Toward war's end the U.S. dollar's place in the global monetary system had been seriously challenged, and the cooperative financial regime that it symbolized since World War II had collapsed.

For Vietnam, the struggle, despite its horrendous costs, proved to be a political success because it finally resulted in the ousting of foreign powers from its soil and united the country under an independent national government. As a war of national liberation, the Vietnam war demonstrated that a highly committed population could eventually expel a less committed intervention force, despite the latter's superior military power. The tragedy, however, was that it ever should have happened.

For the United States, the only redeeming features of this war (besides the unintended infusion of Vietnamese refugees into American society) were the lessons it provided about matching means with goals, about questioning the basis of U.S. foreign policy, and about better understanding the circumstances into which the country interferes. The price paid for these lessons, however, was too high. Over 50,000 Americans lost their lives (and over twice that number were casualties) in a futile struggle to save the integrity of a series of regimes that never had the support of their own people. The American public came to seriously question and doubt its government, a "credibility gap" developing between what people were being told and what they were witnessing via live television coverage. Allies to the United States distanced themselves from U.S. policy in Vietnam and pressured the leading power in the world to alter its course. Enemies of U. S. hegemony reveled in its failure, and some hoped to exploit what came to be known after the U.S. withdrawal as the "Vietnam syndrome"—the apparent paralysis of U.S. military policy abroad.[2]

The obvious question about this episode in international politics as we look back over the 20th century is *why?* The United States was unquestionably the most powerful nation in the world and supposedly the country most committed to the democratic self-determination of other nations after the Second World War. Why did it choose to embroil itself in a conflict halfway around the world against its own anticolonial principles, and why couldn't it change the course of events once it had become involved? What does this tell us about the motivations of our leaders and about the goals that they set? Where does power lie in international conflict? This David and Goliath story tells us a great deal about why international conflicts occur and why policy makers succeed and fail in projecting national power. The case study that follows examines the origins and consequences of U.S. involvement in Vietnam and reveals that "pivotal decisions" can and do have negative and far-reaching consequences.

....

THE ATLANTIC CHARTER AND U.S. PLANS FOR A POST-WORLD WAR II ORDER

Several months before the United States entered the Second World War, President Franklin Roosevelt already had mapped out what he thought the postwar world should look like. Convinced, like President Wilson had been after World War I, that the imperial rivalries of the great powers perpetuated conflict, he sought a postwar arrangement with the other major nations that would put an end to colonialism and establish a system of collective security. He also hoped this new era would open the way for the democratic self-determination of new nations formerly dominated by their European or Asian conquerors. The breakup of the old imperial relationships would open the way for freer U.S. access to trade in these areas, and economic motives were partially driving the administration's policy. However, equally important was the fact that Roosevelt and his advisers were convinced, on both practical and moral grounds, that the self-determination of peoples long subjugated under the yolk of imperialism would encourage peace, prosperity, and global stability. Nowhere were Roosevelt's intentions more clear than in Indochina, where French colonial control was particularly harsh and exploitative. In a number of communications with his advisers and others Roosevelt registered his disgust with French imperialism in Southeast Asia and vowed that the United States would reject the maintenance of a French presence in the region once the war was over.[3]

When Roosevelt met with British Prime Minister Winston Churchill on a ship in the Atlantic Ocean in August of 1941, he carried with him a set of principles for guiding postwar policy that he thought the two Atlantic powers should discuss. In the midst of a struggle for his country's very existence Prime Minister Churchill was hoping that this summit with President Roosevelt would result in a U.S. pledge of assistance that would turn the tides of war away from the advantage of the Nazis and toward eventual victory for Britain. President Roosevelt was clearly sympathetic and very worried that without substantial U.S. aid Britain would not be able to hold out against German attacks. He had for some time been trying to convince a reluctant Congress that the United States should come to the aid of the British.

However, Roosevelt was also aware that perhaps for the first time in history the United States had the leverage to pressure Britain into agreeing to the U.S. prescription for a new character for the global system. Freer trade (especially an end to the British imperial preference system that had proved so discriminatory in the interwar period), self-determination for the inhabitants of colonial possessions, and a collective security system were U.S. foreign policy goals. If the United States was to agree to extend significant amounts of military aid to Britain that would result in the defeat of the Nazi behemoth, its President wanted to ensure that the U.S. blueprint for a postwar order would be the one that would be followed.

Prime Minister Churchill, although desperate for a commitment from the U.S. administration to join Britain in waging war against Nazi Germany, was not enthused about the anti-imperial orientation of the U.S. plan, especially the statement that "guaranteed equal access to world wealth to 'all States, great or small, victor or vanquished.'"[4] He managed to get a reluctant Roosevelt to agree to a modification of the language, substituting the provision that "equal access would be guaranteed only 'with due respect for . . . existing obligations.'"[5] In a great show of solidarity, the two leaders signed the historic "Atlantic Charter," a document pledging their respective countries to cooperation in the war effort and in shaping the postwar world. Still prominent in the Atlantic Charter was the commitment of support for the self determination of all nations, including those currently under colonial domination, as is revealed in the following excerpts:

> First, [The United States and Britain] seek no aggrandizement, territorial or other.
>
> Second, they desire to see no territorial changes that do not accord with the freely expressed wishes of the peoples concerned.
>
> Third, they respect the right of all peoples to choose the form of government under which they will live; and they wish to see sovereign rights and self-government restored to those who have been forcibly deprived of them.
>
> Fourth, they will endeavor, with due respect for their existing obligations, to further the enjoyment by all States, great or small, victor or vanquished, of access, on equal terms, to the trade and to the raw materials of the world which are need for their economic prosperity.[6]

When the Japanese attack on Pearl Harbor on December 7, 1941, brought the United States directly into the war, the country was guided by these goals. Once the Axis powers were defeated, the United States would then be able to pursue its political objective of creating a different, more cooperative and democratic world order.

SOUTHEAST ASIA

In the French colonies of Southeast Asia Roosevelt's plan for the postwar dismantling of imperial holdings was met with great enthusiasm by those groups and individuals who had long agitated for independence. Having consolidated its control over the region by the early 1890s, France divided Indochina into different units. France ruled the southern part, Chochin China, directly as a colony of France from the capital of Saigon; central Vietnam, called Annam, and northern Vietnam, called Tonkin, along with Cambodia and Laos were held under indirect rule.[7]

France imposed a highly repressive regime that extracted wealth for the French patricians and shared benefits only with a tiny local elite. Disparities in wealth widened under French colonial rule as French land holdings expanded at the expense of the peasantry, and the local elite allied themselves with the French colonialists. Indigenous Buddhism was repressed, while Catholicism was favored among the elite, creating deep cultural divisions between the rulers and the masses. Under these circumstances poverty and resentment became mutually reinforcing causes of alienation between the people and their colonial masters. Moreover, the French colonial authorities were especially brutal in maintaining their control. Strikes, demonstrations, and other forms of political protest were met with savage retaliations that included indiscriminate executions of thousands of people by the French military. According to one account, following a wave of insurrections led by Communist rebels in 1930, the French

> brought in legionnaires, other troops, and a horde of security police and suppressed the soviets with extreme brutality. An estimated 10,000 Vietnamese, many of whom had taken no part in the rebellion, were killed and another 50,000 were deported. Many others suffered assault, rape, robbery and unjust imprisonment.[8]

Therefore, by 1941 when the Atlantic Charter was unveiled, the anticolonial nationalists in the region, who had been hoping for independence, were encouraged that the world's preeminent power was endorsing the principle of self-determination as a goal of postwar policy.

HO CHI MINH

No one followed Roosevelt's statements with more optimism and enthusiasm than did Ho Chi Minh, a Vietnamese nationalist and Communist who in 1941 had organized in northern Vietnam the Viet Minh, a revolutionary party committed to the unification of Vietnam and its independence from French (and from September 1940, Japanese) imperialism. Ho Chi Minh is the most famous of many pseudonyms taken by this man who was born in 1890 as Nguyen Sinh Cung in the northern Tonkin region of Vietnam. His father, a partially educated farmer who on his own persevered in his studies to achieve a Mandarin degree and a position as a teacher, educated his son and imbued him with a distaste for French colonial rule and the Mandarin elite who kowtowed to it.[9] Ho (as he would call himself much later) was himself a dissenter and a self-educated scholar in his own right. He learned several languages including French, Cantonese, and English, and he was very well read. He was also an adventurer, who spent many years traveling and observing other cultures and political systems, including a trip to the United States in 1913, and many years in Europe, particularly Paris. Generally he worked at menial jobs to support himself while he studied political philosophy and revolution.

Although his early life and thinking are not well documented, it is clear that, while Ho opposed everything about the French colonial regime in Indochina, he was quite taken with many aspects of French society and philosophy, particularly the principles of the French Revolution. Similarly, he was inspired by the American War for Independence and the human rights it championed. In remembering his visit to New York City he recounted

> how he and a shipmate made a long and . . . adventurous journey [to] Chinatown, where they had talked in Cantonese to migrants who still spoke hardly a word of English. What had stood out in his mind was that all these Chinese living in the heart of a Western capital and surrounded by millions of Westerners nevertheless had equal rights and privileges in law if not always in fact.[10]

In 1917 Ho became a Communist, persuaded by Lenin's analysis of colonialism, and attracted to the Marxist call for revolution of the masses against the exploiting class. Like Mao Tse-tung in China, he realized that Marxism had to be modified to the circumstances of the peasantry in Asia, but he saw it as a guiding philosophy for achieving self-determination for his people. He was particularly interested in communism as a vehicle for revolution against the imperialist occupation of his home country. Calling himself "a professional revolutionary," Ho made clear to all those with whom he associated that "the passion of his life [was] a free Vietnam."[11] As one of his biographers has explained,

> Before Ho read Marx or Lenin he understood only that the French had conquered his country and were keeping his compatriots in subjection. He saw that all efforts to combat French supremacy were ruthlessly put down and that every such uprising would fail unless a new method could be applied and outside help obtained. It was to seek such methods and such help that he had gone out into the world.[12]

After some time spent in Moscow during the 1920s to develop his understanding of Marxist-Leninist strategy and the tactics of revolution, Ho became convinced that only single-minded perseverance and violent revolution could wrest Vietnam away from the French. Fully allied with the Communist International, Ho left Europe for Asia to begin his struggle against imperialism. Spending most of his time in China, Ho trained other revolutionaries and began the long process of developing a Communist-structured nationalist movement in Vietnam. By the 1930s Ho had become such a powerful figure in the political opposition to the French regime that he was condemned to death in absentia, and whatever forays he later made into Vietnam had to be done in disguise and always with the specter of capture and execution looming over him.

It wasn't until January 1941 (as far as historians can determine) when Ho actually returned to his native Vietnam after 30 years in exile. Apparently motivated by a desire to join and assist the resistance against the Japanese in northern Vietnam and emboldened by overtures from Chinese nationalist leader Chiang Kai-shek, who saw some merit in encouraging all anti-Japanese activity in the region, Ho set up a guerrilla base in China on the border with Vietnam. From this base he traveled into Vietnam and helped create the Viet Minh (The League for Vietnamese Independence), which he hoped would appeal to "Patriots of all ages and all types, intellectuals, peasants, workers, businessmen, soldiers."[13] He also organized Vietnamese exiles living in southern China into guerrilla bands whose mission was to fight the occupying Japanese. After the United States entered the war in December, Ho "went to their headquarters in Kun-ming [China] and obtained from the Americans the weapons and instructors he needed for the fight against the Japanese who had become their common enemy."[14]

However, his Communist activities and associations still put him at risk in China, where Chiang Kai-shek and his warlord allies continued to work against Mao Tse-tung and his Communist adherents despite a public agreement to collaborate against the Japanese since their invasion of China in 1937. Locally, there was considerable mistrust of the Viet Minh, which the warlords viewed as a competitor to their own domination of northern Vietnam if the Japanese were successfully repelled. On one of his visits back to China in 1942 Ho was arrested and spent a year and a half in a Chinese prison. It appears that he was finally released to resume his guerrilla leadership activity when the local warlord was persuaded that alliance with the Viet Minh in the resistance effort was, at least for the moment, more valuable than it was a threat. In fact, upon his release, Ho was provided a monthly subsidy by the Chinese to help his Viet Minh obtain supplies and further the development of the anti-Japanese effort.[15]

THE VIET MINH, THE UNITED STATES, AND WORLD WAR II

Influenced by Lenin, the Viet Minh's platform was a practical adaptation of Marxist revolutionary principles to the conditions of the Vietnamese peasantry. Strongest in the north where Ho Chi Minh organized and directed it, the Viet Minh became an effective network and organization for nationalist activity and guerrilla warfare against the Japanese, who had dominated the French colonial regime since September 1940 when the Japanese army garrisoned 50,000 troops in the country and threatened full occupation if the regime did not succumb to Japanese control.

In the previous June of that same year, when the Nazi military swept into northern France and forced the capitulation of the government in Paris, a group of French leaders led by Marshall Pétain negotiated an arrangement with Hitler to save southern France from direct occupation. Setting up a collaborationist regime in Vichy, France, Pétain avoided a Nazi takeover, but submitted his region of governance to oversight and virtual control by the Nazi regime. For many onlookers this ignoble and precipitous defeat by the Nazis, coupled with a willingness on the part of Pétain's government to collaborate, represented a terrible failure on the part of the French—a willingness to cooperate instead of to fight that was cowardly and self-serving. Whether a fair assessment or not, this was reportedly the view taken by President Roosevelt, a man never enamored with the French, who saw in these unfortunate actions proof of the corrupt and self-centered nature of French leadership.[16]

Shortly following the collapse and subsequent collaboration of Vichy France with Nazi Germany, French colonial authorities were confronted by an ultimatum from the Japanese, who were entering Southeast Asia in search of resources for their own military and economic expansion. In no position to resist, given the collaboration of their home government with the Nazi allies of the Japanese and the absence of assistance from Britain and the United States, the Vichy colonial authorities in Vietnam capitulated. In exchange for Japanese domination of economic and foreign affairs, the Vichy colonialists retained administrative control over the colonies.[17]

The capitulation of the French authorities in Southeast Asia fueled President Roosevelt's prejudices regarding the French, hardening his already stated view that once the war was won France should be forced to give up its colonial presence in Indochina. Moreover, as late as February 1944, when the United States and Britain were preparing for the Normandy invasion that would begin the liberation of France, Roosevelt made clear his view in a conversation with Undersecretary of State Edward Stettinius, that "no French troops whatever should be used in operations in Indochina." Even after France was liberated in the summer of 1944 and again officially joined the Allies in the final defeat of Germany, it was not to be allowed to reestablish itself in Indochina. Following the defeat of Japan, Roosevelt stated firmly, an international trusteeship (not including France) should be established to oversee Vietnam's transition to self-government.[18] The President conveyed this position to the British as well. Recounting his conversation with British ambassador Halifax, he told Secretary of State Cordell Hull in January 1944 that

> [I] told him . . . that it was perfectly true that I had, for over a year, expressed the opinion that Indo-China should not got back to France . . . it should be administered by an international trusteeship. France has had the country . . . one hundred years, and the people are worse off than they were at the beginning.[19]

During the course of the war, even though the United States maintained diplomatic relations with the Vichy government, its dealings were kept to a minimum and treated with caution. After the United States was drawn into the war against Japan, it did cultivate, along with Britain, intelligence contacts within the Vichy colonial government in Vietnam. Its purpose was to obtain information regarding Japanese troop movements as part of its effort to support the Chinese military resistance against the Japanese.

This relationship with select French colonial authorities lasted until Japan seized direct control of Vietnam from the French administrators in March 1945. The Japanese coup made it impossible for Allied forces to use their old informants within the French colonial government. Therefore, the Office of Strategic Services (OSS), the intelligence wing of the U.S. military during the war, sought to develop its contacts with other organized groups in Vietnam who might be able to supply information on Japanese troop locations and provide help in rescuing downed U.S. pilots.

In the meantime, the Viet Minh in northern Vietnam were becoming a significant resistance force, as the population increasingly supported this indigenous nationalist group first against French-Japanese collaboration and then against direct Japanese rule. In their search for an alternative to their Vichy agents in Vietnam, U.S. officials had begun to focus on the Viet Minh, whose operations in the countryside kept them outside the control of the Japanese and uniquely able to secure both information and downed pilots.[20] The United States had already hoped that the Viet Minh would be a useful ally against Japanese forces in the area, and the OSS began dropping supplies directly to Ho's newly formed Army of Liberation in 1944. When Japan removed the French from administrative control of the country in March 1945, the Viet Minh and Ho Chi Minh's Army of Liberation became key agents of the allied effort against Japan.

Joined by OSS agents who coordinated intelligence activities, Ho's guerrilla army was provided arms and other supplies by the United States and encouraged to join the final struggle against the Japanese army in the region.[21] A close relationship developed between the American officers and Ho Chi Minh during the months that they worked side by side. The Americans became very sympathetic with the plight of the Viet Minh in their long-term struggle for independence, and they reported to Washington that the Vietnamese would resist any effort to include the French in the final reoccupation of territory wrested from the Japanese.[22] However, during the last few months of the war, a number of events occurred that complicated official Allied treatment of their Viet Minh partners.

The first event was the successful liberation of France by the United States, Britain, and their other allies (including the Free French forces led by Charles de Gaulle) in the summer of 1944. A new government under Charles de Gaulle's leadership had been established in France, and it was considered a partner of the Allied powers in their defeat of Germany. This legitimization of France as one of the victors in the war created an ambiguous situation in Asia, where British and American military leaders disagreed on its status in the ongoing war effort there. The British included French authorities in its plans for the area, while the Americans were reluctant to allow it a role in accordance with Roosevelt's long-held views.

However, under pressure from the British, the State Department's European office, and military advisers, Roosevelt apparently began to "soften his anticolonial position." This was at first in evidence at the Yalta summit in February 1945, "where the Allies agreed that only colonies surrendered 'voluntarily' by the colonial powers would be subject to the trusteeship plan. In mid-March, the president confided . . . that he would agree to allow the French to return to Indochina if they promised eventual independence." He later authorized U.S. forces in China to provide "air support for the French fighting the Japanese in Indochina."[23] This new approach, while not constituting an abandonment of earlier policy, did create confusion about what U.S. policy was toward the region. The United States wanted whatever help it could muster against the Japanese in Asia, and there was mounting pressure for the development of stronger relations with France in Europe.

The second event compounded this confusion. On April 12, 1945, President Roosevelt died suddenly, and the vision he had for the future of Vietnam was lost with his passing. It became evident that the new administration under Harry Truman was uncertain what its policy should be regarding Vietnam's fate, and given Roosevelt's recent modifications of his anti-French attitude, the plan for Vietnam's self-determination fell by the wayside. In its place was considerable confusion. On the one hand, many people involved in foreign policy planning, as well as many of the military officials most familiar with the situation in Indochina, continued to believe that the United States should not encourage the return of French colonialism to the area. On the other hand, emerging concerns about the need for French cooperation in the postwar peace settlements were supplanting this moral commitment. This shift was demonstrated by the third event that changed the status of the U.S.-Viet Minh relationship.

This third event was the decision by the Allies to allow France to share in the final defeat of Japan and in the occupation of Vietnam. At Potsdam, a suburb of Berlin, during the last few days of July and the first days of August 1945 the leaders of the Allied powers met to decide the final fate of defeated Germany and to plan the last effort against Japan. At that meeting it was decided that, upon the defeat of Japan, France would be allowed to participate in the occupation of its former colony. Its forces would occupy the region south of the 16th parallel, and Chinese forces would be allowed to occupy the north; no mention was made of the Viet Minh, whose activities were most directly responsible for defeating Japan in the area. By war's end on V-J day August 15, 1945, U.S. policy toward Vietnam remained ambiguous. There remained a strong sentiment in favor of self-determination for this country, yet the new status of France in postwar power politics made the U.S. reluctant to act against its ally.

···

THE END OF WORLD WAR II AND
VIETNAM INDEPENDENCE DECLARED

While the Allies were meeting in Potsdam, the Viet Minh were consolidating their control over much of north and north-central Vietnam. Upon the final surrender of the Japanese army on August 15 the Viet Minh "stepped easily into the power vacuum created by Japan's collapse and the tardy arrival of Allied occupation forces."[24] By August 30 all key governmental positions had been seized by the Viet Minh.

> Everywhere in northern Vietnam local People's Revolutionary Committees took control of the Governmental machinery. In Hanoi the Viet Minh expelled the Tran Trong Kim government, while in Hue on 30 August the Emperor Bao Dai, last descendent of the Nguyen lords of Vietnam [who had been brought back to Vietnam by the Japanese to serve as titular head of the government following the coup in March], abdicated in favor of what would be known as the Democratic Republic of Vietnam.[25]

···

THE DEMOCRATIC REPUBLIC OF VIETNAM
AND U.S. POLICY

On September 2, 1945, in a speech in Hanoi, Ho Chi Minh proclaimed the independence of Vietnam. Standing on the platform with him were the OSS officers who had worked alongside him in the final defeat of the Japanese army in Vietnam, and in his address, titled the "Declaration of Independence of the Democratic Republic of Vietnam," he quoted directly from the American Declaration of Independence: "All men are created equal. They are endowed by the Creator with certain unalienable Rights; among these are Life, Liberty, and the pursuit of Happiness." He then added his endorsement and interpretation. "This immortal statement was made in the Declaration of Independence of the United States of American in 1776. In a broader sense, this means: All the peoples on the earth are equal from birth, all the peoples have right to live, to be happy and free." Finally, he traced the crimes against the Vietnamese people by the French colonialists and recounted recent history, saying, "The French have fled, the Japanese have capitulated, Emperor Bao Dai has abdicated. Our people have broken the chains which for nearly a century have fettered them and have won independence for the Fatherland." Unequivocal in his resolve he declared: "The whole Vietnamese people, animated by a common purpose, are determined to fight to the bitter end against any attempt by the French colonialists to reconquer their country. . . . The entire Vietnamese people are determined to mobilize all their physical and mental strength, to sacrifice their lives and property in order to safeguard their independence and liberty."[26]

France, for its part, was unwilling to allow control to slip easily to the Viet Minh, and it opposed the unilateral declaration of independence. During the months following the proclamation of the Democratic Republic of Vietnam, the U.S. government attempted to "ride the fence" in its policy toward the country. Several appeals for support were made to President Truman from Ho Chi Minh, but his efforts were rewarded with silence, despite State Department reports that the Vietnamese expected the United States to provide aid in accordance with the commitments espoused in the Atlantic Charter, and despite impassioned appeals from the OSS officers who had fought side by side with Ho.[27] In February 1946, when the Chinese (having moved their forces into northern Vietnam during the fall of 1945) proposed a "joint Chinese-American mediation of the Franco–Viet Minh dispute," the United States rejected it.[28] Yet at the same time the Truman administration refused to authorize U.S. military support for the French in Indochina.

In the meantime the French and the Chinese, now the official occupying forces in the aftermath of Japanese evacuation from the area, signed their own treaty, which provided for the withdrawal of Chinese troops from northern Indochina. Realizing that this was his best opportunity to get the French to agree to the existence of his new government, Ho negotiated a compromise arrangement with France, which most observers agreed required a highly conciliatory approach. This arrangement provided for the recognition by France of the Democratic Republic of Vietnam in Tonkin as a "free state having its own government, its own parliament, its own army and its own finances, forming a part of the Indo-China Federation and of the French Union."[29] The possibility of the unification of Tonkin with the other two regions of Vietnam was to be decided at a later date by plebiscite.

However, almost immediately fighting erupted between the French and the Viet Minh, and Ho Chi Minh returned to his original claim of a "wholly independent Vietnam." Although Ho traveled to Paris to negotiate for his country's independence, the French continued to resist. By 1947 all-out warfare had erupted as the French launched a major offensive against the Viet Minh and the Viet Minh responded with the guerrilla tactics they had developed during World War II.[30]

THE UNITED STATES SHIFTS ITS POLICY IN FAVOR OF FRANCE

It is at this point that U.S. policy began to move from ambiguity to clear-cut support for the French against the Viet Minh. While many American policy makers remained unsympathetic with French colonialism, it soon became evident that in the emerging cold war environment, they also were more concerned about the spread of communism than they were about allowing the French to retain their colonies. Having announced the Truman Doctrine in March 1947, the President committed the United States to the containment of communism. This new foreign-policy preoccupation replaced whatever had been left of the goals embodied in the Atlantic Charter and focused American attention on the need to quash Communist movements of any kind regardless of whether they were a vehicle of nationalism or not.

Enlisting deposed Emperor Bao Dai, whose own hopes for an independent Vietnam were encouraged with a promise of eventual independence, the French created a puppet regime in Saigon in 1949. The reaction in Washington to this situation was decidedly mixed. The Bureau of Far East Affairs within the State Department was wary of the new French arrangement, worrying that a commitment to recognize and support the Bao Dai regime would take the United States "into a very bad mess."[31] Increasingly, however, the growing preoccupation with European affairs, and the desire to court the French into supporting U.S. policies there, plus the mounting fear about the spread of communism, overshadowed the concerns expressed by those most familiar with Vietnam.

Besides, 1949 proved to be a particularly eventful year for American foreign policy. The North Atlantic Treaty Organization was founded between the United States and its Atlantic partners in a display of solidarity against potential Soviet aggression in Europe. This supplanted efforts by the French to form a Europe-only defensive alliance. Secondly, the U.S.-backed Federal Republic of Germany was created from the Western zones of occupation, causing considerable consternation in France, which remained wary of the reconstruction of a German polity that someday might be rearmed. Finally, 1949 marked the takeover in China by Communist forces under the leadership of Mao Tse-tung and the defeat of wartime ally Chiang Kai-shek. Given these historic events, there was little sympathy in the United States for supporting Ho's nationalist struggle. His adherence to communism, even though nationalistic in orientation, made his government an unacceptable alternative to French colonialism.

Consequently, a number of considerations made the Truman administration take steps to change its Indochina policy. First, French reluctance about U.S. policy in Europe, which centered on a U.S.-led military alliance and on the reconstruction of West Germany as the cornerstone of economic recovery policy, had to be overcome. French cooperation was needed for U.S. policy to go forward in Europe. In addition, the French government could ill afford the Indochina war along with the demands of European recovery. Under the circumstances France asked for, and received, a pledge of assistance from the United States for its ongoing struggle in Vietnam. Policy makers in Washington were persuaded that American assistance in Vietnam was a necessary trade for French cooperation in the European recovery program.

Secondly, the "loss" of China to communism was a dark event for the Truman administration. Branded as having a weak policy toward communism abroad and indicted during the Senate McCarthy hearings for harboring Communists in the State Department, the administration was under pressure to exhibit its hard-line attitude toward Communist expansion.[32] In particular, its policies in Asia had come under scrutiny, and there was increasing right-wing pressure for a definite stand against Vietnamese communism.

Thirdly, in January of 1950 both the newly founded People's Republic of China and the Soviet Union formally recognized the Democratic Republic of Vietnam, convincing Secretary of State Dean Acheson and others that Ho Chi Minh was nothing more than "an agent of world Communism [who preached] Indo-China for the Kremlin and not Indo-China for the Indo-Chinese."[33] Acheson argued that the recognition "reveal[ed] Ho in his true colors as the mortal enemy of native independence in Indo-China."[34] On February 4, 1950, following Acheson's urgent recommendation, President Truman recognized the Bao Dai regime, taking the first step toward endorsing and materially supporting the French in the region, yet all the while aware that the Bao Dai government was a powerless puppet under the control of the French.

The Korean War, which erupted in June of 1950, fueled the demand in U.S. foreign policy circles for a deeper commitment to the French in Vietnam, as policy makers became convinced that "the loss of any single country [of southeast Asia] would probably lead to relatively swift submission to or an alignment with communism by remaining countries. . . ."[35] Furthermore, the Truman administration's growing concern with the recovery of the Japanese economy was creating a strong argument for the development of Southeast Asia as an important area for Japanese trade.[36] These two factors led to an even stronger interest in the maintenance of a non-Communist regime in Vietnam that could participate in the economic development of Southeast Asia and help the area resist further Communist expansion. As a consequence aid to the French regime was increased substantially. By the end of the year the United States had provided $33 million in military and economic aid.[37]

PRESIDENT EISENHOWER TAKES THE REINS FROM THE FRENCH

When President Dwight Eisenhower succeeded Truman as president in 1953, he faced the dual challenges in Asia of winning the U.S. war in Korea and of supporting the French in their ever deepening war with the Vietnamese. Largely inheriting the Truman administration's policy toward Vietnam, Eisenhower continued to pour aid to the French in hopes of thwarting a communist victory. Between 1950 and 1954 France received $3.6 billion in aid, much of which went to its effort in Indochina.[38] Despite U.S. aid, however, the French military found itself increasingly on the defensive in its struggle against the Viet Minh, and discussions in Washington regarding the region focused on what measures the United States could take to prevent a Communist takeover. Generally, the administration, the Joint Chiefs, and Congress all opposed direct intervention by the United States, hoping that U.S. aid would be enough. In 1954, however, the French military suffered a crippling defeat in a battle at the frontier outpost of Dien Bien Phu. Following this catastrophic event the French government decided enough was enough and announced that it would enter into peace negotiations and withdraw its forces. The United States found itself faced with the question of what direction it would now follow with regard to the future of the region.

Opposed to any negotiated settlement that would result in advantages for the Viet Minh, the United States was skeptical about the 1954 Geneva Conference, which aimed at settling the nine-year conflict between the French and the Democratic Republic of Vietnam. The conference was attended by representatives from the United States, Britain, France, Russia, and China, as well as Laos, Cambodia, and the Viet Minh. Despite the fact that Ho Chi Minh's forces controlled three-fourths of the country, there was considerable concern that the United States might intervene to replace the French and that this would perpetuate and widen the conflict. Therefore, the other great powers "feared . . . that they, too, might be drawn into the war—and that eventually it might become a World War. So they used their combined influence at Geneva to try to bring about peace in Indochina."[39]

While the declaration that resulted from the Geneva Conference regarding the future of Vietnam was not an unequivocal statement of support for the Viet Minh (and was therefore received with disappointment by Ho Chi Minh), it was still perceived by U.S. leaders as unacceptable. Basically the declaration had three main provisions. First, "Vietnam was to be temporarily divided into two zones . . . at the 17th parallel," emphasizing that the division "should not in any way be interpreted as constituting a political boundary."[40] The division was to facilitate the separation and regrouping of military forces on their respective sides of the boundary. This division was also aimed at allowing French forces, officials, and Vietnamese allied with the French to collect themselves and arrange for evacuation if so desired. The two areas were to be administered separately "until the country was reunited."[41] Secondly, there would be an internationally supervised election throughout the whole of Vietnam to determine the type of government desired by the people. It was to take place within two years. Thirdly, "until the country was reunited, neither zone would receive any military aid from outside, or make any alliances."[42]

Knowing that elections in Vietnam likely would result in support for the Viet Minh, the Eisenhower administration refused to vote for the Geneva Conference declaration. Working behind the scenes, Washington had already been scheming toward the creation of a new government in Saigon that might have the political legitimacy to compete with Ho Chi Minh. Even before the Geneva Conference was completed the United States had "persuaded the French to allow Bao Dai to appoint Ngo Dinh Diem as his prime minister and to get the emperor to agree to stay in Europe's spas while Diem returned to Saigon to run the south. By July 7, 1954, Diem had a fully organized cabinet in place," and the Republic of South Vietnam was proclaimed.[43]

The reason the Eisenhower administration selected Diem to head a government in South Vietnam was that he had established himself as anti-French and anti-Communist (and his collaboration with the Japanese during World War II seemed not to be of any concern in this coldwar environment), and he had years of experience within Bao Dai's earlier cabinets. Most recently he had spent 1951 through 1953 in the United States. Despite his anti-French credentials he was a member of the Catholic elite and an authoritarian who had little contact with, or sympathy for, the masses. Evidence suggests that the United States was not well enough acquainted with him to realize this until later, when it became clear that his family and "cronies" would run the government with a ruthless disregard for Vietnamese society.[44]

Plagued immediately by a massive refugee problem, as over 800,000 people fled the north, the Diem regime sought assistance from the United States. The Eisenhower administration was quick to respond with $323 million in Diem's first year in office.[45] Then, despite a rocky relationship with the United States, as U.S. officials became more and more aware that Diem would not be able to effectively achieve public support, the Eisenhower administration followed through on its commitment to Diem to help create and train a new army for the Republic of South Vietnam.[46] By 1956 the French had withdrawn all their remaining forces from Vietnam, the elections that were to have been scheduled that year were prevented by the unilateral proclamation of the new South

Vietnamese regime, and the United States had begun to directly support a noncommunist alternative to Ho Chi Minh's government. The baton had been passed from the French to the Americans. The Diem regime and its army were now the creation of the United States, and their preservation and success became a U.S. concern. The struggle was not for the perpetuation of a colonial empire, as it had been for France; it was now a struggle to hold the line against Communist expansion. The lessons learned by France in its recent attempts to maintain control in the face of highly determined Viet Minh forces were lost on Washington, which seemed increasingly blind to the nationalistic motivations of the Vietnamese people and unwilling to face the inadequacies of the government it had installed in Saigon.

CONCLUSION

By the end of the decade the United States had 1,500 military advisers in South Vietnam, and between 1955 and 1961 it provided $1 billion in military and economic aid. When the Kennedy administration assumed control of Southeast Asian policy, it was trapped by the same mind-set that had reversed U.S. policy after the war and had persuaded the Eisenhower administration to ignore the Geneva declaration and sponsor a nondemocratic regime in the South. Convinced that the Diem regime would topple without a substantial increase in U.S. aid, but, like Eisenhower, reluctant to launch a massive military intervention, President Kennedy continued to escalate U.S. involvement through more and more aid and advisers. By the end of 1962 there were 11,000 U.S. military advisers in South Vietnam and by the end of 1964, 23,000.[47]

Still, however, the Communist forces in Vietnam kept the Army of South Vietnam on the defensive, and the South Vietnamese government's success in the political battle for public support was equally bleak. Pressure was growing for the United States to take more direct control of the military defense of the regime, while also trying to get that regime to become more responsive to its own people. This paradoxical state of affairs confronted Lyndon Johnson when he became president following Kennedy's assassination in November 1963, and he too seemed committed to the outlook taken by his predecessors. Within three days of taking the oath of office he issued the following directive on Vietnam:

> It remains the central object of the United States in South Vietnam to assist the people and government of the country to win their contest against the externally directed and supported Communist conspiracy. The test of all U.S. decisions and actions in this area should be the effectiveness of their contribution to this purpose.[48]

By placing U.S. credibility on the line in this battle against Communist expansion, which he believed was directed from Moscow and China, Johnson increased the stakes. Withdrawal had not been a viable alternative for U.S. policy in Vietnam since 1954, but under Johnson's leadership it became unthinkable because it would signify defeat in the larger coldwar conflict. Now the war had to be *won* before the United States could withdraw. Otherwise, according to Johnson, the United States would be committing the same appeasement in Southeast Asia that the European nations had committed in their agreement with Hitler in Munich in 1936.[49] Given this belief, South Vietnam could not be allowed to fall to the Communists without strengthening the hands of the Soviets and Chinese and seriously weakening the United States in its role as leader of the noncommunist world.

In August 1964 the Johnson administration secured from Congress a resolution that supported the President "in his determination to take all necessary measures to prevent further aggression."[50] Thus, with this blanket approval, the first U.S. ground troops were sent to South Vietnam in 1965, beginning the war between U.S. forces and Ho Chi Minh's supporters that would last for 10 more years and would alter forever the generation that fought it.

Discussion Questions

1. What circumstances led the United States military to treat Vietnamese Communist leader Ho Chi Minh as an ally during World War II?
2. What circumstances led the United States to change its policy toward Ho Chi Minh?
3. How was Vietnam divided, and how did the U.S. government use this division as a justification for its military intervention?
4. How was policy toward Vietnam affected by the transition from Franklin Roosevelt as president to Harry Truman as president?
5. Were U.S. policy makers from Truman to Lyndon Johnson correct in their assumption that the battle for liberation in Vietnam was really the result of Soviet expansionism?
6. What does this case tell us about how foreign policy orientations change?

Notes

1. U.S. estimates of Vietnamese killed (included North and South) between 1965 and 1972 range from about 1,000,000 to about 1,500,000. In addition, out of an 18 million population, some 6 to 7 million people became refugees. Gabriel Kolko, *Anatomy of a War: Vietnam, the United States and the Modern Historical Experience* (New York: The New Press, 1994), pp. 200–201.
2. The most infamous example of this was when Iraq's Saddam Hussein miscalculated that the United States would not risk war in the Persian Gulf to roll back Iraqi aggression against Kuwait in 1990–91.
3. Ronald H. Specter, *Advice and Support: The Early Years of the U.S. Army in Vietnam 1941–1960* (New York: The Free Press, 1985), p. 22.
4. Walter LaFeber, *The American Age: U.S. Foreign Policy at Home and Abroad Since 1896*, vol. 2 (New York: W.W. Norton, 1994), pp. 400–401.

5. Ibid., p. 401.

6. Text of the Atlantic Charter quoted from the memoirs of Winston S. Churchill, *The Grand Alliance* (New York: Bantam Books, 1962), pp. 374–375.

7. Specter, *Advice and Support,* p. 9.

8. Ibid., p. 13.

9. Charles Fenn, *Ho Chi Min: A Biographical Introduction* (New York: Charles Scribner's Sons, 1973), pp. 6–22.

10. Ibid., p. 26.

11. Ibid., p. 39.

12. Ibid., p. 43.

13. Ibid., p. 68.

14. Jean Sainteny, *Ho Chi Minh and His Vietnam: A Personal Memoir,* trans. from the French by Herman Briffault (Chicago: Cowles Book Company, 1972), pp.37–38.

15. Specter, *Advice and Support,* pp. 37–38.

16. Ibid., p. 23.

17. Specter, *Advice and Support,* p. 18.

18. U.S. Department of State, *Foreign Relations of the United States 1944,* vol. 5, pubn. 7859 (1969), p. 1206.

19. Specter, *Advice and Support,* p. 22.

20. American diplomats and military officials seemed generally unaware of Ho Chi Minh's organization until 1945 when they became motivated by the Japanese coup to find alternatives to Vichy agents. Specter, *Advice and Support,* pp. 39–40.

21. John T. McAllister, *Vietnam: The Origins of Revolution* (New York: Alfred A. Knopf, 1969), pp. 161–165.

22. Specter, *Advice and Support,* pp. 57–58.

23. Andrew J. Rotter, *The Path to Vietnam: Origins of the American Commitment to Southeast Asia* (Ithaca: Cornell University Press, 1987), p. 93.

24. Specter, *Advice and Support,* p. 55.

25. Ibid., pp. 55–56.

26. Ho Chi Minh, "Declaration of Independence of the Democratic Republic of Viet-Nam (September 2, 1945)," George Katsiaficas, ed. *Vietnam Documents: American and Vietnamese Views of the War* (New York: M.E. Sharpe, 1992), pp. 7–8.

27. U.S. Department of State, *Foreign Relations of the United States 1946,* vol. 8, pubn. 8554 (1971), pp. 17–19.

28. Specter, *Advice and Support,* pp. 77–78.

29. Ibid., p. 78.

30. Ibid.

31. Ibid., p. 95.

32. Rotter, *The Path to Vietnam,* pp. 170–171.

33. Ibid., p. 172.

34. Ibid.

35. Specter, quoting a National Security Council Memorandum of 1952, *Advice and Support,* p. 194.

36. Ibid., p. 6.

37. Ibid., p. 127.

38. Kolko, *Anatomy of a War,* p. 1.

39. Benjamin Spock and M. Zimmerman, "How We Got Involved—the Vietnamese and the French," in Katsiaficas, ed., *Vietnam Documents,* p. 40.

40. Quoting the declaration, Ibid., p. 41.

41. Ibid.

42. Ibid.

43. Kolko, *Anatomy of a War,* pp. 82–83. Note that the Geneva declaration was issued on July 21!

44. Ibid., p. 84.

45. Ibid.

46. Specter, *Advice and Support,* p. 220.

47. Kolko, *Anatomy of a War,* p. 113.

48. National Security Action Memorandum 273 issued by McGeorge Bundy, November 26, 1963. Quoted in Gareth Porter, ed. *Vietnam: The Definitive Documentation of Human Decisions,* vol. 2 (Stanfordville, N.Y.: Earl M. Coleman Enterprises, 1979), p. 22.

49. Lyndon Baines Johnson, *The Vantage Point: Perspectives of the Presidency 1963–1969* (New York: Holt, Rinehart, and Winston, 1971), pp. 147–148.

50. "The Gulf of Tonkin Resolution, August 7, 1964" quoted in Katsiaficas, ed., *Vietnam Documents,* pp. 52–53.

PART II

UNDERSTANDING CURRENT FORCES IN INTERNATIONAL POLITICS

New Directions and New Challenges

CHAPTER 7

TAKING THE INITIATIVE

The Canada–U.S. Free Trade Agreement and the North American Free Trade Agreement

....

INTRODUCTION

In the realm of international political-economic relations the predictability of trade flows has become one of the most important priorities of businesses and governments alike. Since the creation of GATT in 1947, the world's trade has multiplied exponentially, contributing significantly to the economic development and prosperity of most of the nations of the world. However, imports and exports do not flow easily across borders at all times. Often, protectionist interests react against the importation of goods, perhaps because they compete against domestically produced goods, perhaps because they have been unfairly traded, or perhaps because they pose some kind of health or safety concern, and governments in turn respond to the pressure from those interests. Thus, at any given time one might pick up the newspaper and read about a brewing dispute between the United States and one of its trading partners, or about negotiations to improve their trading relationship. One of the most significant post-GATT trade developments was the Canada–United

States Free Trade Agreement, which in turn lay the foundation for the more far-reaching North American Free Trade Agreement that also included Mexico. Outside of the European Union it is the most important free trade arrangement in the world.

Former Canadian prime minister Pierre Elliott Trudeau often described Canada's relationship with the United States as analogous to that of a mouse sleeping with an elephant. The elephant hardly notices the mouse, but the mouse constantly is aware of every move the elephant makes! A huge country in geographical area, Canada is relatively small in population terms. Its 26 million people, most of whom live within 200 miles of the U.S. border, often feel overwhelmed and dominated by their superpower neighbor to the south. With 260 million people and the largest national economy in the world, the United States has posed challenges to, and opportunities for, Canadians who desire economic vitality, but who also strive for some degree of economic and cultural independence from the American behemoth. In fact, much of the history of this bilateral relationship is characterized by Canadian governmental efforts to limit U.S. economic influence in the Canadian market. For decades Canada has attempted to diversify its international trade so that it could limit its dependency on the United States. Thus, trade with the United States has always been very controversial, and even within the multilateral forum for reducing trade barriers (the General Agreement on Tariffs and Trade), Canada generally avoided making concessions that would make Canadian industry vulnerable to U.S. competition.

For many observers of Canadian politics, both within and outside Canada, it came as somewhat of a surprise in 1985 when the Canadian government departed from past foreign economic policy patterns and proposed a free trade agreement with the United States. The resulting bilateral arrangement drastically lowered Canadian tariffs (U.S. tariffs were already relatively low for Canadian products), established a set of rules and norms for governing trade between the two signatories, and in 1994 became the foundation for a North American Free Trade Agreement (NAFTA) that included Mexico. Within 10 years of the free trade initiative in Canada, the dynamics and politics of investment and trade in North America had been significantly altered.

How did this radical change in Canadian foreign economic policy come about? Why would a nation, preoccupied with maintaining its economic and cultural independence from the United States, decide to eliminate much of its market protection and embrace free trade with the very nation of which it was so wary? The following case study examines the circumstances that led Canada to alter its policy toward the United States, demonstrating that even in a highly asymmetrical economic relationship a smaller nation can set the agenda.

ECONOMIC RELATIONS PRIOR TO 1985

Canadian economic policy has historically been dominated by the dual goals of benefiting from participation in the global economy without opening its borders to unrestricted competition from its economically powerful neighbor, the United States. This resulted in a foreign trade and investment policy that was characterized by governmental regulation and relatively high protection. If the Canadian government did not manage its economic relations with the United States, it was argued, larger, more competitive firms from south of the border would either drive Canadian producers out of business or merely absorb them directly. In order to retain the independent viability of Canadian businesses, the Canadian government would have to erect and maintain restrictions that protected domestic production and investment from foreign encroachments. Between 1879, when the National Policy for Canada was adopted, and 1985, when the radically new free trade direction was taken, Canada had generally pursued a nationalistic policy aimed at developing Canada's own indigenous industrial base within the walls of protection. Despite efforts in 1911 and again in 1947 to pursue more hospitable trade relations with the United States, the National Policy, which consisted of protecting Canadian business, industry, and agriculture, dominated the bilateral economic relationship for over a century.[1] Although limited bilateral tariff reductions were negotiated in the 1930s and multilateral trade negotiations resulted in tariff reductions under the General Agreement on Tariffs and Trade (GATT) for three and a half decades following World War II, the character of Canada's trade policy with the United States remained decidedly protectionist. As one observer explains,

> U.S. average tariffs on dutiable imports . . . from Canada [in the 1980s] were about 1 percent. . . . By comparison Canadian average tariffs on dutiable imports . . . averaged about 9 to 10 percent. . . . As a trade-dependent middle power, Canada . . . supported multilateral trade liberalization under the GATT, but it had always managed to pursue multilateralism without losing the margin of protection inherent in the National Policy of 1987.[2]

Even the 1965 Canada–U.S. Automobile Agreement (Auto-Pact), which opened Canadian auto firms to U.S. investment and the Canadian market to U.S. exports, consisted of governmentally managed arrangements ensuring that significant portions of North American production would be located in Canada to the benefit of the Canadian economy and Canadian workers.[3] The Canadian argument was that if Canadians were going to buy automobiles from the big automakers in Detroit, then they should also be allowed to participate in their manufacture, thus securing jobs and other economic benefits besides consumption.

Generally, the Canadian government's approach was to channel U.S. investment by imposing restrictions aimed at encouraging industrial capability. For economic development purposes this was considered vital. Canada's agricultural and resource-based economy has made it much more vulnerable to the vagaries of the international marketplace, forcing it to share many of the less desirable features of the economies of lesser developed, resource-based countries. Consequently, the Canadian government and its business interests have pursued the goal of diversifying Canada's economic base to include substantial activity in manufacturing and processing. From a development point of view this policy was a smashing success. "During the 1960s, for example, manufactured goods dramatically increased the share of total Canadian exports to 30 percent from 8 percent."[4] Because much of this increase was due to manufacturing in the auto industry, the 1965 pact with the United States automakers was largely responsible for this impressive growth. Success in this area meant that a number of Canadian efforts to encourage industry were linked to foreign direct investment deals with U.S. firms.

This approach to investment and trade became a systematic policy after 1973 when Canada adopted the Foreign Investment Review Act (FIRA), which "institutionalized a process for obtaining 'commitments' from direct foreign investors to improve the economic benefits that Canada derives." Specifically, these requirements included "target levels for export, value added, and employment."[5] If foreign firms wanted to invest in Canada, they would be required to meet these specific targets, which were aimed at ensuring that Canadian workers, suppliers, and trade balances would benefit. This was followed in 1980 by the National Energy Program (NEP), which regulated the energy industry and set strict limits on foreign ownership in the lucrative oil and natural gas sectors. Irritants to United States businesses who wanted to establish or expand operations in Canada, FIRA and the NEP were decried by the U.S. government as unfair policies that discriminated against foreign firms and discouraged transborder economic activity to the detriment of American firms. Their implementation marked a low point in post–World War II economic relations between the two countries.

Ironically, despite Canada's industrial policy, its historical commitment to resisting free trade, and its restrictions on investment, by the early 1980s it was even more dependent than ever on the U.S. trade relationship. In 1984 over 75 percent of Canadian exports were destined for the U.S. market, and nearly 72 percent of Canadian imports came from the United States![6] Additionally, the foreign investment policies of the Trudeau governments had produced some negative effects, while not producing the kind of invigoration of domestic Canadian industry that had been intended. Besides alienating the United States, these policies had forced a "large drop in foreign investment in Canada, which fell from an average of C$684 million in 1970–75 to C$372 million in 1976–80."[7] When recession gripped the global economy between 1981 and 1982, many critics of Canada's restrictive economic policies blamed these approaches for the recession's severity in Canada.

A NEW APPROACH

In the wake of this debate, an opportunity for policy revision was beginning to open for those individuals and groups who for years had advocated more liberal trade in the face of overwhelming nationalistic opposition. Even within the government there was some interest in approaching the United States about the possibility of negotiating certain sectoral free trade agreements.[8] However, these stopped far short of advocating general free trade; instead, the proposals were aimed at opening trade only in those sectors where Canadian industries were clearly competitive with U.S. industries. Still, these ideas demonstrated that even in official governmental circles, where the Liberal Party had long advocated protectionist approaches to trade, the value of Canada–U.S. trade could not be sacrificed completely to nationalistic preferences regarding economic autonomy.

The opportunity to consider a more open approach toward the United States was enhanced when the results of an in-depth inquiry into the "long-term economic potential, prospects and challenges facing the Canadian federation" were published by a specially delegated royal commission in 1985.[9] Interestingly, this Royal Commission on the Economic Union and Development Prospects for Canada (commonly known as the Macdonald Commission in reference to the commission's chairman, Donald S. Macdonald) had been established in 1982 under the Trudeau government and charged with investigating the circumstances that framed Canada's prospects as a federation and as a vital economic entity. In the words of the report, the commission was also charged with "assessing whether the Canada we know today, built as it has been upon the incremental changes of the past, is well positioned for the major challenges ahead. Because Canada is going to have to adapt to meet a much more competitive world environment, the commission's role was also to look at Canada's position in that broader context."[10]

In establishing the context within which Canada's future would be shaped, the Macdonald Commission examined Canada's economic situation and carried out a systematic study of its relationships with other nations in the global economy. It arrived at several important conclusions regarding the opportunities and limits facing Canadian policy makers. First it noted that, despite Canada's activity in GATT and a determined effort to diversify its external economic relations, Canada had actually increased its dependency on the United States. It reported that "the merchandise exports going to the United States increased from 59.8 to 76.3 percent from 1954 to 1984, while the percentage of [Canada's] merchandise imports from the United States remained level at 72 percent."[11] It also pointed out the fact that not only was Canada significantly trade dependent (28.2 percent of GNP compared with an OECD average of 19.8 percent), it was the most dependent of all OECD countries for its export market on a single country (the United States). As the commission explained, "We suffer from interdependence without security in a context wherein our dependence on the U.S. market is not reciprocated by an equivalent American dependence on the Canadian market."[12]

Moreover, the commission explained, as U.S. industry suffered increasingly from the competitive challenges of other nations in recent years, it pressed the U.S. government to impose a range of protectionist and retaliatory measures against the flood of imports. Given Canada's dependence on the American market, this unilateral protectionist trend in U.S. policy was particularly alarming. What the commission called "the insecurity of access" was rising for Canadian producers as the United States resorted to non-tariff barriers (NTBs) to protect its own industries from competition. In addition to creating uncertainty for Canadian exporters, this insecurity of access, they argued, was having two other undesirable effects on the Canadian economic situation. First, it was prompting Canadian manufacturers and service providers to move production to the United States in order to escape the export difficulties caused by U.S. NTBs; and second, it was making rationalization of industry (the restructuring of industry to respond to the competitive demands of the international marketplace) difficult to pursue. After all, how could Canadian industry plan for certain export markets when unpredictable protectionism (and not market forces) in the United States disrupted their access to American consumers.

These observations were nothing new to the Canadian public. Obviously, it had been this very dependency and vulnerability that had prompted national governmental efforts like the National Policy, Auto-Pact, and FIRA. However, it was the commission's conclusions about this unique economic context that were a clear departure from past policies. Rather than recommend yet another inward-looking, nationalistic policy aimed at protecting Canadian industry from American competition, the Macdonald Commission offered a radically different recommendation. Given Canada's dependency on the United States market and given its past inability to diversify its trade partners, the Macdonald Commission argued, it would be Canada's best option to make the most of its existing circumstances. Canada should embrace the bilateral relationship in a free trade arrangement, but it should be an agreement that would provide greater certainty for Canadian producers by ensuring more predictability for Canadian exports.

The commission estimated that if Canada and the United States achieved a free trade agreement, the free trade effects would stimulate gross national product growth by 3 to 8 percent. Such economic growth had not been experienced since the 1960s, and the prospects of renewed economic vitality were very attractive. Although it recognized that the gains from increased trade with the United States would be accompanied by the associated costs of economic adjustment, the commission considered such adjustments to be positive for the long-term health of Canadian industry. In fact, it focused its recommendation on the importance of altering the general thrust of Canadian economic policy from protectionism to free market competition:

> Free trade is the main instrument in this Commission's approach to industrial policy. It is based on the same intellectual thrust which governs Commissioners' approach to domestic economic policy: that the role of governments is not to retard competitive market forces, but to complement them by positive adjustment measures.[13]

This independent commission, charged by the Trudeau government in 1982 with assessing the state of the Canadian federation and its prospects for economic development, had ironically encouraged the Canadian people in its report in 1985 to embark in a different direction from that which had been pursued by successive Trudeau governments. Coupled with public dissatisfaction over the performance of the Canadian economy, the recommendations of this highly visible and much respected group of Canadian experts created momentum for a new free trade debate.

This came at a crucial juncture in Canadian politics. Nearly one year prior to the official release of the Macdonald Commission report, national elections had resulted in a noteworthy change in Canadian government. The Progressive Conservatives won a strong majority in the House of Commons in September 1984, and their party leader, Brian Mulroney, became prime minister. Except for a brief nine-month period in 1979–80 the Conservative Party had not held the prime ministership since 1963. In 1984 it successfully drew voters away from the Liberal Party, especially those who had become disaffected with the Liberals over FIRA , the NEP, and general discomfort with economic conditions. While Mulroney did not have a particularly strong policy agenda when his party assumed the reins of government, he did pursue generally a more free market approach to the economy than had been followed by the Liberals. This "included a policy of privatization of public corporations, deregulation and tax measures aimed at encouraging increased investment."[14] Thus, when the Macdonald

Commission's report was issued, it "was embraced by the Conservative government of Brian Mulroney because it reflected the philosophy and broader concerns of that government."[15]

TAKING THE INITIATIVE

The Mulroney government issued its own report regarding the future of Canadian industry, competitiveness, and economic growth. This report, *Competitiveness and Security: Directions for Canada's International Relations,* noted, "Our dependence on trade means that we are economically secure only if we are internationally competitive." It concluded that "the messages are clear. Our economic interests require us to be competitive; we must trade if we are to prosper."[16] Following the recommendation of the Macdonald Commission regarding the need to open trade with the United States in order to achieve international competitiveness (as well as to secure more predictable conditions for Canadian trade), the Mulroney government announced in September 1985 its intention to pursue a bilateral free trade agreement with the United States. The rationale behind this announcement was consistent with the Macdonald Commission's report:

> The government claimed that the Free Trade Agreement would bring long-term economic benefits for the country, securing access to the American market, creating the opportunity for economic rationalization and creating a mechanism for resolving trade disputes with the United States.[17]

This was a bold new initiative on the party of the Mulroney government. Clearly it was guided by an overarching economic philosophy that placed confidence in the market's ability to increase the competitive capability of Canadian industry, and thus its long-term vigor in the international economy. This new policy orientation was buttressed by the work of a nonpartisan commission of experts from across Canada, which lent broad-based legitimacy to the Conservative Party's platform. However, specific domestic circumstances made it possible for the Conservatives to markedly shift economic policy direction away from the patterns of the past. The recession, western provincial disaffection with the NEP, splintering of the Liberal Party, and strengthening of the Conservatives in Quebec all contributed to the ability of the Mulroney government to launch Canada in a new foreign economic policy direction. The new Conservative government drastically changed FIRA and the NEP to make Canada more hospitable to foreign investment, and it announced its plan to pursue even freer policies toward the United States.

Even so, entrenched patterns of behavior are difficult to break. Despite the convincing arguments about the benefits of free trade, many groups were fearful about the costs associated with free trade adjustment. Worried that less competitive industries would be put out of business and local jobs would be lost, a heated debate ensued around the character that the free trade agreement should have. Familiar arguments surfaced about the need to protect Canadian culture from being overwhelmed by U.S.

businesses, products, and practices. To many, the free trade initiative posed a genuine threat to the unique aspects of Canadian culture and society.

Not wanting their initiative to lose momentum in the midst of this debate, the Mulroney government stressed the importance of free market principles for disciplining Canadian industry so that it could survive (and in fact thrive) in the world economy. It observed that the competitive challenge came not only from the United States but also from a whole new range of economic actors that were becoming very successful at penetrating Canada's domestic market. If Canada hoped to be competitive in the next century, it would have to subject its industry to the marketplace. Moreover, if Canada wanted to benefit from economies of scale, it had to enhance its export role in the most logical place for Canadian products—the United States.

The Conservative government also stressed the importance of a Canada–U.S. free trade agreement for protecting Canadian exporters from the vagaries of U.S. NTBs—especially in the guise of claims against alleged unfair trading practices. These so-called retaliations against Canadian exports were very disruptive because they required long, drawn-out investigation and determination procedures that increased uncertainty and raised costs for Canadian exporters, even if in the end U.S. administrative law determined that the exporters had not violated U.S. regulations.

This had become particularly troublesome for Canadian exporters charged with having received subsidies from the government to assist their export enterprises. Because export subsidies are generally illegal under the GATT and U.S. countervailing duty law, claims against alleged export subsidies had always been a method employed by U.S. producers to curtail Canadian export competition. However, with passage of the 1979 Trade Agreements Act in the United States, it became much easier for American producers to initiate trade disruptive petitions against Canadian exporters. Designed to protect U.S. producers from the competitive advantages that subsidies from foreign governments often provided, U.S. countervailing duty law allowed American producers to file petitions against imports that they believed benefited from foreign government subsidies. Once filed, the petition complaints were investigated to determine whether competition from the imported products were causing the plaintiff injury. Then, if an affirmative determination regarding injury was made, a further investigation of whether the exporter benefited from an illegal subsidy was carried out.

Sometimes U.S. investigations would determine that the Canadian export was not in violation of U.S. law, and at other times the investigation would support the American domestic producer's claim. However, in the latter situation the fairness of the U.S. determination was often called into question. For example, certain "upstream" subsidies, which were very similar to the kinds of subsidies enjoyed by U.S. producers, would be singled out as creating unfair competitive advantages for Canadian producers. Yet, even though Canadian producers and government representatives would cry foul, there was no procedure that they could follow to appeal the U.S. decision.

Once the decision was made, a countervailing duty would be imposed against the imported product, raising its price in the American market and reducing its competitiveness there. The duty would be calculated by the United States to offset any advantage that the U.S. International Trade Commission had determined existed from the alleged subsidy, yet there was no recourse for Canada to overturn what it considered to be an unfair decision. Moreover, because the United States and Canada disagreed over what constituted an unfair subsidy in the first place, and because U.S. producers were increasingly resorting to countervailing duty claims to obtain protection from Canadian exports, this issue became a chronic and worrisome problem in their bilateral trading relationship.

Observers of U.S. trade policy also charged that the countervailing duty petitions were part of a larger movement within U.S. industry to exploit U.S. trade law as much as possible to secure protection from free trade commitments. Canada was by no means the only victim of U.S. protectionist tendencies during the early 1980s. Japan, the newly industrialized countries of East Asia, the European Community, and Latin American nations were all being targeted by claims in the United States that their goods were either being dumped at prices below cost of production or were being unfairly subsidized. However, given Canada's grossly asymmetrical trade dependence on the United States, the trend was particularly alarming for Canadian producers who were so dependent on the U.S. market.

Given this concern about the insecurity of access to the U.S. market under current circumstances, the Mulroney government also saw promise in a U.S.–Canada free trade agreement for limiting Canada's vulnerability. They believed that the best way to guarantee that Canadian producers would not be subjected to the vicissitudes of American protectionism would be to include specific agreements on fair trade rules, dispute settlement, and bilateral arbitration. The Canadian public was assured that any Canada–U.S. free trade agreement would include guarantees that American "fair" trade enforcement procedures would no longer be allowed to disrupt legitimate Canadian exports. The "security of access" argument that had been a prominent feature of the Macdonald Commission's report became the centerpiece of the Mulroney government's promise to its public regarding an agreement with the United States. Thus,

> [o]ne of Canada's principal objectives in the free trade negotiation was to secure its access to the U.S. market, that is, to reduce the impact of U.S. trade remedies, especially countervailing duties on Canadian products, either directly by negotiating an exception to U.S. trade law, or indirectly by creating a dispute settlement system that would circumvent those laws. During the negotiation, security of access (or dispute settlement, which it boiled down to) became the paramount objective of the Canadian side because it was the one area where Canada was unquestioningly the demandeurand thus in a position to 'get something' from the negotiation.[18]

When Canada formally approached the United States with its proposal for a bilateral free trade agreement, it did so with a clear agenda: a strong commitment to achieving competitiveness for Canadian industry and secure access to the huge American market of over 250 million people. It wanted the bilateral agreement to be comprehensive in nature, arguing that if Canadian producers could achieve "world-competitive costs" via participation in a genuine Canada–U.S. market, they would be well positioned to compete on a worldwide basis. Additionally, while Canada wanted a mutual lowering of tariffs, it also expected the agreement to "reduce non-tariff barriers and clarify their applicability" so that future trade would be governed by predictable and mutually acceptable rules of behavior.[19] If successful, the Canada–U.S free trade agreement would force Canadian firms to be more competitive. It would reduce the temptation for Canadian firms to move south of the border to escape the uncertainties of trade across the border, and it would provide clear and fair means of dispute settlement.

On May 21, 1986, preliminary discussions between Canada and the United States launched the negotiations for the Canada–U.S. Free Trade Agreement that was eventually signed by Prime Minister Mulroney and President Ronald Reagan in October 1987. There were disappointments on both sides of the border and considerable debate within Canada about this bold new direction in foreign economic policy. Even so, in 1988 the House of Commons ratified the agreement, following the U.S. Congress in signaling its support for an important new direction in bilateral trade relations.

FROM CAFTA TO NAFTA

Observing the emergence of this new trading arrangement between the United States and Canada, the Mexican government under Carlos Salinas considered its extension to Mexico to be of vital interest. Like Mulroney, Salinas's motivation for tying Mexico to the United States in a free trade area consisted of a desire to kindle the embers of the struggling Mexican economy, and also like Mulroney, Salinas was very interested in turning Mexico away from a long tradition of protectionism and national economic management and toward a new era of market liberalism and free trade. Specifically, the Mexican government was interested in a free trade agreement that would "improve industrial productivity both by exposing Mexican business to foreign competition and by encouraging foreigners to invest in Mexico."[20] Following on the heels of the Mexican decision to join GATT in 1986, this new direction in trade and investment policy was notable, especially since protectionism against American economic domination was deeply embedded in Mexico's political tradition, as was a heavily managed domestic economy.

This shift had a lot to do with the state of the Mexican economy by the middle of the 1980s. It had become clear to many top economic officials in the country that the old patterns of price controls, trade and investment restrictions, and government control had outlived their usefulness. By the middle of the decade, Mexico had begun to dismantle some of its most restrictive economic structures and to slowly welcome investment and free market forces. This was quite successful, encouraging Mexican exports and specifically increasing trade with the United States (between 1986 and 1991 non-oil exports had grown by 95 percent and total exports by 140 percent, with the vast majority of that trade with the United States).[21] As one set of analysts put it, the time seemed right to do more to encourage productivity and economic growth: "Mexico has reached a stage in which it needs a more active involvement of foreign capital and technology if it is to sustain the economic progress that has been made. NAFTA is seen as a primary means of achieving that objective by increasing the confidence of international corporations in the stability and growth potential of the Mexican economy."[22] In 1990 Salinas saw in his proposed North American Free Trade Agreement (NAFTA) an opportunity to institutionalize the economic reforms that were already under way, and he also believed that the time was right for securing the support of the United States for such an arrangement. In the wake of the successful ratification of the Canada–United States Free Trade Agreement, the U.S. government was espousing the value of reinvigorating its free trade efforts, and Congress seemed willing to go along. Given these hospitable circumstances in Washington, the NAFTA proposal looked promising.

The Bush administration was indeed receptive, seizing upon the idea with enthusiasm, because it offered yet another avenue for encouraging U.S. trade and investment, and it facilitated the administration's goal of restructuring "the American political economy according to laissez-faire principles of deregulation, liberalization, and privatization."[23] Despite the fact that trade with Mexico constituted only 2 percent of total U.S. trade, the idea of a potential new market appealed to the business sector. Moreover, the regional free trade concept was gaining ascendancy in Washington, as policy makers observed the impressive regional integration being undertaken in Europe. The idea that the United States could benefit from its own regional arrangements, in addition to its global agreements under the GATT, was gaining popularity. Therefore, the Bush administration entered into negotiations with enthusiasm, and the Clinton administration that followed in 1993 was similarly supportive.

The public hearing and congressional ratification process, however, did take considerably longer than it had for the Canada–U.S. Free Trade Agreement. The disparity in level of economic development between Mexico on the one hand and the United States and Canada on the other contributed significantly to the controversy. Many people were worried that there would be a rush of factories relocating to Mexico because of lower wages and lax safety and environmental requirements, and that jobs would be lost. Others worried that the weaker enforcement of environmental protection in Mexico would encourage deliberate pollution and degradation south of the border. However, the anti-NAFTA lobby was relatively small compared to the pro-NAFTA effort. The Mexican government and an impressive number of American companies threw themselves into convincing Congress that the agreement should pass. In fact, U.S. firms "separately formed one of the largest private sector lobbying groups ever; the Coalition for Trade Expansion quickly attracted a membership of more than 500 companies, trade associations, coalitions, and lobbying associations to voice support for approval of NAFTA."[24] In 1994 their work paid off. Congress ratified the agreement, creating the second most significant regional trading area in the world and binding both Canada and Mexico with the United States in a commitment to freer trade and investment policies and demonstrating that at least in this issue area and at this time in history smaller states could successfully influence their own political economic direction as well as that of their larger and more influential neighbor.

....

CONCLUSION

This case demonstrates that even states with smaller markets can influence the structure of international trade arrangements. It shows that bold initiatives that reverse years of restrictive trade policy are possible when there is a strong enough domestic momentum for change, coupled with a hospitable international environment. Thus, when Mulroney government sought to build upon the assessments of the Macdonald Commission regarding the future of Canadian economic growth and stability, it exploited a window of opportunity in both domestic politics and in its relations with the United States. This was similarly true for the Mexican government in its bid to join a larger North American Free Trade Agreement.

The Canada–U.S. free trade agreement also emerged as an indictment of the GATT regime which had governed international trade (regional and otherwise) for nearly 40 years. Canadian and American officials alike hoped that the new regional trade agreement would solve the inadequacies of the GATT. For Canadians, it was their hope for a more binding dispute-resolution process that motivated a separate agreement, and for the Americans, it was a broader interest in more liberal Canadian markets. While neither side got everything it had been looking for in a regional arrangement, the initiative marked a new approach to bilateral (and later trilateral) trade in North America.

Discussion Questions

1. What has been Canada's historical dilemma regarding trade policy, and how does it illustrate the challenges of economic interdependence?
2. What domestic circumstances in, and international challenges to, Canada prompted the Mulroney government to seek a new trade initiative with the United States?
3. What is a free trade area, and how might it encourage regional economic development?
4. Why do nations enter into regional free trade agreements when global free trade is supposed to be the norm?
5. What does the emergence of this regional trade arrangement tell us about the limitations of the global trading system as it was established in 1948?

Notes

1. Gilbert R. Winham, *Trading with Canada: The Canada–U.S. Free Trade Agreement* (New York: Priority Press, 1988), pp. 4–6.
2. Ibid., p. 16.
3. Carolyn Rhodes, *Reciprocity, U.S. Trade Policy and the GATT Regime* (Ithaca: Cornell University Press, 1993), pp. 185–187.
4. Richard G. Libsey and Murray G. Smith, *Taking the Initiative: Canada's Trade Options in a Turbulent World* (Toronto: C. D. Howe Institute, 1985), pp. 14–15.
5. Willis C. Armstrong, Louise S. Armstrong, and Francis O. Wilcox, eds., *Canada and the United States: Dependence and Divergence* (Cambridge: Ballinger Press, 1982), p. 104.

6. Margaret Biggs, "An International Perspective," in Robert M. Stern, Philip H. Trezise, and John Whalley, eds., *Perspectives on a U.S.–Canadian Free Trade Agreement* (Washington, D.C.: Brookings, 1987), pp. 134–136.

7. Winham, *Trading With Canada,* p. 58.

8. These ideas were circulated in a 1983 discussion paper of the Department of External Affairs entitled *Canadian Trade Policy for the 1980s* noted by B. W. Wilkinson, "Some Comments on Canada–U.S. Free Trade," in Whalley et al., eds., *Canada-United States Free Trade,* p. 100.

9. Royal Commission on the Economic Union and Development Prospects for Canada, *Report: Vol. I* (Ottawa: Minister of Supply and Services Canada), p. v.

10. Ibid., p. xvii.

11. Ibid., p. 58.

12. Ibid., p. 59.

13. Ibid., p. 60.

14. George C. Perlin, "The Progressive Conservative Party: An Assessment of the Significance of Its Victories in the Elections of 1984 and 1988," in Hugh G. Thorburn, ed., *Party Politics in Canada* (Scarborough, Ontario: Prentice-Hall Canada, 1991), p. 309.

15. Winham, *Trading With Canada,* p. 19.

16. Ibid.

17. Perlin, "The Progressive Conservative Party," p. 310.

18. Winham, *Trading With Canada,* p. 38.

19. Lipsey and Smith, *Taking the Initiative,* p. 80.

20. Bruce E. Moon, *Dilemmas of International Trade* (Boulder: Westview Press, 1996), p. 136.

21. Nora Lustig, Barry P. Bosworth, and Robert Z. Lawrence, "Introduction," *North American Free Trade* (Washington, D.C.: Brookings, 1992), p. 8.

22. Ibid., pp. 8–9.

23. Moon, *Dilemmas,* p. 138.

24. Stephen D. Cohen, *The Making of United States International Economic Policy: Principles, Problems, and Proposals for Reform* (Westport: Praeger, 1994), p. 136.

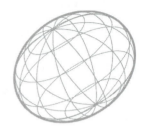

CHAPTER 8

GERMAN UNIFICATION AND THE END OF THE COLD WAR

....

INTRODUCTION

The unification of Germany in 1990 marked the end of 45 years of political and military confrontation between the United States and the Soviet Union. In symbolic terms and in harsh reality Germany's division into two states after World War II—the Western-oriented German Federal Republic (FRG) and the Soviet-oriented German Democratic Republic (GDR)—represented the very essence of the cold war in Europe. Western fears about Soviet socialist expansionism and Soviet fears about hostile capitalist encirclement compelled each side to renege on cooperative Allied agreements about the treatment of defeated Germany and to move in their own defensive directions. Particularly troublesome was the occupation and division of Berlin. An enclave within the territory of East Germany, West Berlin became a test of the U.S. commitment in Europe and a constant frustration to Soviet officials, who resented its existence and continually pressed for its incorporation into East Germany. The construction of the Berlin Wall in 1961 added a physical barrier between East and West that became synonymous with the phrase "Iron Curtain" coined by Winston Churchill in 1946. Crisis after crisis between the two superpowers centered on disputes over Berlin, bringing the world to the brink of nuclear confrontation during the cold war and reminding everyone that until both sides could either peacefully accept the other's existence or until one side gave way, the potential for starting World War III seemed to be greatest in Germany, where conventional and nuclear weaponry and hundreds of thousands of troops warily eyed each other across a hostile border. That this scenario was eclipsed by the peaceful reunification of Germany in 1990 remains one of the great wonders of this century. This chapter examines the circumstances that led to Germany's reunification, exploring the historical background, shifting systemic factors, and key leadership decisions that made it possible.

....

HISTORICAL BACKGROUND

In 1945, a few months after the Nazis surrendered unconditionally, the wartime allied powers met at Potsdam, a suburb of Berlin, to determine Germany's fate and to plan a course of action for the shared occupation and "denazification" of the German nation. The "Four Powers Agreement" that resulted from this conference specified that the Allies would indefinitely retain sovereign control over the affairs of Germany and that occupation of German territory would be shared by the United States, the Soviet Union, Great Britain, and France. The agreement also provided for joint occupation by the Allies of Berlin, Germany's historic capital, even though it lay within the Soviet zone of occupation. Occupation of Germany as a whole and Berlin in particular was to occur under a common Allied authority with dismemberment of Germany into smaller units (each under the respective authority of one of the Allies) for the purpose of local administration.

However, by 1947 it became clear that wartime Allied cooperation had seriously eroded, as the Soviet Union and the United States became more worried about each other as potential adversaries than they were about some shared potential threat from Germany. Disagreement after disagreement and confrontation after confrontation created a chasm between the two, convincing Washington that it needed to alter its policies toward Germany (see chapter 4). Thus, the United States made a drastic shift away from the plans it had made for Germany during the war. It moved quickly and dramatically to reconstruct the Western zones of occupation rather than to continue to punish them, to tutor them in the principles of liberal democracy rather than impede their political development, and to make preparations for the creation of a (mostly) sovereign state in western Germany that would be allied with the capitalist West and serve as a bastion against Soviet socialist expansion in Central Europe.

The rift between the Western Allies and the Soviet Union over the breakdown in the administration of postwar Germany was manifested most dramatically by the Berlin blockade, which the Soviets imposed in June 1948. The Soviets argued that the "Western powers had violated wartime and postwar agreements providing for unified allied administration of Germany as a whole through moving to set up a separate government for West Germany, and had thereby also undermined the legal basis of their right to participate in the administration of Berlin." Furthermore, they argued, "Berlin lies in the center of the Soviet zone and is part of that zone."[1] Avoiding a direct confrontation with the Soviets by instituting along with Britain an airlift (consisting of nearly 250,000 flights over a period of 11 months) to supply West Berlin, the United States demonstrated its resolve to protect the Western zones and its refusal to recognize Soviet territorial control.

When Western access to Berlin was restored in May 1949, the only accomplishment was de facto in nature—Eastern and Western zones would remain divided. Solidifying the division of Germany between East and West, the Federal Republic of Germany was created in 1949 with a liberal democratic constitution known as the

"Basic Law" (the name reflecting the fact that West Germany's sovereignty remained ultimately in the hands of the Western Allies). Shortly thereafter, the Soviets announced the creation of the German Democratic Republic. The emergence of two separate Germanys, each developing under the influence of its respective sponsor, came to represent East-West competition and conflict in the heart of Europe. This was especially true after 1955, when the Federal Republic of Germany was allowed to rearm as a member of the North Atlantic Treaty Organization (NATO) and the GDR followed a similar route within the newly created Warsaw Pact.

The two different economic and governmental models presented stark contrasts for the German people, and this was manifested between 1949 and 1961 in a mass exodus from the GDR of over two and a half million people, most of them through the "escape hatch" provided by West Berlin.[2] In a desperate effort to close that escape route, which was draining East Germany of some of its most educated and skilled people, the East German government headed by Walter Ulbricht convinced the Soviets to back construction of the notorious Berlin Wall between Eastern and Western zones in 1961.[3] This barbed wire and concrete barrier in Berlin, so much like a prison wall, became the symbol of cold war divisions everywhere.

During the 1960s conflict between East and West invariably raised the issue of Berlin's status. During the Cuban Missile Crisis in October 1962, U.S. policy makers were convinced that action on the part of the United States against Soviet forces in Cuba would certainly be met with action against West Berlin by the Soviets. West Berlin as a potential hostage of the Eastern bloc was a constant source of concern for the U.S. foreign policy establishment and even more so for the Bonn government. Whenever tensions escalated between East and West, the security and freedom of West Berlin became a serious question.

WITHER A DIVIDED GERMANY?

Within Germany, the status of the two separate German states was evolving as a subplot in the larger story about competition between the United States and the Soviet Union. As West Germany gained more of a role for itself in international relations (especially as a key participant within the European Economic Community), East Germany also sought greater latitude in governing its own affairs. In particular, the East German government wanted more direct control over West German access to West Berlin, hoping to achieve legitimacy for its own authority (rather than be treated as a mere puppet of the Soviet Union). Little progress on this front was achieved; however, the effort on the part of the German Democratic Republic to assert its sovereignty did indicate that the existence of two German states since 1949 was beginning to create expectations within their governments that it was becoming time for them to have more independence from their respective mentors—to be treated (and to treat each other) as sovereign entities with the rights of other nation-states. These expectations were encouraged in the early 1970s as the United States and the Soviet Union entered a period of détente in their relationship. Concerned with finding an end to the Vietnam War and with achieving cooperation in the area of arms control, the United States had begun to cultivate better relations with the Soviets.

In this climate of reduced tensions the chancellor of West Germany, Willy Brandt, whose Social Democratic Party was elected into power in coalition with the Free Democratic Party in 1969, pursued his own policy of détente toward East Germany and the Soviet Union known as *Ostpolitik*. This initiative was based upon the fundamental premise that acceptance of two German states as a practical matter would facilitate cooperation and help to end unproductive antagonisms. Overtures from West Germany were fairly well received within the GDR, where the leadership for two decades had been attempting to convince the rest of the world of the legitimacy of the German Democratic Republic as a sovereign state. In East Berlin it was hoped that negotiations with the government of the Federal Republic would result in official recognition of GDR sovereignty. While Brandt stopped short of offering full diplomatic recognition of the GDR as a separate sovereign nation, he was willing to renounce past hostilities and enter into a new era of East-West cooperation.

To facilitate trade, allow freer movement of people across the shared border, and create a general climate of peaceful relations—but not to end the West German commitment to eventual reunification—were Bonn's goals.[4] These fundamental differences in goals between the GDR and the FRG plagued negotiations between the two governments, but each side seemed to consider the gains from mutual accommodation to be worth the failure to fully resolve them. In December 1972 the so-called Basic Treaty was signed. This accord was historic in that it involved direct agreements between the two Germanys, and many onlookers assumed that it was the precursor to what the East German government ultimately wanted—independence and sovereign recognition for each German state. Within West Germany, however, few were willing to see the treaty in those terms. Political pressure, especially from the right, remained high against accepting the indefinite existence of two separate Germanys, and although diplomatic successes, such as those achieving easier travel across the border for relatives, were met with enthusiasm, the long cultivated policy within West Germany of expecting eventual unification impeded significant progress toward full, separate sovereignty.

Still, despite the rhetoric, by the mid-1980s no one on either side of the border took seriously prospects for unification. The Basic Treaty, while facilitating increased contacts between East and West Germany, had done so with the expectation that normalized relations required at least a degree of mutual recognition and acceptance. And even though there were diehards within West Germany who swore that they would never accept the legitimacy of two separate Germanys, cold war divisions continued to make de facto acceptance a necessity.

Furthermore, the broader international context within which German relations operated had deteriorated considerably since the early 1970s when the United States and the Soviet Union had been interested in détente, and this decline in superpower relations contributed to a sense of pessimism about what had been accomplished under the Brandt government. With the election of Ronald Reagan to the U.S. presidency in 1980, the cold war intensified, and tensions between East and West again escalated. The earlier refusal of the U.S. Congress to ratify the second Strategic Arms Limitation Agreement (SALT II), along with the administration's deployments of Intermediate Nuclear Force (INF) missiles in Western Europe and Reagan's space-based Strategic Defense Initiative (SDI), marked a renewed era of distrust and a renewed effort to raise the ante

against the Soviet military threat. Responding to U.S. INF deployments in Europe, the Soviets attempted to sow seeds of mistrust within the NATO alliance with a campaign to encourage antinuclear demonstrations, to discredit U.S. motives, and to threaten a hard-line response. However, although there were some political successes among left-wing groups within NATO countries, the Soviet campaign failed to divide the alliance at the official level. In fact, as one observer described, "Instead of wedging the NATO nations away from the United States, Moscow's hard-line position served to consolidate the Western allies in Europe."[5] Thus, by the end of Reagan's first administration in 1984 it appeared that cold war divisions were as rigid as they had ever been.

In this climate of superpower tension, prospects for German reunification seemed especially remote. Reflecting in 1984 upon the fate of Germany's boundaries, Willy Brandt, whose tenure as chancellor between 1969 and 1974 had become synonymous with *Ostpolitik,* showed some exasperation with those who continued to hold such hopes. Unable to break away from West German pressures to maintain the official policy favoring eventual unification when he was in office, 10 years later he appeared impatient with the rigidity of official FRG policy regarding East Germany. He argued that,

> [a]ll fruitless discussion about how open the German question is should be ended. It doesn't bring us anything. As the Basic Treaty specifies, we should cultivate as good relations as we can with the GDR, a state that is very much different from our own, but which is just as sovereign and independent as any other state in the Warsaw Pact. We should look for commonalities in spite of and within the division.[6]

On the East German side the long-standing attitude that two Germanys would indeed persist was reflected in the rather smug statement (also in a 1984 speech) by Erich Honecker, first secretary and later general secretary of the GDR's ruling Socialist Unity Party (SED) of the GDR, from 1971 to 1989:

> Both German states have a vital, common interest in preserving peace. . . . Now that "reunification" has proven to be a big illusion, their differences over the German question have the drama of a dream, which occasionally recurs, but is gone once one wakes up.[7]

Ironically, Honecker's sarcasm about the elusiveness of West German wishful thinking and Willy Brandt's equally "realistic" assessment of the prospects of German reunification, before the decade closed, would be proved totally wrong.

....

THE END OF THE COLD WAR AND THE ROLE OF THE SOVIET UNION

What neither Honecker nor Brandt—or anyone else for that matter—could have foreseen were the swift, dramatic changes that would take place over the next few years

within the Soviet bloc. At a time when U.S.–Soviet tensions were at their highest since the Cuban Missile Crisis, many on both sides were beginning to wonder if confrontation was becoming inevitable. Arms control negotiations had been bogged down for years, and the ever escalating arms race was threatening to spin out of control. Entering political leadership of the Soviet Union at this critical moment in 1985 was Mikhail S. Gorbachev, a 54-year-old agricultural economist who had moved up the ranks of the Soviet Communist Party but whose distinction was (unlike his predecessors) that he was not of the Stalinist era, nor, as it soon became apparent, of the Stalinist mind-set.

After this relatively young and energetic leader had been in office for a short time, it became clear to observers that he had in mind a radical agenda for the Soviet Union. Convinced that his country could no longer sustain the economic effort necessary to continue the arms race with the United States, and equally convinced that the United States and the USSR were headed perilously toward the precipice of nuclear confrontation if something were not done to alter that course, he launched a campaign to reform both domestic and foreign policy orientations. At the domestic level these reforms were targeted toward refashioning the economy into a more competitive and innovative environment. This "restructuring" policy (or *perestroika,* as it became known worldwide) was geared toward adapting the state-planned economy into a more market-oriented (and hopefully a more vibrant) economy.

Ideologically, this effort to move the Soviet Union away from its Stalinist phase was based on Gorbachev's belief that Lenin, just before his death, had realized the necessity of loosening the application of socialist tenets in order to achieve economic development. Always a committed Communist, Gorbachev never rejected the Marxist-Leninist roots of the Soviet Union. Instead, he argued that it had been Stalin, not Lenin, who had condemned the Soviet Union to an unworkable, moribund economic and political system, and that in fact Lenin's more flexible view guided his own proposals for reform. Noting this in his memoirs, Gorbachev claimed that

> [g]ravely ill, Lenin was deeply concerned for the future of socialism. He perceived the lurking dangers for the new system. We, too, must understand this concern. He saw that socialism was encountering enormous problems and that it had to contend with a great deal of what the bourgeois revolution had failed to accomplish. Hence the utilization of methods which did not seem to be intrinsic to socialism itself, or, at least, diverged in some respects from generally accepted classical notions of socialist development.[8]

Gorbachev, therefore, saw his reforms as an extension of Leninist doctrine, not as an affront to socialist principles in general. Furthermore, he argued, the direction that the Soviet Union had taken after the death of Lenin had been influenced not only by Stalinist harshness but also by the necessities of surviving World War II and the hostility of a capitalist world. In this environment, he claimed, the Soviet model of economic and political development became distorted. As he explained,

> The specific situation in the country made us accept forms and methods of socialist construction corresponding to the historical conditions. But those forms

were canonized, idealized and turned into dogma. Hence the emasculated image of socialism, the exaggerated centralism in management, the neglect for the rich variety of human interests, the underestimation of the active part people play in public life, and the pronounced egalitarian tendencies. . . . The threat of war, the bloodiest and the most devastating wars in a history which would have been difficult even without them and the two postwar rehabilitation efforts all naturally gave rise to strict centralism in management. As a result, the democratic basis of our management system shrank.[9]

Committed to expanding that democratic base, Gorbachev also introduced another policy associated with *perestroika* known as *glasnost,* which aimed at "opening" Soviet society to dissent, discussion, and ideas from outside. As one contemporary analysis reported, *glasnost* in particular had far-reaching implications for the direction of Soviet policy:

> *[G]lasnost* has opened up new areas of information, fostered intense debate over fundamental issues, stimulated a critical appraisal of Soviet history, expanded the scope of human rights, encouraged cultural innovation, and reduced the pervasive fear in Soviet society. In terms of fostering openness, since 1986 when *glasnost* was initiated, the atmosphere in the Soviet Union has been substantially changed. *Glasnost* has extended the range of policy options considered, diversified the participants in the policy debate and forced discussion of heretofore restricted subjects into the "fishbowl" of publicity.[10]

While viewed from the West with a healthy dose of skepticism, Gorbachev's reforms were being watched with a great deal of interest.

In addition, Gorbachev's willingness to seek better relations with U.S. President Ronald Reagan at the summit in Geneva in the fall of 1985 and to consider a far-reaching agreement (at the follow-up summit in Reykjavík in 1986) to eliminate intermediate nuclear forces in Europe began to convince even the most suspicious that a very different policy orientation was sweeping the Soviet Union. Interestingly, President Reagan, whose first administration between 1981 and 1984 had been especially hostile to any type of arms control agreement with the Soviet Union, became personally convinced of the sincerity of the new Soviet leader, and the United States began to be more receptive to Gorbachev's overtures and more open to his ideas.

In a speech in Moscow in February 1987 Gorbachev's views about nuclear weapons were laid before the world. He indicted the strategic defense doctrine that had propelled the nuclear arms race for over 40 years and defended the breakthrough at Reykjavík.

> What happened in Reykjavík irreversibly changed the nature and essence of the debate about the future world. However, some people were scared by the new opportunities and are now trying to make a fast retreat. But attractive as the past may be, there is no returning to it. I am sure mankind can and will quite soon free itself of the chains of nuclear weapons. . . . The new political outlook is bound to raise civilization to a qualitatively new level. This alone serves to show that this is not a one-off adjustment of position but a methodology for conducting international affairs.

There is probably no one in this hall or elsewhere who considers nuclear weapons harmless. However, quite a few people sincerely believe that they are an evil necessary to prevent a greater, evil war. This is the viewpoint underlying the doctrine of nuclear deterrence.

Let me say the following.

First, even if we stick to this doctrine, we will have to admit that the "nuclear safeguard" is not 100 per cent effective and not without a time line. This doctrine can at any moment become a death sentence for mankind. The bigger the nuclear arsenals, the less the chances are that they will remain "obedient."[11]

Compelled by his own belief that the nuclear arms race had become too dangerous, and encouraged by President Reagan's shared concern at the Reykjavík summit, Gorbachev made the reduction of nuclear arsenals his highest priority. His commitment and his willingness to accommodate, rather than confront, U.S. concerns led to a major new agreement with the United States. Despite Gorbachev's ongoing misgivings about President Reagan's Strategic Defense Initiative, which the President refused to put on the bargaining table, the historic INF agreement was signed in December 1987.

This agreement was truly the first of its kind in Soviet–U.S. arms negotiations. Rather than limiting the future development of nuclear weaponry, as had been the approach to previous arms control agreements, this agreement pledged both sides to the destruction of their medium- and intermediate-range nuclear arsenals in Europe and the pledge to build no more. The destruction of U.S. weapons was verified by on-site inspectors from the Soviet Union, and the destruction of Soviet weapons verified by U.S. inspectors, heretofore an unimaginable arrangement between such archenemies. Within two short years, the very character of the superpower rivalry had taken a dramatic turn away from hostility and mistrust toward cooperation and mutual interest.

This new orientation was also evident in the Soviet Union's shifting posture toward territorial defense. In fact, the very definition of defense for the Soviet Union in Europe underwent substantial revision during the 1980s. Up to that time military policy had been predicated since World War II on the belief that if military confrontation occurred with the West, combat must occur as far westward as possible, with the Soviet Union pressing its advantage quickly and hopefully preemptively. Experience had been a brutal teacher with regard to this principle in both world wars, as well as in the war with Napoleon. No one in the Soviet Union wanted to suffer again the terrible losses that conflict on Soviet territory would entail if yet another war came to pass. Consequently, for 40 years Soviet military strategy in Europe had involved the forward basing of hundreds of thousands of Soviet troops and control of the Eastern European territory that lay between them and the mother country.

However, during 1982–83, even before Gorbachev came to power, the Soviet military decided that a somewhat different orientation was necessary if the Soviet Union was to avoid a disaster with the West. It concluded that circumstances had become too dangerous to risk war in the first place. The potential for confrontation with the United States had become too probable and the threat of escalation all the way to nuclear war from such a confrontation was too great to ever let it happen. Consequently, by the time Gorbachev came to power, Soviet strategic planning no longer rested on the objective of prevailing in a confrontation with the West and moving quickly to seize the advantage (hopefully keeping the war as far from Soviet territory as possible). Such a policy, the Soviet military leadership argued, had become counterproductive in the Reagan-era climate of hostility, in the current confrontational posture of NATO and Warsaw Pact forces, and in the existence of a combined nuclear arsenal of over 50,000 warheads. To address this concern, a new military posture—much more self-consciously defensive and cautious—was assumed in Europe. This new policy was based on the objective of avoiding escalation of a regional war to world war and meant in practical terms that if a crisis did erupt in Europe, Soviet forces would actually fall back rather than press forward, thus signaling NATO of their defensive, rather than offensive, intentions and hopefully prevent a crisis from escalating out of control.[12]

While U.S. policy makers were slow to recognize this change, it was fundamental to the emerging cooperative attitude on the part of Soviet leadership with regard to the Soviet Union's military policy in general, and in Europe in particular. After Gorbachev came to power, the concept of Soviet defense changed even more. Arguing that the Soviet Union would actually be safer if forces were reduced, the new military doctrine was based upon the concept of "reasonable sufficiency." This concept reflected the belief that the arms race—both nuclear and conventional—had become too dangerous and costly. It was defined by Defense Minister Iazov in 1987:

> When we speak about maintaining the armed forces, our military potential, within the limits of reasonable sufficiency, we mean that at the present stage the essence of adequacy for the strategic nuclear forces of the Soviet Union is determined by the necessity of preventing an unpunished nuclear attack in any, even the most unfavorable, circumstances. As far as conventional weapons are concerned, sufficiency refers to a quantity and quality of forces and arms which would be enough to reliably guarantee the collective defense of the socialist community.[13]

While all students of international security recognize that "defensive" and "offensive" forces may well be a matter of interpretation, it became clear in the years that followed that Soviet policy makers were sincere in their transformation of Soviet military orientation into a defensive posture. This was manifested initially in Soviet proposals for NATO–Warsaw Pact arms and troop reductions before the Warsaw Pact Political Consultative Committee in Budapest in 1986, and subsequently before the committee in 1987 in Berlin and in 1988 in Warsaw. The so-called Mutual and Balanced Force Reduction Talks based in Vienna for years had produced no progress, mostly because the Warsaw Pact had adamantly refused to reduce troop numbers and conventional forces, and NATO had refused to allow Eastern bloc conventional advantages to make Western Europe vulnerable. That impasse had in large part contributed to the INF deployments, as NATO sought security through nuclear means when it feared the conventional superiority of the Warsaw Pact. Consequently, these new proposals marked a dramatic shift in direction in Warsaw Pact policy. They included "a broad range of arms reductions . . . [and] an initial cut of between 100,000 and 150,000 troops from each side" with additional cuts to follow later.[14] Moreover, the Soviet Union proposed that on-site verification—like that agreed for the INF Treaty—would provide a confidence-boosting element to the reduction of conventional forces.

....

GORBACHEV, THE TWO GERMAN STATES, AND EAST GERMANY'S DEMISE

Beyond the realm of the arms race, Gorbachev's commitment to reform, as well as his keen interest in the roles that trade and Western technology could play in Soviet economic development, led him to seek better ties with the rest of the world in general, and with Western Europe in particular. Nowhere was interest in the new Soviet outlook higher than in West Germany, which, between 1986 and 1988, signed a series of cooperative agreements with Gorbachev's government, including arrangements for environmental protection, nuclear safety (in the wake of the 1986 Chernobyl disaster), maritime safety, and scientific and technological cooperation. "In addition, more than thirty new contracts with West German firms were signed."[15] In October 1988 Chancellor Helmut Kohl visited Moscow, signaling a bold new direction in West German–Soviet relations. The visit represented for the Soviet Union a recognition that West Germany was key to its larger policy of détente toward the West, and it demonstrated Bonn's interest in playing a significant role in courting the new policy.

With regard to the German unification and Berlin issues, the "rapprochement, however, did not imply a shift in the Soviet approach. During Kohl's visit, Gorbachev emphasized that Germany's division was the result of specific historical developments. Any attempt to change the situation or to pursue 'unrealistic policies,' he said, would be 'an unpredictable and even dangerous business.' "[16] However, despite these vocal admonitions against altering the status quo between the two German states, there were indications that Gorbachev's position regarding the future direction of German sovereignty was changing. In a 1987 reaction to West German President Richard von Weizacker's claim that German unity must prevail, Gorbachev responded that the two Germanys with two different political and economic systems were a postwar reality. However, he went on to say that it "would be left to history to decide" what might come to pass in a hundred years.[17] Perhaps more telling than this cryptic remark was the fact that Gorbachev was asking advisers to study the German question and its role in the new Soviet foreign policy. Out of this examination were a number of suggestions, including the proposal that if Soviet troops (some 350,000) were withdrawn from East Germany, relations with West Germany would become considerably more cooperative. There was even talk about the desirability of dismantling the Berlin Wall.[18]

To observers one of the most significant signs that relations between East and West were undergoing phenomenal change was the visit by Gorbachev to Bonn in June 1989. Received with great enthusiasm by the German public, Gorbachev represented the potential for a new future for Germany, whose destiny may no longer be divided by rival antagonists. Highly successful in terms of public relations, his visit culminated in a very important joint statement between the Federal Republic and the Soviet Union, which foreshadowed events of the coming months. Insisted upon by the Kohl government, this Joint Declaration recognized "the 'right of all peoples and states' to freely determine their destiny and 'the respect for the right of peoples to self-determination.' "[19] This statement did not represent a Soviet endorsement of West German hopes for unification. On the contrary, Gorbachev "continued to stress the 'realities' of the existence of two German states, noting that 'time would take care of the rest.'"[20] Still, it was Gorbachev's apparent willingness to accept the eventuality of unification—if, indeed, the people of both German states at some point chose to move in that direction—that was such a remarkable development.

At the time, few politicians within the Federal Republic (except for the radical minority, who had always pressed for unification despite the international climate) were willing to suggest that West Germany attempt to alter the status quo. Instead, most political figures saw this new Soviet attitude as an opportunity to engage in a new *Ostpolitik* toward East Germany and to urge the government of the German Democratic Republic to institute political and economic reform. In this more cooperative environment Kohl's government offered a number of assistance and cooperation arrangements to the Honecker government in East Berlin to encourage reform and increased flexibility toward the West.

Meanwhile, throughout Eastern Europe the effects of Gorbachev's new foreign policy were being felt. The proposals made for Warsaw Pact force reductions proved to be only the beginning of a new policy for the region. The Brezhnev Doctrine, which had stressed the expectation that Eastern European countries conform to the Soviet model and obey Soviet doctrine, was rejected in favor of a new tolerance for self-determination and diversity. This was expressed in a speech by Politburo Secretary Yegor Ligachev during a trip to Hungary in 1987: [e]very country looks for solutions independently, not as in the past. It is not true that Moscow's conductor's baton, or Moscow's hand is in everything. . . . Every nation has a right to its own way.[21] While Soviet leadership made it clear that it continued to expect its neighbors to improve upon the socialist model—not reject it outright—this new approach toward Eastern Europe appeared to be an invitation to the people of the region to democratically choose the path they would follow in the future. The implication of this policy was that these people might choose not to adhere to socialism at all.

Nowhere was this possibility more likely than in East Germany, whose special historical circumstances made it especially susceptible to revisionist thinking, and among the East German public Gorbachev's policies were welcomed with enthusiasm. However, the East German government had serious misgivings about the implications of reform. Honecker was very worried that Gorbachev's invitation to openness and debate would unleash too many demands for change, especially among the intellectual community. Moreover, if reforms took a free-market, democratic direction, then the very identity of the East German state would be lost. As one analyst has explained,

> Gorbachev's calls for reform presented particularly acute problems for the GDR because they threatened to undermine the very rationale for its existence. The GDR, as East German ideologist Otto Reinhold argued, could only exist as an "anti-fascist, socialist alternative to the Federal Republic." A capitalist GDR would have little reason to exist as a separate state. Hence the strategy of the East German leadership, he warned, had to be uncompromisingly aimed at "solidifying the socialist order" in the GDR.[22]

Consequently, the Honecker regime went to great pains to claim legitimacy for the existing East German socialist model in its effort to avoid pressures for reform.

Antidemocratic and reactionary, the East German government stubbornly held to its own course despite Soviet displeasure and domestic public outcry. However, by 1989 the failure of the Honecker regime to respond to public demands for reform was increasingly criticized both within and outside the GDR, and more and more East German citizens joined the call for reform. In the wake of public demonstrations in Leipzig in January, 80 participants were arrested, further delegitimizing the government's position and inflaming the public. Demands for freedom of movement were particularly shrill, and while the East German parliament did legislate policies to liberalize travel regulations, they fell far short of public expectations. The one outcome, however, was that by July 1989 over 46,000 GDR citizens were able legally to emigrate to West Germany—a very large number considering the red tape involved in securing permission under the new legislation.[23] In fact, in August the West German mission in West Berlin was forced to close its doors due to the overwhelming number of applicants for emigration.

In the meantime reforms in neighboring satellite states were also playing a role in East Germany's fate. Thousands of would-be emigrants fled to the West German embassies in Prague and Budapest in hopes of circumventing the bureaucratic bottleneck in Berlin. Then, in May the Hungarian government began to dismantle its border with Austria, and by September it began to allow GDR citizens to cross Hungary into Austria. This action opened a new escape hatch for East German citizens wanting to emigrate to West Germany via Austria. By the fall of 1989 the domestic situation in East Germany had become a crisis as GDR citizens left the country in droves. The Honecker regime condemned the Hungarian government for its irresponsible behavior, but massive demonstrations in East Germany made clear the public's disdain for the position taken by their government.[24]

In the midst of this crisis, in October Honecker was removed from office, and a new government was declared under the leadership of Egon Krenz. Hopeful that reform might preserve the East German state, Krenz offered amnesty to those who had fled the country illegally, and moved to institute a range of new democratically oriented policies. On November 9 his government announced new visa requirements, which the public interpreted as opening the way for total free movement from East into West Germany. That night in a euphoric and raucous display of freedom, Berliners from both sides of the border danced on the Berlin Wall and crossed freely back and forth from one side to the other! The following day GDR citizens poured across the border into West Berlin, marking the beginning of a new era in postwar German history.

KOHL'S INITIATIVE AND FOUR POWER REACTIONS

Events had occurred so rapidly between the 1987 statements by Soviet leaders about the value of open debate and national self-expression to the fall of the Berlin Wall in November 1989 that no one was prepared for the challenges those events posed for East-West relations generally and for Germany's destiny in particular. Clearly, Gorbachev had hoped that the end of the Honecker regime would bring about a new direction in East German political development. However, the fall of the Berlin Wall created mounting pressure in West Germany for a policy that could take advantage of these new circumstances. Less than three weeks after the wall fell, Chancellor Helmut Kohl announced his "10-point plan" for German unity. Fearing that if he failed to seize the initiative regarding the future of East Germany, the Four Powers (who retained ultimate sovereign control over postwar Germany since the agreements at Potsdam) might settle on some kind of diplomatic solution that could "stabilize East Germany in pursuit of a two-nation solution," he moved quickly.[25] Motivated by this concern, he outlined a plan for a set of cooperative arrangements predicated on the emergence of a democratic East Germany and that laid forth the prospect of "confederative structures" in the near term and federation potentially in the long term.[26] In East Germany Kohl's proposals regarding confederation were welcomed by the Krenz government, as long as the "sovereignty of the GDR remained intact."[27]

Among the Four Powers, reactions were mixed. The U.S. government under the presidency of George Bush was quick to support the principle of democratic unification. Only a week before, West German Foreign Minister Genscher was told by President Bush that the situation was one in which Bonn must take the lead, saying that the German question was really a "matter for the Germans."[28] What the Bush administration did stress was that if unification did eventually happen, it "should occur in the context of Germany's continued commitment to NATO and to an increasingly integrated European Community."[29] This attitude about the structure for German unification was embedded in the Bush administration's vision for a post-cold-war environment in which

a new architecture was needed for a new era and that this new structure must accomplish two main purposes. First, there must be an "opportunity to overcome through peace and freedom the division of Berlin and of Germany." Second, "the architecture should reflect that America's security—politically, militarily and economically—remains linked to Europe's security."[30]

Furthermore, this new approach would require "new missions for NATO, including a shift in the alliance toward arms control and other cooperative structures in Europe and closer alliance cooperation on regional conflicts."[31] This shift in U.S. attitude toward European security was a positive gesture to the Soviet Union, reassuring Gorbachev that NATO, although slow in fully appreciating the changes that had occurred in Soviet policy, was now demonstrating a commitment to respond in kind. In reaction to the U.S. position, Chancellor Kohl was firm that a future unified Germany would not be a neutral. He argued that its status within the NATO alliance and within the European Community would be preserved.

Britain's attitude toward unification was less warm than that of the United States. Despite a very strong and positive relationship, especially regarding NATO, the British government under Margaret Thatcher was somewhat cool to the notion of a united Germany. In February 1990 Prime Minister Thatcher told Parliament that a "lengthy transition period" would be necessary before unity could be contemplated. A few days later she admonished that, "You cannot just ignore the history of this century as if it did not happen and say 'we are going to unify and everything else will have to be worked out afterwards.' That is not the way."[32]

The French position was in many respects guided by the fact that the Franco-German axis had been the pivot point for the integration of Western Europe within the European Community. The original impetus for European integration—the containment of West Germany within a supranational framework for peaceful economic cooperation—placed France in a uniquely influential role regarding Germany's future. The very institution that was created to originally contain West Germany's potential was in 1990 robust and institutionally well developed and therefore could continue in its role toward a unified Germany. Cited by President Bush as an important player in the larger framework for a unified Germany, the European Community afforded France a degree of comfort, and it was to this organization that France eventually turned to develop its policy toward German unification.

Although French President Francois Mitterand had initially tried to encourage the Soviets to support the Krenz regime and to forestall the prospects of German unification, he seemed to realize the fact that events within Germany had assumed a dynamic of their own that democratic means would be unable to curtail. Faced with this reality, Mitterand in December 1989 joined with other European Community heads of state and governments in advocating deeper integration. Chancellor Kohl proved to be sensitive to the concerns of his neighbors and went to great lengths to reassure them that Germany's ambitions lay within a peaceful European Community. In April 1990 he joined Mitterand "in calling for a political union, involving a deeper cooperation among the Twelve [member states] on foreign policy and security issues."[33]

The Soviet Union also proved to be more supportive of German integration within the European Community and within NATO than anyone predicted. NATO membership for a unified Germany did provoke considerable concern within the Soviet Union. Gorbachev was genuinely concerned about the possible threat it might pose to Soviet security, and debate among Soviet leadership was highly critical. Thus, while the so-called 2 + 4 talks had been a general success in terms of endorsing German unification, misgivings remained about the specific circumstances within which it would occur.[34]

In July 1990 critical talks between Kohl and Gorbachev resulted in a breakthrough. Gorbachev gave his approval for Germany's full membership in the NATO alliance. In exchange Kohl agreed to reduce the size of the German army and to finance the withdrawal of Soviet troops from East Germany. In addition, he pledged that Germany would "renounce the production of nuclear, biological and chemical weapons, and . . . forgo the stationing of nuclear weapons or foreign troops on the former GDR's territory as long as Soviet troops were on East German soil."[35] Coming on the heals of a NATO summit in London that pledged the Atlantic alliance to a more cooperative stance toward arms control, this agreement reflected Gorbachev's belief that the West was indeed responding in kind and that German unification would actually "contribute to a reduction of the military threat facing the Soviet Union."[36]

....

CONCLUSION

With this Soviet endorsement for German unification to take place under the existing structures of the Federal Republic, events proceeded even more rapidly. On August 31 the GDR and the Federal Republic of Germany signed the unification treaty in East Berlin, and on December 2 elections were held, marking the first time since the Nazi dictatorship that democratic all-German elections had occurred. Just barely over a year after the Berlin Wall—that notorious and deadly symbol of the cold war—had fallen, divided Germany was no more. Gorbachev's reforms, Kohl's initiatives, Bush's encouragement, and the institutions created after World War II to structure West European cooperation and integration had come together to produce the democratic transition of a once divided Europe.

Discussion Questions

1. Why is German unification considered the event that marked the end of the cold war that had raged in Europe since 1946?
2. Why was it necessary for the Allies from World War II to formally agree to German unification, and what did this mean for German sovereignty?
3. How did unilateral actions on the part of Soviet Premier Gorbachev lead to a thaw in the cold war?
4. How could the migration of East German residents to West Germany occur despite the Berlin Wall, and how did this migration affect East German policy?
5. How important in changing history was the willingness of the West German government under Helmut Kohl to press for immediate unification?
6. Why did German unification usher in a new era in international and European politics?

Notes

1. Jonathan Dean, "The Future of Berlin," in Edwina Moreton, ed., *Germany Between East and West* (Cambridge: Cambridge University Press, 1989), p. 159.
2. A. James MacAdams, *Germany Divided: From the Wall to Reunification* (Princeton: Princeton University Press, 1993), p. 5
3. Dean, "The Future of Berlin," p. 162.
4. MacAdams, p. 79.
5. Thomas H. Naylor, *The Gorbachev Strategy: Opening the Closed Society* (Lexington, MA: D. C. Heath, 1988).
6. MacAdams, p. 134.
7. Ibid.
8. Mikhail Gorbachev, *Perestroika: New Thinking for Our Country and the World* (New York: Harper and Row, 1987), p. 26.
9. Ibid., pp. 45–46.
10. The Aspen Strategy Group, *The Soviet Challenge in the Gorbachev Era: Western Perceptions and Policy Recommendations* (Lantham, MD: University Press of America, 1989), pp. 1–2.

11. Mikhail Gorbachev, "For the Sake of Preserving Human Civilization," speech before the participants in the international forum "For a Nuclear-free World; For the Survival of Humanity," Moscow, 16 February 1987. Robert Maxwell, ed., *Gorbachev: Speeches and Writings,* vol. 2 (Oxford: Pergamon Press, 1987), p. 156.

12. Michael MccGwire, *Perestroika and Soviet National Security* (Washington, D.C.: Brookings, 1990).

13. Linton H. Bishop, "Soviet National Security Policy Under Gorbachev," in William Green Miller, ed., *Toward a More Civil Society? The USSR Under Mikhail Sergeevich Gorbachev* (New York: Harper and Row, 1989), p. 222.

14. Ibid., pp. 232–233.

15. F. Stephen Larrabee, "Moscow and the German Question," in Dirk Verheyen and Christian Soe, eds., *The Germans and Their Neighbors* (Boulder: Westview Press, 1993), p. 213.

16. Ibid., p. 214.

17. Ibid.

18. Ibid.

19. Ibid.

20. Ibid., pp. 214–215.

21. Quoted in Aspen Strategy Group, *The Soviet Challenge,* pp. 70–71.

22. Larrabee, "Moscow and the German Question," in Verheyen and Soe, *The Germans,* pp. 215– 216.

23. Jonathan Osmond, *German Reunification: A Reference Guide and Commentary* (Harlow: Longman, 1992), p. 4.

24. Ibid.

25. Stephen F. Szabo, *The Diplomacy of German Unification* (New York: St. Martin's Press, 1992), p. 39.

26. Ibid., p. 40.

27. Ibid.

28. Ibid., p. 41.

29. Bush's statement at the NATO summit meeting in December 1989 quoted in Ibid., p. 42.

30. Ibid., pp. 42–43.

31. Ibid., p. 43.

32. Anthony Glees, "The British and the Germans: From Enemies to Partners," in Verheyen and Soe, *The Germans,* p. 52.

33. Ann-Marie LeGloannec, "France, Germany and the New Europe," in Verheyen and Soe, *The Germans,* p. 26.

34. 2 + 4 refers to the formula for negotiation of German unity. The 2 German states negotiated the terms of their plan for unification, but still were subject to the Four Powers' consideration. At a meeting in Ottawa on February 14, 1990, the two German foreign ministers and the foreign ministers from the United States, Soviet Union, France, and Britain met to endorse a general plan for unification.

35. "Moscow and the German Question," in Verheyen and Soe, *The Germans,* p. 219.

36. Ibid., pp. 219–220.

37. Text copied from Szabo, *The Diplomacy of German Unification,* pp. 129–134.

Appendix

....

TEXT OF TREATY ON THE FINAL SETTLEMENT WITH RESPECT TO GERMANY[37]

The Federal Republic of Germany, the German Democratic Republic, the French Republic, the Union of Soviet Socialist Republics, the United Kingdom of Great Britain and Northern Ireland and the United States of America,

Conscious of the fact that their peoples have been living together in peace since 1945;

Mindful of the recent historic changes in Europe which make it possible to overcome the division of the continent;

Having regarded to the rights and responsibilities of the Four Powers relating to Berlin and to Germany as a whole, and the corresponding wartime and post-war agreements and decisions of the Four Powers;

Resolved in accordance with their obligations under the Charter of the United Nations to develop friendly relations among nations based on respect for the principle of equal rights and self-determination of peoples, and to take other appropriate measures to strengthen universal peace;

Recalling the principles of the Final Act of the Conference on Security and Co-operation in Europe, signed in Helsinki;

Recognizing that those principles have laid foundations for the establishment of a just and lasting peaceful order in Europe;

Determined to take account of everyone's security interests;

Convinced of the need finally to overcome antagonism and to develop cooperation in Europe;

Confirming their readiness to reinforce security, in particular by adopting effective arms control, disarmament and confidence-building measures; their willingness not to regard each other as adversaries but to work for a relationship of trust and cooperation; and accordingly their readiness to consider positively setting up appropriate institutional arrangements within the framework of the Conference on Security and Cooperation in Europe;

Welcoming the fact that the German people, freely exercising their right of self-determination, have expressed their will to bring about the unity of Germany as a state so that they will be able to serve the peace of the world as an equal and sovereign partner in a united Europe;

Convinced that the unification of Germany as a state with definitive borders is a significant contribution to peace and stability in Europe;

Intending to conclude the final settlement with respect to Germany;

Recognizing that thereby, and with the unification of Germany as a democratic and peaceful state, the rights and responsibilities of the Four Powers relating to Berlin and to Germany as a whole lose their function;

Represented by their Ministers for Foreign Affairs who, in accordance with the Ottawa Declaration of February 13, 1990, met in Bonn on May 5, 1990, in Berlin on June 22, 1990, in Paris on July 17, 1990, with the participation of the Minister for Foreign Affairs of the Republic of Poland, and in Moscow on September 12, 1990;

Have agreed as follows:

ARTICLE I

(1) The united Germany shall comprise the territory of the Federal Republic of Germany, the German Democratic Republic and the whole of Berlin. Its external borders shall be the borders of the Federal Republic of Germany and the German Democratic Republic and shall be definitive from the date on which the present Treaty comes into force. The confirmation of the definitive nature of the borders of the united Germany is an essential element of the peaceful order in Europe.

(2) The united Germany and the Republic of Poland shall confirm the existing border between them in a treaty that is binding under international law.

(3) The united Germany has no territorial claims whatsoever against other states and shall not assert any in the future.

(4) The Governments of the Federal Republic of Germany and the German Democratic Republic shall ensure that the constitution of the united Germany does not contain any provision incompatible with these principles. This applies accordingly to the provisions laid down in the preamble, the second sentence of Article 23, and Article 146 of the Basic Law for the Federal Republic of Germany.

(5) The Governments of the French Republic, the Union of Soviet Socialist Republics, the United Kingdom of Great Britain and Northern Ireland, and the United States of America take formal note of the corresponding commitments and declarations by the Governments of the Federal Republic of Germany and the German Democratic Republic and declare that their implementation will confirm the definitive nature of the united Germany's borders.

ARTICLE 2

The governments of the Federal Republic of Germany and the German Democratic Republic reaffirm their declarations that only peace will emanate from German soil. According to the constitution of the united Germany, acts tending to and undertaken with the intent to disturb the peaceful relations between nations, especially to prepare for aggressive war, are unconstitutional and a punishable offense. The governments of the Federal Republic of Germany and the German Democratic Republic declare that the united Germany will never employ any of its weapons except in accordance with its constitution and the Charter of the United Nations.

ARTICLE 3

(1) The Governments of the Federal Republic of Germany and the German Democratic Republic reaffirm their renunciation of the manufacture and possession of and control over nuclear, biological and chemical weapons. They declare that the united Germany, too, will abide by these commitments. In particular, rights and obligations arising from the Treaty on the Non-Proliferation of Nuclear Weapons of July 1, 1968, will continue to apply to the united Germany.

(2) The government of the Federal Republic of Germany, acting in full agreement with the Government of the German Democratic Republic, made the following statement on August 30, 1990, in Vienna at the Negotiations on Conventional Armed Forces in Europe:

The Government of the Federal Republic of Germany undertakes to reduce the personnel strength of the armed forces of the united Germany to 370,000 (ground, air, and naval forces) within three to four years. This reduction will commence on the entry into force of the first CFE agreement. Within the scope of this overall ceiling no more than 345,000 will belong to the ground and air forces which, pursuant to the agreed mandate, alone are the subject of the Negotiations on Conventional Armed Forces in Europe. The federal government regards its commitment to reduce ground and air forces as a significant German contribution to the reduction of conventional armed forces in Europe. It assumes that in follow-on negotiations the other participants in the negotiations, too, will render their contribution to enhancing security and stability in Europe, including measures to limit personnel strengths.

The government of the German Democratic Republic has expressly associated itself with this statement.

(3) The governments of the French Republic, the Union of Soviet Socialist Republics, the United Kingdom of Great Britain and Northern Ireland, and the United States of America take note of these statements by the governments of the Federal Republic of Germany and the German Democratic Republic.

ARTICLE 4

(I) The governments of the Federal Republic of Germany, the German Democratic Republic, and the Union of Soviet Socialist Republics state that the united Germany and the Union of Soviet Socialist Republics will settle by treaty the conditions for and the duration of the presence of Soviet armed forces on the territory of the present German Democratic Republic and of Berlin, as well as the conduct of the withdrawal of these armed forces which will be completed by the end of 1994, in connection with the implementation of the undertaking of the Federal Republic of Germany and the German Democratic Republic referred to in paragraph 2 of Article 3 of the present treaty.

(2) The governments of the French Republic, the United Kingdom of Great Britain and Northern Ireland and the United States of America take note of this statement.

ARTICLE 5

(l) Until the completion of the withdrawal of the Soviet armed forces from the territory of the present German Democratic Republic and of Berlin in accordance with Article 4 of the present treaty, only German territorial defense units which are not integrated into the alliance structures to which German armed forces in the rest of German territory are assigned will be stationed in that territory as armed forces of the united Germany. During that period and subject to the provisions of paragraph 2 of this Article, armed forces of other states will not be stationed in that territory or carry out any other military activity there.

(2) For the duration of the presence of Soviet armed forces in the territory of the present German Democratic Republic and of Berlin, armed forces of the French Republic, the United Kingdom of Great Britain and Northern Ireland, and the United States of America will, upon German request, remain stationed in Berlin by agreement to this effect between the government of the united Germany and the governments of the states concerned. The number of troops and the amount of equipment of all non-German armed forces stationed in Berlin will not be greater than at the time of signature of the present treaty. New categories of weapons will not be introduced there by non-German armed forces. The government of the united Germany will conclude with the governments of those states which have armed forces stationed in Berlin treaties with conditions which are fair taking account of the relations existing with the states concerned.

(3) Following the completion of the withdrawal of the Soviet armed forces from the territory of the present German Democratic Republic and of Berlin, units of German armed forces assigned to military alliance structures in the same way as those in the rest of German territory may also be stationed in that part of Germany, but without nuclear weapon carriers. This does not apply to conventional weapon systems which may have other capabilities in addition to conventional ones but which in that part of Germany are equipped for a conventional role and designated only for such. Foreign armed forces and nuclear weapons or their carriers will not be stationed in that part of Germany or deployed there.

ARTICLE 6

The right of the united Germany to belong to alliances, with all the rights and responsibilities arising therefrom, shall not be affected by the present treaty.

ARTICLE 7

(1) The French Republic, the Union of Soviet Socialist Republics, the United Kingdom of Great Britain and Northern Ireland and the United States of America hereby terminate their right and responsibilities relating to Berlin and to Germany as a whole. As a result, the corresponding, related quadripartite agreements, decisions and practices are terminated and all related Four Power institutions are dissolved.

(2) The united Germany shall have accordingly full sovereignty over its internal and external affairs.

ARTICLE 8

(I) The present treaty is subject to ratification or acceptance as soon as possible. On the German side it will be ratified by the united Germany. The treaty will therefore apply to the united Germany.

(2) The instruments of ratification or acceptance shall be deposited with the government of the united Germany. That government shall inform the governments of the other contracting parties of the deposit of each instrument of ratification or acceptance.

ARTICLE 9

The present Treaty shall enter into force for the united Germany, the French Republic, the Union of Soviet Socialist Republics, the United Kingdom of Great Britain and Northern Ireland and the United States of America on the date of deposit of the last instrument of ratification or acceptance by these states.

ARTICLE 10

The original of the present treaty, of which the English, French, German and Russian texts are equally authentic, shall be deposited with the government of the Federal Republic of Germany, which shall transmit certified true copies to the governments of the other contracting parties.

Agreed Minute To The Treaty On The Final Settlement With Respect To Germany Of September 12, 1990

Any questions with respect to the application of the word "deployed" as used in the last sentence of paragraph 3 of Article 5 will be decided by the government of the united Germany in a reasonable and responsible way taking into account the security interests of each contracting party as set forth in the preamble.

For the Federal Republic of Germany
Hans-Dietrich Genscher

For the German Democratic Republic
Lothar de Maiziere

For the French Republic
Roland Dumas

For the Union of Soviet Socialist Republics
Eduard Shevardnadze

For the United Kingdom of Great Britain and Northern Ireland
Douglas Hurd

For the United States of America
James W. Baker III

CHAPTER 9

U.S. HEGEMONIC DECLINE

A New Status for Japan in U.S.–Japan Trade Relations

INTRODUCTION

Given the economic and military dominance of the United States in world affairs following the end of the Second World War II, one of the most noteworthy developments of the second half of the 20th century was the relative decline of U.S. economic influence and the impact this had on a wide range of postwar relationships and institutions. In no area was the erosion of the U.S. dominant position more evident than in trade, where United States exports after the 1970s could no longer keep pace with its growing appetite for imports, and where a mounting deficit in the 1980s and early '90s reached historic proportions. And, nowhere was this shift in economic interdependence more profound than in the U.S.–Japan relationship. Between 1945 and 1990 the United States had gone from the world's largest creditor to its largest debtor, and Japan had gone from total dependence on U.S. economic aid and military protection to the U.S.'s largest source of credit and a significant supplier of defense finance. The United States had, over a period of four decades, become Japan's most willing customer, amassing its largest trade deficit in history, and much of that deficit with Japan. Increasingly preoccupied with how to protect its industry from Japanese competition, the United States resorted to a number of ploys to restrict imports from Japan without violating the General Agreement on Tariffs and Trade (that it had created with the purpose of encouraging and maintaining free trade in 1947). Moreover, it also used a number of threats to force Japan to open its market to U.S. goods. This discriminatory and protectionist activity on the part of the United States marked a fundamental shift in U.S. leadership since World War II. No longer willing to absorb the costs of creating and maintaining the free trade system it had set up after the end of the war, the United States was acting more and more like a "normal" nation and less and less like the hegemonic power it had been decades earlier.

This case study examines the changes that took place in the U.S.–Japan relationship in the 1980s and early 1990s as a consequence of growing Japanese economic power and declining U.S. economic influence. It provides a brief history of the relationship as it developed after World War II. It then traces the emergence of trade conflict in the 1980s, providing a more detailed review of two specific trade negotiations that demonstrate that new constraints on U.S. influence had reined in its ability to dominate economic relations.

HISTORY OF THE U.S.–JAPAN RELATIONSHIP

During the occupation of Japan between 1945 and 1952, the United States introduced a range of policies aimed at ensuring "that Japan will not again become a menace to the United States or to the peace and security of the world."[1] These policies included the dismantling of Japan's military forces, land reform, the breakup of economic conglomerates, and the creation of a new democratic constitution. However, by 1947, U.S. policy makers had decided that some of the plans for the reform of Japanese society were too harsh, especially given rising U.S. concern over Soviet power and Communist expansion. New intentions regarding Japan emerged from the Truman administration's decision to contain Communist influence, including a more supportive attitude toward traditional Japanese economic practices and a commitment to Japanese defense.

Instead of pursuing its plans for radical reform of the Japanese economic system, the United States decided to rebuild the country's economy and allow the *zaibatsu* (the Japanese conglomerates) to maintain their dominant role, rather than risk economic upheaval and the Communist agitation that might result. Thus, growing out of a desire by U.S. leaders to contain Soviet communism and rebuild the global capitalist economy, the United States moved away from its original policy for Japan, which included drastic reform of its oligopolistic economic structures, and toward the encouragement of recovery and economic development. U.S. policy toward Japan also included opening American markets to Japanese goods in the early 1950s and securing the entrance of Japan as a signatory to the General Agreement on Tariffs and Trade (GATT) in 1955.

In addition to its policy of development aid and open markets for Japanese exports, the United States had also pledged to provide Japan with military protection in the wake of Japanese constitutional restrictions on its military force and in the environment of the heightening cold war. This became especially important to American policy makers after the Communists prevailed in the Chinese civil war in 1949. In 1953 the Mutual Security Treaty was concluded between the United States and Japan. It guaranteed Japan's security through a strong U.S. military presence in the region and through the U.S. nuclear umbrella. This dependence on the United States for defense allowed Japan to concentrate its foreign-policy efforts on expanding trade and investment opportunities abroad. In return, the United States had access to Japanese ports and military bases on Japanese soil. This proved critical to U.S. policy when war erupted on the Korean peninsula in 1950 and U.S. involvement intensified in Vietnam through the 1950s and '60s.

For Japan, the special economic/security relationship that developed with the United States following the end of World War II proved pivotal in its pursuit of economic development and international security. As one analyst described it, "Japan's approach to the issue of security has been that of an expanding international trading company, not that of a nation-state. The Japanese [became] a major global economic force and the preeminent power in the East Asian region."[2] This was accomplished, not through military domination, as had been the goals of the Japanese empire during the 1930s and '40s, but through economic interdependence and the American security umbrella. In the meantime, Japan energetically pursued a policy of export-led growth, taking advantage of foreign markets (especially the U.S. market) to raise production levels and enter new areas of product development.

While Japanese exporters had relatively free access to the U.S. economy, however, the Japanese government continued to protect its industry from foreign competition. By the 1960s resentment began to build against Japanese imports in the United States as American producers felt the pinch of Japanese competition, and the perception developed that Japan was enjoying unequal advantages in the bilateral trade relationship. Still, U.S. foreign policy priorities continued to emphasize the importance of Japan as a capitalist bulwark against Communist influence in East Asia, and U.S. economic policy generally remained liberal.[3]

By the end of the 1960s Japanese exports had helped the country achieve full prosperity, and significant market shares were being captured around the world by Japanese products. For the first time in the postwar U.S.–Japan trading relationship, Japanese competition was causing economic concerns for American producers in a number of sectors. A decade later Japanese steel, automobiles, and electronics held strong positions in the global marketplace. In particular, U.S. consumers were attracted to Japanese goods, enjoying the highly competitive and desirable products offered by Japanese industry. For example, in the automotive sector alone, Japanese producers had captured over 20 percent of the U.S. market by 1980.[4] While this situation was welcomed by many consumers, it created strong pressure on Congress to take protectionist action. American firms, competing for their traditional market share, were suffering serious difficulties in the face of Japanese competition.

A secondary concern for U.S. producers was the fact that the Japanese market remained substantially closed to foreign imports, despite Japan's participation in three rounds of GATT trade negotiations. Even though Japan had eliminated most of its tariffs and quantitative restrictions as a result of its GATT commitment, a number of "structural" factors (including the oligopolistic nature of industry and a strictly managed distribution system) within the Japanese economic system continued to impede imports. U.S. imports of Japanese goods skyrocketed during the 1980s while Japanese imports of U.S. goods remained insignificant. As the U.S. trade deficit grew to historical proportions, largely propelled by this trade imbalance with Japan, pressure mounted in Congress to force some changes in the bilateral trade situation.

Throughout the 1980s and into the early 1990s a recurring theme in congressional debates was whether Japanese exports should continue to have such free access to the U.S. market while Japan remained virtually closed to most U.S. goods. The competitive vigor of the Japanese economy stood in stark contrast with the relatively weak position of the United States, which was not only suffering its largest trade imbalance in history but also its largest federal budgetary deficit. In this new position of economic vulnerability, the United States attempted to slow the shift in economic advantage to Japan and also attempted to force Japan to take more responsibility in fostering a mutually beneficial trading relationship. The 1980s was filled with case after case of U.S. pressure on Japan to restrain its exports to the United States and case after case of Japanese acquiescence. Exports of automobiles, steel, and electronics were all limited "voluntarily" by Japan in an effort to placate the United States and thus avoid more restrictive actions being threatened by the U.S. Congress. However, even with the voluntary export restraints (VERs), the bilateral trade imbalance continued to grow in Japan's favor, and Congress began to demand that Japan buy more American goods. A few special agreements on U.S. exports to Japan were reached, and again the Japanese government attempted to placate U.S. politicians with tangible, albeit limited, market access.

....

SHIFTING ROLES IN WEALTH AND POWER

However, it was becoming clear to observers on both sides of the Pacific that the traditional roles played by the United States and Japan in the postwar political economy were beginning to change. Not only was Japan a formidable economic competitor with the United States, U.S. trade and budgetary deficits (the latter requiring huge sums of borrowing from investors at home and abroad) put the United States in a much less advantageous position in continuing to pressure Japan to modify its economic practices to accommodate U.S. competition problems. The fact that Japan's economic position in the world had changed substantially during the previous few decades, coupled with the fact that the United States was experiencing relative economic decline, caused many analysts to speculate about a new relationship for these traditional trading/security partners in the global economy. In both countries there was considerable discussion about whether Japan would be willing to continue to cooperate with U.S. demands when its own bargaining position was becoming stronger and American leverage was becoming weaker.

This debate was heard more frequently as the end of the cold war signaled an end to the special place for Japan in U.S. security policy in East Asia, and observers in Japan and the United States wondered whether the Japanese government would decide that it could no longer assume that the post–World War II security arrangement that had guaranteed Japanese defense would endure. A number of voices in the United States were arguing that Japan should shoulder more of its own defense, given its wealthy position in the global economy. Increasingly, the traditional relationship between the United States and Japan, where Japan could forgo security concerns in favor of economic development, and where U.S. policy makers would overlook Japanese advantages in trade and investment opportunities in the interest of their larger commitment to the security alliance with Japanese, was being called into question.

At the heart of the discussion was the shift in relative economic power that had been occurring since Japan began the process of reconstruction after World War II. By 1990, substantial shifts in wealth, productivity, and comparative advantage between the United States and Japan had created conditions under which past patterns of influence and responses to that influence were being challenged. Relative economic power had become approximate enough that both nations found themselves in positions to exploit the other's vulnerabilities in a wide range of circumstances, despite the fact that power in the traditional security alliance remained weighted in favor of the United States.

Measures of the two nations' respective trade balances at the time are particularly telling. While Japan registered a $64.2 billion trade *surplus* overall for 1990, the United States posted a $101.9 billion trade *deficit,* and 45 percent of the total U.S. trade deficit was with Japan.[5] Other statistics are also indicative of the two nations' relative economic positions in 1990. While the total gross national product of the United States was $5,234 billion, Japan's was just over half that at $2,835 billion; however, *per capita* GNP in the United States was $20,938 compared with $23,031 in Japan. Savings as a percent of household after-tax income in the United States was 5.4 percent compared with Japan at 16.8 percent.[6] Producers competing in the global marketplace were much less concerned about U.S. competition than they were about Japanese competition. As an external threat to traditional manufacturing and marketing practices in industrialized countries around the world, Japan's comparative advantage had a well-known role in motivating numerous reactions from protectionism to domestic industrial reinvigoration.

In 1990 Japanese banking and securities dominated much of the world's financial market, and the United States was particularly dependent upon Japanese capital investment for deficit financing. Between 1983 and 1988, the United States imported $700 billion, much of it from Japan, in order to finance the twin deficits it had amassed in trade and the federal budget.[7] In fact, Japan had been the world's largest creditor since 1985.[8] U.S. dependence on Japanese capital put Japan in a much stronger bargaining position than before. The high degree of interdependence that characterized Japanese–U.S. relations from the end of the war had been shifting in Japan's favor, providing it with more economic leverage than was available in the past.

In security matters, previous policy approaches were also being questioned. After 1981, the Japanese government began responding to U.S. demands that Japan pick up more costs of regional defense, including responsibility for defending its sea lanes up to 1,000 miles from shore. In 1985, Japan adopted a growth-oriented defense policy to meet these demands, and by 1987 the Japanese government suspended the ceiling on national expenditures for defense, allowing spending to exceed 1 percent of GNP for the first time in its postwar history.[9] Highly controversial in Japan, this willingness on the part of the Japanese government to shoulder more of its own defense burden marked a new era in U.S.–Japan relations. While the United States still dominated Japanese defense policy, it was now asking Japan to provide for more of its own military resources.

This in turn began to fuel demands in Japan that Japanese industry benefit from new ventures in defense production.

Furthermore, the end of the cold war was also creating new attitudes regarding U.S.–Japan relations. Firmly entrenched in the post–World War II bipolar alliance system, previous Japan–U.S. relations had been patterned on the United States setting the policy agenda and Japan accommodating. However, changes in the international system, where bipolar competition between the United States and the Soviet Union no longer dominated international relations, had altered the security environment that had necessitated this pattern of behavior. The relationship between the United States and the Soviet Union differed fundamentally in 1990 from the previous 45 years of military competition. Soviet leader Mikhail Gorbachev's arms control and disarmament initiatives, as well as his willingness to alter Soviet security policy, had transformed the post–World War II political system, including the stabilizing bipolar alliances. Without the external threat that made the particular U.S.–Japan security relationship necessary, the character of the alliance came under even more pressure to change.

On the U.S. side of the Pacific, domestic opinion was also reacting to international changes in wealth and power. Demands for burden-sharing, as well as concerns about other U.S. economic interests such as market share, were emerging from American concerns over its relative economic decline. These concerns were based, at least in part, on a strong perception within the United States that Japan was a free rider on U.S. defense arrangements and U.S. open markets and that the United States could no longer afford this relationship.

....

BILATERAL TRADE RELATIONS IN A NEW ECONOMIC/SECURITY ENVIRONMENT

In this new environment, trade relations between Japan and the United States became more strained than they had ever been in the postwar period. Two areas in particular fueled conflict in the relationship and demonstrated that changes had occurred in U.S. influence with its most reliable postwar ally. The first was with regard to Japanese interest in producing a new advanced fighter aircraft, a development that could mean yet another potential shift in comparative advantage away from U.S. producers and toward Japanese producers. The second involved new U.S. legislation that demanded that Japan open its market through major structural changes in its domestic economic system or suffer severe trade penalties in retaliation. An exploration of each of these two areas of trade relations tells us a great deal about the changed economic circumstances surrounding the relationship and the new constraints faced by the United States in bargaining with Japan.

THE FSX CONTROVERSY

Increasingly, Japanese industry was insisting that it be allowed to benefit from its government's new burden-sharing role in defense. Wanting to move into the aeronautics industry, for example, Japanese producers pressed the government to contract with them for new military aircraft. If this venture into the high-technology realm of military aeronautics proved successful, Japanese industry could take part in a potentially lucrative market, where demand for advanced aircraft generally benefited only U.S.- and European-based producers. Such proposals were observed in the United States with dismay as American defense contractors worried that yet another U.S. industry would find itself facing Japanese competition in years to come.

The controversy began in 1984 when the Japanese government decided to replace its 1960 F-1 jet fighter, an aircraft that was domestically produced in Japan but that had limited capabilities in both range and weaponry. The Japan Defense Agency (JDA) decided to expand the role and ability of the next generation fighter and sought to replace the F-1 with a long-range, more sophisticated version. Design plans for the proposed "multipurpose aircraft" included modifications for "air combat capability," adding sea-lane surveillance and antiship combat ability in accordance with Japan's pledge to the United States to defend sea lanes to 1,000 miles.[10] The aircraft, which came to be known as the FSX (fighter support experimental aircraft) soon became the subject of heated debate and intense lobbying.

Initially, the JDA, Japan's Air Self-Defense Force, and the Ministry of International Trade and Industry (MITI) wanted to produce the fighter domestically.[11] There appeared to be two primary motivations for this position. The first centered on the desire to reduce Japanese reliance on the United States for weapons and aircraft and to build Japan's aviation industry. This would also allow Japan to "retain the market share developed by the production of the F-1s," which the new fighter was to replace.[12] The second reason the Defense Agency wanted indigenous development was to increase the application of Japanese advanced technology "in the production of weapons."[13] As one analyst noted, "Both the ministry and the ordnance industry viewed the FSX project as the last chance in this century to rebuild the Japanese aviation industry."[14]

Mitsubishi Heavy Industries, along with four other Japanese companies, lobbied for domestic development of the FSX. Meanwhile, the JDA and Ministry of Foreign Affairs inquired about the possibility of an international arrangement within which Japanese industry could benefit from access to existing advanced technology elsewhere. Specifically addressed were questions of possible modifications and/or licensing agreements for technical assistance or coproduction of three foreign-produced aircraft. The American F-16 and F/A-18, produced by General Dynamics and McDonnell Douglas, respectively, as well as the European Tornado produced by the British, French, and German Panvia Aircraft, were selected for consideration.[15]

Eight months later, the JDA sent a study group to McDonnell Douglas and General Dynamics, both of which expressed interest in the project to codevelop the FSX. As a consequence of this meeting, the JDA study group recommended consideration of a Japanese–U.S. joint venture. This sparked heated controversy within the Japanese Defense community. The JDA report and study group recommendation were seen as the first setback for Japanese proponents of domestic development. They saw the reports as evidence that the United States had begun to apply pressure on Japan to coproduce the FSX with American contractors rather than produce the aircraft alone. This had indeed been the case. U.S. demands for a role in the project, stiffening since 1986, were making it difficult for Japanese officials to favor the domestic option.[16] Pressure in the United

States emanated from concerns about the impact of a unilateral Japanese production effort in the field of advanced aeronautics. U.S. defense contractors raised objections that American aircraft companies would be denied entrance into yet another commercial sector of the Japanese market and, potentially more troublesome, would have to face Japanese competition in third markets where the United States clearly held the lead.

Early in 1987, the Reagan administration and several members of Congress began openly pressuring the Japanese government to pursue joint development of the FSX, using an American fighter as the baseline aircraft for modifications. In April, the U.S. Department of Defense dispatched a study group to Japan, which proposed that Japan adopt or modify the U.S. F-15, F-16, or F-18 fighter.[17] In June, when Japanese press reports indicated that the country's domestic development plans were favored in terms of development costs and performance, Secretary of Defense Casper Weinberger visited Japan, pressing hard for a cooperative production arrangement. In October, Weinberger's plan for joint development of the FSX was accepted. The Japanese Defense Agency adopted General Dynamic's F-16C fuselage as the baseline aircraft for the FSX, with wing modifications and the addition of new electronics. Japanese firms would benefit from the best in American technology in this sector in exchange for codevelopment and production.

By spring 1988, however, Congress was seriously questioning the value of the arrangement. During Senate Armed Services Committee hearings, members worried that the United States was subsidizing foreign development of advanced weapons to the possible detriment of America's aerospace industry. Their argument was that any arrangement that allowed the transfer of American technology to Japan would, in the long term, prove counterproductive because American advanced technology would improve Japan's ability to compete in a business sector where the United States was the current market leader.

The committee made its point by inserting into its recommended version of the FY 1989 Defense Authorization bill a provision mandating that the secretary of defense consult with the secretary of commerce to negotiate the final terms of the FSX arrangement. This action stressed congressional sentiment concerning the commercial implications of U.S.–Japan defense-related agreements and signaled a fundamental change in foreign policy priorities. Over the next seven months, FSX negotiations continued, culminating in a classified Memorandum of Understanding (MOU) that was signed on 29 November 1988. This outlined general terms for work-share as well as for cooperative technology arrangements. Although the deal guaranteed General Dynamics and its U.S. subcontractors 35 to 45 percent of the development work share at an estimated budget of $1.2 billion, the agreement left many unresolved details. Furthermore, the memorandum included no guarantee that U.S. firms would receive approximately the same share of the production contract as they did in the development contract.[18] In January 1989, a detailed licensing agreement for technical assistance was signed between Japan's Mitsubishi Heavy Industries and General Dynamics, but Congress remained dissatisfied with provisions concerning production and technology shares.

By spring 1989, cabinet offices in the new Bush administration were lining up either for or against the arrangement. The Pentagon, in alliance with the Japanese government, was pressing for early approval of the licensed transfer of F-16 production information to Mitsubishi. Japanese officials anxiously sought the technical data from

General Dynamics in order to begin awarding contracts to Japanese industry before the end of the fiscal year on 31 March 1989.[19] The Pentagon wanted to ensure that U.S.–Japan "security interdependence" would not be threatened by delays. Joined by the State Department, which had participated in the FSX negotiations, the Department of Defense feared that a "long review would push Japan to produce the plane on its own . . . leaving American firms without a financial or technological share in the project.[20] They were worried that antagonists in Congress would press Japan into a unilateralist position, arguing that the United States' "goal is to maintain security interdependence with Japan, not to drive them to an independent defense position."[21] The perception in the United States—that Japan would retaliate in such a way—reflected the belief in Washington that Japanese capabilities made this a credible possibility.

Even within the Pentagon, however, economic and military issues were less distinct than in the past, and many were concerned that the joint venture would make Japan a competitor in one of "the few areas where the U.S. can keep the trade balance with Japan in the black."[22] Elsewhere in the administration, the economic dimension of the issue was paramount. Both Commerce Secretary Mosbacher and U.S. Trade Representative Hills demanded that commercial repercussions from the joint venture be taken seriously by U.S. policy. These overlapping economic and military interests rapidly pushed the FSX issue to the top of the Bush administration's agenda, with the executive agencies increasingly at odds. While the Pentagon argued that national security issues should take precedence over economic concerns, Commerce and the U.S. Trade Representative maintained that economic concerns should be a significant part of the calculus.

Moreover, the FSX issue immediately received renewed congressional criticism just when the Japanese government and U.S. Pentagon had begun to press for final approval of the joint venture arrangements. In early February, a Senate resolution was introduced that expressed Senate reservations about the FSX deal and called for a 60-day interagency review before the technical licensing agreement was sent to Congress for formal notification. Five days later, members of the House wrote President Bush, threatening to introduce legislation that would disapprove of the arrangements if modifications of the FSX plans and written Japanese assurances were not forthcoming.[23] It was becoming clear that the bilateral security relationship could no longer be assumed to overshadow economic concerns.

Largely in response to Congress, the Department of Commerce and the Office of the U.S. Trade Representative wanted a 60- to 90-day delay to review the venture's effect on trade. This was finally secured from the National Security Council on the grounds that the FSX licensing and technical assistance agreement between General Dynamics and Mitsubishi lacked specification.[24] During discussions, the cabinet debate became heated over the proposed FSX plans. While National Security Adviser Scowcroft and Secretary of State Baker argued that the joint agreement should proceed without modification, U.S. Trade Representative Hills vehemently argued that the project be scrapped and that the Japanese be persuaded to purchase American F-16s "off the shelf." The Commerce Department held that they could abide by the agreements as long as security measures were adopted to protect the most crucial U.S. design secrets.[25] As a result of these discussions, Mosbacher was assured that the Commerce Department would be included "at the start of any new negotiations involving the exchange of military or technology secrets," which apparently assuaged his concerns and formed the basis of an interagency agreement that was forwarded to the president.[26]

In March, President Bush proposed these FSX agreement modifications to Japanese government officials. His position was that he would approve the FSX codevelopment plans reached by the Reagan administration on the condition that the Japanese accept new "clarifications." The new terms specified (1) tighter restrictions on the transfer of technology (specifically at issue were tighter restrictions on "sourcing codes" for F-16 flight control technology and weaponry) and (2) a guarantee that General Dynamics would receive a share of the estimated $5 billion that Japan proposed to spend on FSX production.[27]

In Japan, the Bush administration's demands for "clarifications" were met with resentment; many saw the new terms as an attempt to significantly alter an agreement that they believed had already been reached. Japanese officials viewed the proposed changes as a U.S. power play, an attempt to renege on a foreign-policy agreement reached under a previous administration. The Bush proposal "led to sharp expressions of irritation and bitterness among Japanese officials."[28] In response to the Bush administration's demands, Director General of Defense Kichiro Tazawa stated "that Bush should respect what has been agreed to . . . the FSX agreement should not be changed, and we want to ensure that it is not."[29] Other Japanese officials warned of repercussions, noting that some Japanese defense industry people had suggested that Japan walk away from the deal and develop the plane individually.[30]

A week later U.S. and Japanese officials met in Washington, D.C., to try to reach a compromise. At this time, Japan's vice minister of defense, Seiko Nishihiro, as well the Japanese ambassador, Nobuo Matsunaga, met with Secretary of State Baker, Secretary of Commerce Moshbacher, and National Security Adviser Scrowcroft in an effort to reach agreement. While negotiations were under way, reports indicated that a right-wing group within the LDP, led by the lower house member Shizuka Kamei, had filed a petition with Japan's cabinet chief, arguing that Japan should develop the fighter itself in light of U.S. concerns.[31] More and more, the internal Japanese debate focused upon whether the new international system and Japan's position within it continued to warrant kowtowing to U.S. demands. Japanese sovereign interests no longer coincided with those of the United States in the security sphere.[32]

The rising voice of Japanese nationalism and resentment against U.S. constraints did not go unnoticed in Washington, but in the end American negotiators were able to secure acceptable guarantees from the Japanese without driving the Japanese officials away from the table altogether. In April 1989, the United States and Japan agreed to proceed with the $7 billion FSX fighter codevelopment plan. Under the renegotiated terms of the FSX agreement, U.S. companies were assured a 40 percent share in the production work, and Japan agreed to "safeguard" sensitive computer software.[33] In reality, little had changed from the original agreement initialed under the Reagan administration, but sensitive issues such as production share and technology transfer were more firmly pinned down.

The FSX controversy illustrated the changing U.S.–Japan security relationship. Nationalistic interests within Japan wanted to alter the status quo by securing the economic benefits of penetrating the high-technology aeronautics industry. Unilateral production of a new-generation fighter had the potential for removing the United States from the Japanese military market in this area and for creating new competition for American defense industries in markets elsewhere. This raised the FSX from an issue in domestic Japanese politics to an international issue of serious consequence to the United States.

While the U.S. State and Defense departments sought to ensure that joint production would instead be pursued, enabling U.S. industry to benefit from shared technology and profits as well as enabling the government to continue to manage alliance relations, mercantilistic interests in the United States, which feared that the project would aid Japanese industry in its drive into the new aeronautics sector, threatened to derail the plan. Their pressure to force Japan to buy directly from the United States and forgo domestic production had the potential for damaging bilateral relations further, with the risk that the unilateral Japanese option would be pursued with renewed rigor in reaction to American demands.

This new competitive relationship between the United States and Japan, made easier by the receding Soviet threat, demonstrated a change from past patterns of interaction and cooperation. In the United States, the foreign-policy agenda was rearranged to place economic concerns alongside traditional security arrangements. In Japan, the ultimate accommodation to U.S. demands reflected a continued commitment to the bilateral relationship over specific sectoral interests, yet the FSX case demonstrated that given the new competitive economic positions of the two countries, industrial areas previously reserved for the United States because of its preeminent military and high-technology position were now being challenged by Japanese interests. While persuaded by the United States to consider a joint venture with U.S. firms, Japan's position against buying existing technologies from the United States was clear. The compromise joint venture, which was the outcome of bilateral bargaining, included threats by Japan that it would choose unilateral development rather than succumb to U.S. pressures to buy American aircraft off the shelf.

The joint-venture debate in the United States and the ensuing bilateral negotiations also highlighted changes within the United States that indicated a new set of foreign policy priorities. The unconventional involvement of the Commerce Department and the U.S. Trade Representative in hammering out the specifics of the revised FSX agreements signaled a dramatic departure from past approaches to foreign policy. This indicated that no longer could security issues be considered "high politics" while economic issues remained in the realm of so-called "low politics."

SUPER 301 AND STRUCTURAL IMPEDIMENTS NEGOTIATIONS

In the meantime, U.S.–Japan trade relations on another front continued to hold center stage. As noted above, trade conflict between the United States and Japan began to characterize the relationship by the end of the 1960s, when Japanese imports threatened the traditional market shares of American domestic producers. Typically, American industry would press the U.S. government for protection, and the U.S. government—not wanting to violate GATT rules against protectionism—would pressure Japan to restrain its exports to the United States to provide American manufacturers with a measure of relief. Japan would generally accommodate U.S. demands, at least to some extent, and the conflict would subside for the time being. Despite Japanese accommodations, however, the United States became increasingly dissatisfied with Japanese efforts. Especially preoccupied in the late 1980s with the bilateral trade imbalance with Japan, which it tended to blame on unfair Japanese trading practices and nonreciprocal market access, the United States began to press for major revisions in the trading relationship. Past case-by-case negotiations aimed at addressing these grievances proved too cumbersome and limited to those in the United States who were impatient with Japanese liberalization. Consequently, new legislation that mandated retaliation against nations utilizing "unfair" trading practices and illiberal domestic market restrictions was passed in 1988 to provide stronger leverage for U.S. trade negotiators. Amending section 301 of the 1974 Trade Act, Congress strengthened provisions that provided for retaliation against unfair foreign trade practices. Known as "Super 301," the new legislation required that the United States Trade Representative (USTR) carry out investigations of possible unfair foreign practices, enter into negotiations with the foreign government targeted, and if reform was not forthcoming from the negotiations, retaliate against the country involved.[34]

The new section 301 also made the USTR more responsible to Congress and removed some of the president's flexibility, thereby providing USTR with greater retaliatory leverage in trade negotiations in accordance with congressional wishes. Moreover, the transfer of authority to the USTR, which now was responsible to Congress, was a clear signal from Congress that management of U.S. trade relations had become a vital foreign-policy goal and that free riding on U.S. open markets would not be tolerated even by a traditional ally.

Observers and participants agreed that the Super 301 section of the Trade and Competitiveness Act of 1988 was aimed specifically (though not exclusively) at Japan.[35] Congress hoped that if the United States threatened retaliation under section 301, foreign countries would eliminate the trade barriers limiting U.S. market access, U.S. exports would consequently increase, and the trade deficit would decrease as a result. Because the largest bilateral trade imbalance by far was with Japan, the USTR in 1989 named Japan as a "priority country" to be engaged in bilateral negotiations under the Super 301 retaliatory threat. Upon this announcement, the Japanese ambassador, Nabuo Matsunaga, registered his government's dismay at being targeted in such a way and warned that "there may be some domestic backlash in Japan."[36] Increasingly, Japanese internal debate focused—as it had during the FSX controversy—on whether the 30-year pattern of accommodation to U.S. demands should be continued.

The new economic power of Japan and the inability of the United States to cope with its own efficiency and budgetary problems led many to argue that it was time for Japan to pursue a more confrontational strategy, even to the point of retaliating against the United States by cutting back on important purchases of U.S. government bonds.[37] This vulnerability, created by the U.S. debtor position, was evidence of the changing nature of bilateral interdependence and the potential bargaining leverage available to Japan. The much publicized book, *The Japan That Can Say No,* coauthored by Ishihara

Shintaro, former minister of transportation, and Akio Morita, chairman of Sony Corporation, verbalized this emerging viewpoint and worried policy makers in Washington that Japan was indeed prepared to retaliate.[38] When discussions were undertaken in Washington about how to approach putting Japan on the Super 301 list, this point of view was considered. According to one report, "State pointed out that Japan—the country that hard-liners wanted to punish for trade imbalances—was America's most important ally in the Pacific, and a major financial power. Treasury expressed concern that a crackdown might send the dollar plunging and discourage Japanese investors. And Michael J. Boskin, chairman of President Bush's Council of Economic Advisers, warned publicly that Japan's possible retaliation to such tough action could bring on a global recession."[39]

When the decision was taken by Carla Hills, the U.S. Trade Representative, to specify only key troublesome practices, she had scaled down her own hard-line approach, taking into account these concerns. She did so by targeting only six areas of concern (out of some 20 pages of trade barriers listed in the USTR's report used by congressional members in support of the new section 301 provisions) that warranted retaliation if liberalization was not achieved in bilateral negotiations.[40] These included practices in the following areas: Japan's ban on government procurement of foreign satellites, exclusionary procurement of supercomputers, and restrictive standards on wood products.[41]

When the Bush administration announced Japan's place on the Super 301 list, the issue of potential counterretaliation, as well as the overall importance of the bilateral relationship, had thus moderated original U.S. plans. Moreover, when the Japanese government approached the United States on its preference for bilateral negotiations under a different context from that of Super 301, including discussions of U.S. trade barriers as well, the Bush administration agreed. Rather than pursuing the purely coercive strategy mandated by Congress, the USTR as a consequence adopted a more conciliatory approach that allowed consideration of sectoral trade demands within the broader Structural Impediments Initiative also under way.

Diplomatically important for the progress of negotiations as well as for bilateral relations, the new Structural Impediments Initiative (SII) publicly replaced the Super 301 context for trade discussions and included the larger domain of structural impediments to market access, such as anticompetitive and exclusionary business practices. The SII also required the United States to reciprocate by putting on the negotiating table U.S. policies that were having a detrimental impact on U.S. savings rates and budgetary problems. For the first time in formalized bilateral negotiations between the United States and Japan, U.S. policies that affected the bilateral trading relationship were on the agenda.

This appeared to be the result of the fact that Japan had the bargaining leverage to insist that its concerns be aired as well. This willingness on the part of the United States to consider Japanese concerns along with Japan's consideration of American concerns apparently proved to be a successful approach. As one analyst concluded, "Whatever its merits or demerits, this two-track approach bore fruit on this side of the Pacific. This was because the principle of *reciprocity* was recognized early in the preparatory talks between senior American and Japanese officials."[42] This factor became an important lever for Japan's government in domestic politics. Because the Super 301 retaliatory threat was viewed with such hostility in Japan, the broader, reciprocal foundation for bilateral negotiations became important in securing domestic cooperation for the government's later agreements with the United States.

In a series of accords in April 1990, Japan agreed to concessions on imports of satellites, supercomputers, and lumber, and also indicated cooperation in the structural impediments negotiations. Reacting to U.S. threats, Japan had repeated its traditional strategy of allowing the United States to "continue to set the parameters" while "Japan would simply accept them and maximize within their given constraints."[43] This appeared to be the case as well for the SII agreement announced in June. The SII produced a pledge from Japan to encourage more domestic consumerism, increase public services with contracts more open to foreign bidders, and liberalize anticompetitive practices. Most observers agreed that the agreement would deflect congressional grievances against Japan in the near future, as well as open the way for a more liberal market economy in Japan.[44]

One of the most interesting aspects of the SII agreement was the inclusion of U.S. pledges to satisfy certain demands of the Japanese government. While all of these pledges included a high degree of flexibility, Japan utilized the SII framework to influence the United States to address its own structural economic shortcomings. Further, the United States agreed to improve procedures to balance the federal budget; to create tax incentives for family savings; to reduce the capital gains tax rate in order to encourage private investment; to increase federal spending for basic research and development; and to improve the national educational system.

These proposals, already supported to a high degree in Washington, were "aimed . . . at bringing down consumption levels in the United States, raising the savings rate and expanding investments."[45] They were buttressed by detailed suggestions, including a high gasoline tax for funding improvements in the U.S. educational system and advice that U.S. consumers should be limited in their number of credit cards.[46] The Bush administration was not committed to comply with such specifics; however, their intrusive detail indicated how far the Japanese government was willing to go to impress its expectations on the United States, as well as upon its own domestic critics.

This reciprocal approach, sanctioned by U.S. parameters for structural negotiations, marked a new approach to U.S.–Japan trade relations. The United States, which had previously been immune from overt Japanese intervention in its internal affairs, now appeared to recognize the duality of the structural problem along with the importance of bilateral cooperation in solving it. This change was particularly important within Japan, where domestic interests were demanding that old patterns of accommodation be altered to reflect new economic power relations. While the Japanese government had not departed significantly from its past reactive and accommodative approach, the willingness of both governments to discuss U.S. structural problems within formal bilateral negotiations represented a noticeable movement toward a more symmetrical bargaining relationship.

This was driven in part by the fact that the relative economic positions of the United States and Japan had changed so substantially that U.S. economic problems required the cooperation of Japan, its largest creditor and its largest supplier of consumer goods. While a confrontational strategy drove the Section 301 approach, a collaborative strategy propelled the SII approach. The two nations realized that their combined economic power not only made the alliance critical to global economic stability but also made both nations vulnerable to the policies of the other. This highly interdependent and highly important position would demand a more cooperative approach.

Washington recognized that Japan had the capability to utilize its creditor position to retaliate against the United States if the United States pushed its own coercive strategy too far. The degree of Japanese investment in U.S. Treasury bonds had made U.S. officials, particularly in the Treasury, aware of U.S. financial vulnerability to Japanese decisions. Domestic agitation within Japan for such a response added credence to speculations that the Japanese government might exercise power in this area, even though no evidence existed that the Japanese government officially entertained retaliation. Perceptions regarding Japan's capabilities and potential for exercising influence had changed. U.S. officials now considered that Japan might retaliate with its own means of leverage in response to U.S. policy if a cooperative settlement could not be reached. Thus, Japan's *ability* to utilize financial leverage influenced decisions across the Pacific, despite the fact that the Japanese government did not actually adopt this strategy.

CONCLUSION

The relative economic decline of the United States, the end of the cold war, and the rise of new, influential competitors in the global economy affected the ability of the United States to dictate its terms in these two sets of trade negotiations with Japan. Illustrative of the shift that had been occurring over the previous four decades, these cases demonstrate that the hegemonic position enjoyed by the United States at the middle of the century had seriously eroded by the 1980s. This change in relative economic power made it necessary that the United States take into account the bargaining position of more influential trading partners and pursue its foreign-policy goals with a broader view of U.S. interests (which now had to include economic concerns as well as security priorities). By the end of the century, it had become clear that, while U.S. influence remained very significant, it was becoming a more "normal" nation in a multipolar political-economic environment.

Discussion Questions

1. Why have Japanese–U.S. trade relations often been considered a measure of the state of American economic health?
2. Why do many analysts view U.S. protectionism against Japanese trade as indicative of the decline of U.S. hegemonic power?
3. What do the FSX and Structural Impediments Initiative negotiations tell us about the changing influence of the United States in economic relations?

4. Given the fact that the United States led the world in the creation of a free trade order after World War II, why was its behavior toward Japan during the 1980s and early '90s so interesting?
5. Even though official Japanese government ties with the United States remained strong during this period, what was happening to Japanese domestic political attitudes toward U.S. relations?

Notes

1. "United States Initial Postsurrender Policy for Japan," quoted in Donald C. Hellmann, "Japanese Security and Postwar Japanese Foreign Policy," Robert A. Scalapino, ed., *The Foreign Policy of Modern Japan* (Berkeley: University of California Press, 1977), p. 323.
2. Hellmann, "Japanese Security and Postwar Japanese Foreign Policy," p. 325.
3. The exception to this was trade in textiles. As early as 1955 Japan's Ministry for International Trade and Industry had imposed export restraints in response to U.S. requests. See Vinod K. Aggarwal, *Liberal Protectionism: The International Politics of Organized Textile Trade* (Berkeley: University of California Press, 1985), p. 48.
4. Carolyn Rhodes, *Reciprocity, U.S. Trade Policy and the GATT Regime* (Ithaca: Cornell University Press, 1993), p. 158.
5. *The Economist,* September 1–7, 1990, p. 92; *Business America,* April 9, 1990, p. 6.
6. *The Wall Street Journal,* June 13, 1990, p. A8.
7. C. Fred Bergsten, *America in the World Economy: A Strategy for the 1990s* (Washington, D.C.: Institute for International Economics, 1988), p. 39.
8. Kent E. Calder, "Japanese Foreign Economic Policy Formation: Explaining the Reactive State," *World Politics,* 40, no. 4 (July 1988): 520.
9. Stanley R. Sloan, "Defense Burdensharing: U.S. Relations with NATO Allies and Japan," Congressional Research Service Report, Washington, D.C. (June 24, 1988), pp. 38–39.
10. U.S. Congress, Senate, *Congressional Record.* 101st Cong., 1st sess., 135, 74 (June 7, 1989): H. 2368.
11. Otsuki Shinji, "Battle over the FSX; Who Won?" *Japan Quarterly* 35 (April–June 1988), p. 140.
12. Ibid.
13. Ibid.
14. Ibid., p. 142.
15. Ibid., p. 140.
16. Ibid.
17. Ibid., p. 143.
18. Carole A. Shifrin, "General Dynamics Expects to Receive 75% of U.S. Share of FS-X Development Work," *Aviation Week & Space Technology,* May 8, 1989, p. 16.
19. "Japan Approves 5.9% Increase for Defense Spending in 1989," *Aviation Week & Space Technology,* February 6, 1989, p. 22.
20. Elaine Sciolino, "Agencies at Odds on Japan's Role in Fighter Plan," *New York Times,* February 15, 1989, p. A3.

21. Ibid.

22. Ibid.

23. Pat Towell, "U.S.–Japanese Warplane Deal Raises a Welter of Issues," *Congressional Quarterly* 47, no. 10 (March 11, 1989), p. 537; Clyde H. Farnsworth, "Snags in U.S.–Japan Fighter Deal," *New York Times,* March 23, 1989, p. D6; Eduardo Lachica, "Prospect of a Mitsubishi Role in F-16 Fighter Spawns New Round of 'Japanphobia' in Capital," *The Wall Street Journal,* April 10, 1989, p. A16.

24. Michael Mecham, "Technology Concerns Delay Approval of FS-X Agreement," *Aviation Week & Space Technology,* February 20, 1989, p. 16; Elaine Sciolino, "Agencies at Odds on Japan's Role in Fighter Plan," *New York Times,* February 15, 1989, p. A3.

25. Christine Gorman, "A Deal That Nearly Came Undone: Despite Qualms, the U.S. Will Help Japan Build the FSX Jet," *Time,* March 27, 1989, p. 71; "The Rise of the Trade Hawks: They Want Washington to Get Tough with Japan—Starting This Week with the FSX Decision," *Newsweek,* March 13, 1989, pp. 46–47.

26. Gorman, "A Deal That Nearly Came Undone," p. 71.

27. Pat Towell, "Bush Seeking to Modify Deal for Japanese Warplanes," *Congressional Quarterly* 47, no. 12 (March 25, 1989), p. 659.

28. Steven R. Weisman, "Japanese Warn of Repercussions from U.S. Move to Alter Jet Deal," *New York Times,* March 25, 1989, p. A1.

29. Towell, "Bush Seeking to Modify Deal," p. 659.

30. Miho Yoshikawa, "U.S. Balk on FSX Miffs Officials, Industry," *The Japan Economic Journal,* February 18, 1989, pp. 1, 7.

31. "LDP Group Suggests Japan Scrap FSX Accord," *Japanese Economic News,* March 29, 1989.

32. Otsuki Shinji, "The FSX Problem Resolved?" *Japan Quarterly* 37, no. 1 (January–March 1990), p. 73.

33. Barry S. Surman, "Bush Administration Officials Defend Accord With Japan," *Congressional Quarterly* 47, no. 18 (May 6, 1989), p. 1058; Carole A. Shifrin, "General Dynamics Expects to Receive 75% of U.S. Share of FS-X Development Work," pp. 16–18; Bernard Weinraub, "U.S. and Japanese Agree to Proceed on Fighter Plane," *New York Times,* April 29, 1989, p. 1.

34. Stephen D. Cohen, Joel R. Paul, and Robert A. Blecker, *Fundamentals of U.S. Foreign Trade Policy: Economics, Politics, Laws, and Issues* (Boulder: Westview Press, 1996), p. 154.

35. Stephen D. Cohen, et al., *Fundamentals of U.S. Foreign Trade Policy,* p. 190.

36. Raymond J. Ahearn, et al., "Super 301 Action Against Japan, Brazil and India," p. 24.

37. Dries van Agt, "United States–Japan–Europe: The Unholy Trinity," *European Affairs* 4 (Summer 1990), p. 61.

38. Ishihara, Shintaro, *The Japan That Can Say No: Why Japan Will Be First Among Equals* (New York: Simon & Schuster, 1991).

39. Art Pine, "The Toughest Trader of Them All," *Los Angeles Times Magazine,* September 3, 1989, p. 23.

40. Office of the United States Trade Representative, *Report to Congress on Foreign Trade Barriers, 1986 National Trade Estimate* (1986).

41. Stephen D. Cohen, et al., *Fundamentals of U.S. Foreign Trade Policy,* p. 154.

42. Yuichiro Yamagata and David Williams, "Remaking Japan," *Tokyo Business Today,* November 1989 (my italics).

43. Shotaro Yachi, "Beyond Trade Frictions—A New Horizon for U.S.–Japan Economic Relations," *Cornell International Law Journal* 22 (1989), p. 400.

44. David E. Sanger, "U.S. and Japan Set Accord to Rectify Trade Imbalances," *New York Times,* June 29, 1990, p. Al; Clayton Jones, "Japan Hopes to End Trade Friction with Pledges on Economy," *The Christian Science Monitor,* July 2, 1990, p. 4; Dries van Agt, "United States–Japan–Europe," p. 62.

45. Dries van Agt, "United States–Japan–Europe," p. 65.

46. Ibid., p. 5.

CHAPTER 10

THE DISINTEGRATION OF YUGOSLAVIA AND THE PARALYSIS OF THE INTERNATIONAL COMMUNITY

....

INTRODUCTION

In one small region of Europe the 20th century ended much as it had begun: in turmoil and bloodshed and in controversy about how the area should be governed. This region, named Yugoslavia in 1929 for the "south Slavs" who inhabited it, was formed into a nation-state at the end of World War I. Its creation was the culmination of an effort by the victorious Allies to dismantle and punish the Hapsburg Empire, to wrest domination of the region away from the Turks, to hopefully settle the wars that had racked the Balkan region for decades, and to give international recognition to Serbian self-determination (even if this was at the expense of other groups in the area). The right of Serbs scattered throughout the area to live within one sovereign state had long been at the heart of Serbian claims and regional conflict. Even though they would share that state with Croats, Slovenians, Albanians, Hungarians, Muslims, and others, the Serbs would be given the opportunity to dominate the governance of their own country rather than be unwilling subjects, as they had for centuries, of a neighboring empire.[1]

Still, fundamental differences between the Serbs and the other groups, who did not share the Serbian vision for the country and who resented and feared Serbian domination, would be problematic for their coexistence as compatriots. Despite 70 years of shared citizenship the commitment to Yugoslavia as a whole eventually became subjugated to the separate interests of the various groups.

By 1992, not only had Yugoslavia disintegrated as a country, its own citizens found themselves in mortal combat with one another. Different groups pursued their own visions of self-determination at the expense of other groups, and increasingly old fears and animosities flamed territorial competition into war. What began as a civil dispute within

• 153 •

a country, whose governmental system had progressively since the 1950s reflected the diversity and interests of its several regions and peoples, became first a campaign of ethnic cleansing, and then an international battleground of historic proportions. Between 1991 and 1995 the casualties of this conflict had become staggering, especially in the region known as Bosnia-Herzegovina, where Croats, Serbs, and Muslims fought most desperately; 145,000 people had been killed, and 174,000 injured. Two and a half million people were uprooted from their homes and over one million (who had the means or the skills to find employment) fled to sanctuaries abroad. Damage to housing, transportation networks, and the economy was severe. In Sarajevo alone, which suffered a one-thousand-day siege, 10,500 people were killed, 60,000 wounded, and 150,000 fled.[2]

In the meantime, the international community was essentially paralyzed. Watching in dismay as the situation in Yugoslavia began to unravel between 1989 and 1991, Western European nations, as well as the United States, worried that the intrastate conflict would deteriorate. Yet they were ill-prepared and unwilling to intervene in a significant way. They were undergoing their own adjustments to the new world around them. The European Community was considering a major new treaty that would allow the member states to deepen their institutional commitment to unity, including stronger cooperation on foreign policy. They were also working hard to respond to the rapid changes taking place in Europe because of Soviet reforms and German unification.

The United States was equally challenged by the apparent end of the cold war and its implications for U.S. foreign policy in general and U.S. foreign policy toward Europe and the Soviet Union in particular. Moreover, the Iraqi aggression against Kuwait in 1990 had catapulted the United States and its allies into a massive military campaign to repel that aggression and stabilize the oil-rich Persian Gulf region. Events in Yugoslavia seemed less disturbing and certainly less threatening in comparison, and pleas for more attention by those foreign-policy experts most closely associated with the country fell on uninterested ears.[3]

Yugoslavia's neighbors to the east (including the Soviet Union) had their own preoccupations as they broke with Soviet communism and pursued independent economic and political reforms. Thus, even though the foreign-policy advisers of concerned nations were increasingly worried about events in Yugoslavia, those concerns had not become priorities for world leaders. Therefore, on Europe's southern flank, as everyone else was reveling in the end of the cold war and the dawn of a new era of freedom and democracy, a very different scenario was being played out that would cause horrendous suffering and upheaval for the unfortunate people who lived there. It would call into serious question the ability of the international community to respond in an effectual manner to such a crisis. This was especially significant because the end of the cold war had supposedly created a new opportunity for political consensus in international affairs and for a concert of action when circumstances warranted it. The fact that little was done to save the Yugoslavian people from self-destruction meant that the end of the superpower conflict had not ushered in a new era of international responsibility and humanity.

This case study examines the background to the Yugoslavian crisis and circumstances surrounding the outbreak of war. It traces how the intranational conflict escalated into international warfare and demonstrates the difficulties faced by the rest of the international community in deciding how to react. This narrative focuses on events in

Yugoslavia leading to conflict and on decisions by the international community *not* to intervene. It leaves to the reader judgments about what might have been done differently, or whether a different course was politically viable.

....

HISTORICAL BACKGROUND AND DEVELOPMENT OF A UNIQUE POLITICAL, ECONOMIC, AND SOCIAL SYSTEM

A CULTURAL CROSSROADS

Yugoslavia was in almost every way a unique state. Its location in southern Europe at the nexus between East and West is always noted as the most significant feature by historians and commentators. It lies at the junction between Islam and Christianity and between Eastern Orthodox Christianity and Roman Catholicism. Its people come from all three religious and cultural backgrounds. This is reflected in its architecture, cultural symbols, and social patterns, and visitors to the country have always been struck by its rugged natural beauty, its cultural treasures, and rich diversity.

Historically, the region had been fought over and dominated by outsiders. This helps to explain the cultural diversity of the area. Nearly all the people in the region are Slavic in ethnic origin, and two-thirds of them speak Serbo-Croatian. Yet, depending upon the history of a particular area, the people might have adopted Roman Catholicism, Eastern Orthodoxy, or Islam. Their economic status, their social interactions, and their cultural identity evolved over time to make them distinct from each other despite their racial similarity. Still, despite their diversity, there was often peaceful coexistence and mutual tolerance. One analyst in 1996 described it this way:

> The extreme cultural diversity of the South Slavs stems from the fact that they are situated at the cultural crossroads of the Old World. The continental crusts of Rome and Byzantium have been colliding here for a millennium. The subcontinent of Islam dashed at the emerging landmass half a millennium ago. There is a Central European belt (Slovenia, northern Croatia, the Vojvodina) and a Mediterranean belt (the littorals of Slovenia, Croatia, and Montenegro). There is a Muslim belt and an Eastern Orthodox belt. And they used to come together. In Mostar, Herzegovina, before the warlords destroyed it, one was able not too long ago to sip Viennese coffee and read newspapers mounted on wooden frames, listening all along to a muezzin's call in the shadow of a Franciscan church (where the chant was Latinate), and then wander into a fig grove that surrounds a Byzantine-style church (where the chant was Slavonic). None of this was imported for the tourists. It raised no native eyebrows. And it did not prompt intolerance.[4]

Thus, the unique and diverse culture of the region developed with its history, and while religious diversity has played a role in the conflicts that erupted from time to time, some analysts are reluctant to ascribe Yugoslavian conflict to religious differences.[5] This is because the south Slavs coexisted side by side for centuries without the kinds of religious wars that had racked the rest of Europe, and so religious differences alone cannot explain the animosities that exist and the conflict that has occurred. However, other analysts claim that religious and cultural diversity are at the heart of intra-Yugoslavian strife, and although political opportunists may have exploited differences, they could not have done so if strong resentments and fears between groups had not already existed.[6]

One thing that does seem clear is that regardless of a person's religious commitment, his inherited identity has been with a particular religion, so that over the centuries different "ethnic" groups have developed because of their place in the religious/political and social history of the region. A Bosnian Muslim, Slovenian Roman Catholic, or Orthodox Serb may be categorized as such, not by religious practice so much as by association within the group as it historically evolved. In 1952 a formal demographic study determined that 42 percent of all Yugoslavians considered themselves Orthodox; 32 percent considered themselves Roman Catholic; and 12 percent Muslim. More recent countrywide figures are only estimates, but most agree that the main difference with the 1952 statistics is that there has been growth in the Muslim population in comparison with the other two groups.[7]

Still, religious identification is not the only source of distinctiveness in Yugoslavian society. Perhaps the best characterization of the different groups in Yugoslavia is that utilized by Tito's government in his reforms beginning in the 1950s. In his organization of the country, he recognized the existence of different *nationalities,* and the nationalities were constituted in autonomous republics and provinces in order to give political expression to religious, cultural, and ethnic diversity.

To describe this national diversity one must again return to historical evolution. Generally, northwestern Yugoslavia (which included Slovenia and Croatia) was ruled by the Austrian-Hungarian Empire and was Roman Catholic. However, even within this area there were significant differences. Slovenia was more homogeneous than Croatia and had a culture that was profoundly intertwined with that of Vienna. Thus, Slovenia had more direct contact with, and influence from, western Europe. It also had a separate Slovenian language.[8] In Croatia there was a significant Serbian minority that lived in the eastern Krajina region, and its history was punctuated with rivalries between the two nationalities. The rest of Yugoslavia to the southeast was generally dominated by the Ottoman Turks, and most of the people in Kosovo and many in Bosnia-Herzegovina and Montenegro (and in the Sandzak region of Serbia and along the northwest rim of Macedonia) converted to Islam. Their descendants became part of the Muslim nationality, regardless of their religious activity. The majorities within Serbia and Macedonia retained their identity with the Eastern Orthodox church and rebelled from time to time to secure independence from their Ottoman rulers. They resented their fellow Slavs who had been co-opted by the Muslim conquerors and had often benefited—seemingly at the expense of the Serbs—from their willingness to cooperate with the Turkish Empire.

THE NEW YUGOSLAVIAN NATION-STATE

Thus, when Yugoslavia was constituted as a new nation-state in 1918 it was an agglomeration of different nationalities, each with a distinct history and sense of identity.

Originally named the Kingdom of Serbia, Slovenia, and Croatia, it was established as a monarchy under the leadership of the Serbs. Despite their shared Slavic inheritance, a shared root language (Serbo-Croatian), and a history of domination by others, they had many differences. Different religions, distinct historical experiences, different economic conditions, two different alphabets (Roman in the west and Cyrillic in the east), and different dialects served to divide them. Furthermore, animosities and fears from past encounters with each other (and their respective big-power allies) made them wary, if not suspicious, of domination by any group other than their own.

Difficulties immediately arose in the new country. Croats resisted domination of the regime by the Serbs, and constitutionalists (who tended to be non-Serbian) competed with the monarchists (who tended to be Serbian) for power. For its first 20 years Yugoslavian governance was unstable as the key actors involved competed for influence in defining the character of the fledgling nation-state. Furthermore, the rise of fascism in Europe during the period also had a profound influence on the development of Yugoslavian history. After several years of friendly relations with the Italians and Germans during the 1930s, the Yugoslavian government in 1941 became a party to the Axis alliance among Germany, Italy, and Japan. Following a coup against the Yugoslavian regime by opponents to this policy, Germany and Italy invaded Yugoslavia and partitioned the country between themselves and neighboring Bulgaria. Albania, which also included the province of Kosovo, was formed as a separate state under direct Italian and German control, and Croatia, which included Bosnia-Herzegovina, was proclaimed as an independent fascist state.

WORLD WAR II, NAZI OCCUPATION, AND THE RESISTANCE

During the war the pro-Nazi Croatian Ustashe ruled greater Croatia with merciless brutality and repression, carrying out massive extermination policies against Serbs, Gypsies, and Jews who resided within their territory. Moreover, the collaboration of the Roman Catholic Church with the Ustashe demonstrated that religious differences did play a role in the persecution of these minorities. During this period of time, Muslims in Bosnia-Herzegovina were considered Croats and largely cooperated with their rulers, but the other minorities were to be "cleansed" from the region. The numbers of people killed are in dispute, but certainly were horrific—well into the hundreds of thousands. As one Serb resident of Croatia recalled, "The Croatian fascists did not have gas chambers at Jesenovac [the concentration camp 65 miles south of Zagreb]. They had only knives and mallets with which to commit mass murder against the Serbs. The slaughter was chaotic, nobody bothered to keep count."[9] This infamous period in Yugoslavian history left deep scars on the psyche of the Serbs in the region, including those who resided outside Croatia, as well as those who were direct victims of the fascist terror wrought by the Ustashe. A people who had barely had a chance to govern themselves now faced annihilation by fellow Yugoslavs who had allied themselves with the Nazis.

The persecution of minorities during the Nazi occupation inflamed animosities between the Serbs and the Nazi collaborators, and retaliation by Serb nationalists was widespread as they "answered the Croat and Muslim fascists' genocide with their own ethnic massacres of Croats and Muslims."[10] Yet, here also the desire for revenge general-ized reprisals to all non-Serbs, and indiscriminate genocide affected countless numbers of innocent people. It is estimated that the "1941–1945 war in Yugoslavia, simultane-ously a world war, a civil war with interethnic massacres, and a war of national and so-cial liberation, caused more than a million deaths in a Yugoslav population that totalled [sic] about 16 million."[11] Bosnia-Herzegovina bore the brunt of the conflicts and mas-sacres because of its ethnic diversity and because of the strong resistance that formed in the rugged terrain there.

Dedicated to the defeat of the Ustashe and of Nazi and Italian domination of the region, a partisan resistance movement emerged in northern Bosnia in 1942. In the con-text of Croat-Serb conflict this partisan movement was unique in that it was highly ecu-menical, placing the goal of defeating the fascists over interethnic differences. Thus, many Yugoslavs, including "Serbs, Croats, Slovenes, Albanians, Muslims and Jews," to-gether actively resisted the fascists, finding more in common in this cause because of their desire to rid the country of fascist dominance than difference because of their sep-arate nationalities.[12] Encouraged by a Communist-led partisan military effort that used guerrilla tactics against the Nazis and their allies, this resistance movement gained mo-mentum during the war.

Its purpose was both immediate and far-reaching. First, it defined as its task the de-feat of the fascists and the liberation of Yugoslavia from foreign occupation. Secondly, it was organized as a truly multiethnic antifascist movement with a common interest in a future Yugoslavian state. A provisional government, which had a federal-type structure that included leaders from the different regions within Yugoslavia, provided the proto-type for later governmental organization. Communist in orientation, this resistance movement was led by Josip Broz Tito, who had been the key Communist leader in the country since 1937 and who was himself a Croatian and Slovenian by national heritage.

While other resistance organizations were formed during the war, it was Tito's par-tisans who were recognized by the Allies and aided in their military struggle against the Nazis and their fascist partners. Remarkably successful against their enemies, Tito's par-tisans were in a strong position to influence the future direction of their country follow-ing the war. When British Prime Minister Churchill and Soviet leader Stalin met in 1944 to consider their respective spheres of influence in the Balkans upon the defeat of the Nazis, they agreed that Yugoslavia would reemerge as an independent state, and that the Western powers and the Soviets would share influence in the area. This big-power arrangement was reinforced by the fact that Tito's forces successfully liberated Belgrade before the Soviet army could arrive, thus depriving the Soviets of the military occupa-tion that had established their power over the rest of Eastern Europe at the end of World War II.

....

TITO'S YUGOSLAVIA

Under Tito's leadership a new government in Belgrade was formed. The United States was quick to encourage Yugoslavia's independence from the Eastern bloc, and Tito was astute in courting aid from the West without relinquishing his ties to communism. Still, Tito took his country in a very different direction from that dictated by Moscow. Breaking formally with Stalin in 1948, Tito pursued a "middle way" between capitalism and communism. Moreover, he instituted a series of constitutional reforms from the early 1950s onward that created a unique federal political and economic system. These reforms reflected the fact that the people of Yugoslavia had evolved socially, culturally, and economically in distinct ways, and a high degree of local autonomy was encouraged.

As early as 1946 the Yugoslavian constitution recognized the existence of a *multinational* country, even though the reality prior to 1948 was that government was highly centralized according to the Soviet model. During the 1950s and early '60s, however, the multinational concept was developed, and in a uniquely Yugoslavian way. Coinciding with the split with Moscow, Tito introduced a governing structure known as "communal federalism" for the governance of his country. This arrangement allowed extensive latitude on the part of the various republics and provinces that were created to reflect the existence and desire for self-governance of the respective nationalities.[13] Six republics (Serbia, Slovenia, Croatia, Bosnia-Herzegovina, Montenegro, and Macedonia) and two autonomous provinces within Serbia (Vojvodina and Kosovo) were recognized constitutionally. Each territorial entity had its own government structure, and all were loosely tied to the national government, which maintained and directed foreign policy and the armed forces, but which eventually had little direct power over the political and economic structures of the respective regions.

It should be kept in mind, however, that even Tito's efforts to recognize the autonomy of the various nationalities through this type of federal organization could not ensure that political boundaries would fully coincide with the territorial distribution of the nationalities, because (except for Slovenia, where no other significant minorities resided) minority groups were scattered throughout Yugoslavia. Thus, for example, while Serbia was recognized as a republic, Serbs within the Croatian republic resided there as a minority. In the republic of Bosnia-Herzegovina, none of the three nationalities (Croat, Serb, and Muslim) held a majority on its own, and it wasn't until the 1974 constitution that the Bosnian Muslims were recognized as a separate nationality. In Kosovo, an autonomous province within the Serbian Republic, the Albanian Muslims held a strong majority, but increasingly, the minority Serbs backed by the Serbian Republican government dominated and often persecuted the Muslims. Therefore, while communal federalism attempted to grant as much self-governance as possible to the different nationalities, the mixture of peoples across boundaries still begged for centralized citizenship rights that would be universal and guaranteed from Belgrade.

Tito's government never managed to achieve this guarantee, and from time to time nationalist sentiment on the part of minorities flared into conflict between different groups. Some have argued that "only Tito's personal authority and ability to intervene in any matter had counterbalanced the centrifugal force[s]" that characterized Yugoslavia.[14] Others point to the fact that he used his power in the Communist Party to purge individuals who challenged him too much and that he made use of his well-armed military when necessary to restore cooperation.[15] Instead of focusing on universal human rights, Tito's reforms (especially the 1974 constitution) focused more on encouraging the respective republics to manage their own affairs, which often resulted in disparate economic and social achievements. Known as the 4-Ds—democratization, decentraliza-tion, debureaucratization, and destatization (the latter referred to the self-management of state enterprises)—the main thrust of Tito's approach was to set national-level guide-lines for running the country but allow the various regions to essentially govern them-selves.

Tito also worked to involve Yugoslavia in the global economy. He obtained several loans for economic development, and he directed Yugoslavian industry to set the goal of achieving export growth. Generally speaking, as long as external lending could be counted on, the Yugoslavian economy grew significantly, creating new employment op-portunities and urbanizing a country that had been largely agrarian. Some republics were much more successful than others, however. For example, Slovenia, with its West-ern European orientation and higher level of development, proved adept at participating in the international marketplace. Croatia came in second, largely because of the attrac-tion to Western European tourists of the Adriatic coastline. However, Serbia, which was more agrarian and somewhat more backward economically, was less capable of benefit-ing from Tito's open approach to the global economy. Even more impoverished and eco-nomically disadvantaged were Macedonia, Montenegro, and Kosovo.[16] Predictably, resentments developed between regions. Serbia and others resented the fact that Slove-nia was not sharing fully the wealth that it generated from its advantaged position, and Slovenia resented having its economic prospects hampered by the inefficiencies of the rest of Yugoslavia, especially by the 1980s after a huge international debt had been amassed. In addition, a product of industrialization and general economic growth was increasing urbanization.

In Bosnia-Herzegovina this trend had especially interesting results because Serbs and Croatians, who had historically stayed in rural areas, moved to the cities to seek jobs. Consequently, cities such as Sarajevo, which had previously been dominated by Muslims, became highly cosmopolitan and diverse communities where all three major ethnic groups lived in peaceful coexistence. However, when the economy seriously dete-riorated in the 1980s inter-republic resentments fueled internal Bosnian acrimony, where Serbs, in particular, resented the relative prosperity enjoyed by the Muslim mer-chant and professional classes.

One of the more striking features of Yugoslavia by 1980 (the year Tito died) was that its political economy was not unified in any significant way. Each republic pursued its own autarkic economic policies in an effort to preserve investment, industry, and em-ployment for its own residents, and the national government had become virtually pow-erless to intervene to influence investment flows, trade, or labor mobility. Location of industry, still a decision of the state, was decided by republican officials who wanted to benefit their own republic at the expense of the others. No Yugoslavian-wide commit-ment to economic prosperity ever developed. Instead, each territorial unit competed for wealth and consciously attempted to create its own economy, insulated from the economies of the other republics.

While Yugoslavia's neighbors in Western Europe were increasingly integrating their economies through the European Community, Yugoslavia's economy was increasingly fragmented and inefficient. Even as various republics developed their trade with the out-side world, trade barriers between republics multiplied. Between 1970 and 1976, for example, "inter-republican traffic in goods dropped from 27.7 percent to 23.1 percent of social product. In 1981, 66 percent of all trade was intra-regional. 22 percent was inter-regional, and 12 percent was with the rest of the world. Less than 4 percent of investment crossed republican/provincial borders."[17] It was an oddly regressive situation, reflecting the fact that the separate regions found it more important to jealously protect their respective economies than to cooperate in achieving a more efficient and productive economy countrywide.

Furthermore, Tito's approach to the structure of Yugoslavian government also contributed to the production of a highly decentralized system. Under his leadership the autonomy of the republics increased substantially, and national differences increased with it. This pattern became especially apparent during the 1970s and '80s, when Yugoslavia began to face major economic difficulties due to the debt it had accumulated ($20 billion) and the triple-digit inflation that followed.[18] Whenever the central government introduced economic reforms in an attempt to respond to the demands of the international financial community (and in particular the International Monetary Fund), it faced recalcitrant republics that had the power to block its efforts.

The constitution after 1974 placed the majority of power with the republics, at the expense of the central government. The three major national-level institutions reflected this. First, the Collective Presidency was made up of the presidents of the respective republics and autonomous provinces. Presided over by one of the presidents on a fixed rotating basis, this body could make decisions only on a consensual basis. Second, the Chamber of Republics and Provinces consisted of 12 delegates from each of the six republics' assemblies and eight delegates from each of the two autonomous provinces' assemblies. Here, also, for most significant legislation, unanimity of the regional representatives was required. Third, the Federal Chamber, the national parliament of Yugoslavia headed by a prime minister, was also constituted on a regional basis. Thirty delegates from each of the republics and 20 delegates from each of the autonomous provinces made up the parliamentary body, regardless of the population of the respective regions. While most decisions in the Federal Chamber could be taken on the basis of a majority vote, all amendments to the constitution (and most legislation affecting the power of the regions fell in this category) required a two-thirds vote plus unanimous consent of all the republic and provincial legislatures.

Still, any measure that confronted the regions with uncomfortable adjustments— even if not challenging their constitutional power—would be reviewed by the Chamber of the Republics and Provinces and by the Collective Presidency. Therefore, any legislation that might be proposed by the prime minister and Federal Chamber would face the scrutiny of the Presidency and the Chamber of Republics and Provinces. If something threatened the interests of any one of the regions, it would be rejected, even if a broader benefit for the country would have been produced by its adoption.

The political autonomy of the majorities in each of the regions was recognized and reinforced by the Yugoslavian constitution. With the stark exception of the Albanian Muslims in Kosovo, who make up 90 percent of the population, the majority nationalities wielded almost exclusive sovereign control over their domain by the 1980s. In Kosovo, the Republic of Serbia increasingly extended its domination over the province, despite desperate appeals by the Albanian majority to the federal government in Belgrade and to the international community for help. In Bosnia-Herzegovina, where no national group held a majority and where after 1974 the Bosnian Muslims were recognized by the Yugoslavian constitution as being a Yugoslavian "nation" in their own right alongside Serbs and Croats, compromise and transnationality coalitions were often necessary for governance.[19]

Yet, even in Bosnia the undercurrents of ethnic or "national" cohesion and purity tugged at the republic's identity. Croatian nationalists who resided within Bosnia, but along the border with Croatia, often agitated for annexation to the Croatian Republic. In turn, Serbs in the area were fearful of being dominated or expelled yet again by a "greater Croatia" and agitated for unity with Serbia. However, such boundary changes would not have suited everyone, because pockets of Muslims lived amongst the Serbs and Croats and vice versa. Particularly in Bosnia-Herzegovina the congruity of territorial boundaries and ethnic populations could not be assured.

Moreover, the growth in the number and influence of the Muslims worried both the Croats and the Serbs, who watched in dismay as they witnessed Muslim activists demand that Bosnia-Herzegovina be considered their own republic homeland (just as Serbs had Serbia, Croats had Croatia, and so on). In addition they believed that these demands were really a power play by the Islamic religion to dominate the republic. The only merit to this interpretation was the fact that Muslim nationality began to express itself more and more through religious identity, and some religious leaders took advantage of this. As one analyst has explained:

> Recognition of their [Bosnian Muslim] nationhood was expected to have only secular implications, since previously the Bosnian Muslims had shown little religious predilection. However, when they gained national recognition and began to increase their communal self-identification as a nation, their religiosity was concomitantly asserted as a main part of their self-identification and differentiation.[20]

The Bosnian Muslims, while not a majority within Bosnia-Herzegovina, did constitute a plurality. After 1974 this provided them with an avenue toward a highly visible presence in republican government, "because most high-ranking jobs in the republics, as well as in the federal government, were filled according to an ethnic key (apportionment according to the proportion of the national group in the population)."[21] Even though this had been an uphill struggle for them, since nationality status had been very recent, the Muslim leadership made the most of the opportunity. Thus, as Bosnian Croats and Serbs agitated for annexation to their respective "homeland" republics, Bosnian Muslims seized the initiative to try to establish Bosnia-Herzegovina as their own homeland.

For their part, the Bosnian Muslims had always been willing to work in coalitions with the Serbs or the Croats, and outside observers would at first glance consider this a positive attribute in any workable government. However, in Yugoslavia this trait was viewed by Serbs and Croats as opportunistic and exploitative. Just as the Bosnian Muslims had benefited from their conversion to Islam under the Ottoman Empire, so might they benefit from switching from side to side within Bosnian politics. Thus, the national group that recognized the merits and practicality of working in cooperation with the other groups was resented for its willingness to do so!

Therefore, the pattern that seemed to repeat itself again and again in Yugoslavian politics was evident here, in the most plural of all the republics. People never seemed able to break from their separate national identities to share governance in a trusted, co-operative fashion, where all groups and individuals held equal rights and status under the law and equal opportunity within the political economy. Cooperative motives were suspect, and no individual group wanted to lose its influence to another. No genuine sense of common citizenship seemed to take root.

As we can see, Tito's Yugoslavia was a very odd creation. While many boasted that its strength lay in the ability of the country to exist as a multinational association of re-publics and autonomous provinces, its organization and historical development was skewed in favor of fragmentation and against unity. While the constitutional reforms culminating in a highly confederal arrangement in 1974 did reflect the self-determination of the majorities in the respective republics, and thus kept those "nations" together as components of Yugoslavia, the various nations were never participants in a shared vision for Yugoslavia. The role of the Yugoslavian people across groups was neglected. As one analyst noted in 1988, "The citizen is taken as a particle of his 'national community,' and only through that community can he or she obtain or gain any political meaning or legal protection. The fact that Yugoslav federalism is excessively colored by national-cor-poratist elements thwarts democratic political evolution on the basis of citizens' political rights."[22]

POST – TITO ERA

Following Tito's death, a number of crises erupted that had been in the making for some time. First, the economy was increasingly in peril. The huge debt that had been incurred during the Tito years was now becoming a serious burden. Interest payments were ex-tremely high, and the International Monetary Fund was threatening to impose an aus-terity program on the country in order to force improvement of its balance of payments as well as its creditworthiness. However, the weak confederal government that had been Tito's legacy was incapable of implementing serious economic reform. Attempts to do so were met with widespread strikes, and increasingly the republics blamed each other and the federal leadership for the problems they faced.

Second, Kosovo, the autonomous province in the southern tip of Serbia, erupted into civil conflict when the majority Albanians demanded that Kosovo be granted status as a separate republic rather than stay within Serbia as a province, whose so-called au-tonomy was not respected by the Serbian government. International attention began to focus on the Kosovo dilemma, and diplomatic contact with Yugoslavia was increasingly critical over the federal government's handling of the Kosovo situation. This was espe-cially true as the thaw in the cold war emboldened Western leadership to comment upon civil rights matters in Central and Eastern Europe after 1988. It was also a reaction to the harsher tactics employed in Kosovo by Serbia's new president, Slobodan Milose-vic, to purge all agitators for independence from Kosovo's local governing bodies. Hav-ing consolidated his power in Serbia and extending it to neighboring Montenegro by 1988, he was intent upon extinguishing opposition in Kosovo. Slovenia, the most liberal of the republics, also admonished Serbia to refrain from its human rights abuses in Kosovo, but at the same time resisted calls for better redistribution of wealth to the poorest regions (including Kosovo).

For its part, however, the federal government found itself unable to effectively cope with the economic crisis or to intervene in the Kosovo conflict. In 1989 Yugoslavian Prime Minister Markovic launched a drastic austerity program to comply with IMF terms and to try to reform the disastrous economy. His effort was met with immediate resistance by the republics. None wanted to take on the tax burden it included (as well as continue to cope with the inflation that the devalued currency created), and Slovenia (and to a large measure Croatia) was particularly resentful that its relatively sound economy would have to shoulder the lion's share of the burden. Nationalistic impulses were becoming stronger and stronger, as economic difficulties inflamed resentments. Many leading political figures in Slovenia were arguing that Slovenia should break away from the rest of Yugoslavia and pursue its own economic and political destiny. Serbians were arguing publicly for unity, but privately only worried about keeping Croatia in because of its Serbian minority. Apparently motivated by their desire to dominate Yugoslavia, and not by a sense of commitment to the constitution and to their fellow Yugoslavs (including non-Serbs), Serbian leadership rejected the constitutional recognition of Kosovo and Voivodina autonomy, flexing their own power and thumbing their noses at the federal government.

Persecution of the Albanians in Kosovo was bringing more and more criticism on the government in Belgrade by outsiders who continued to think the federal government had the authority to alter the situation. However, it was becoming increasingly clear to long-time observers that republican intransigence in general and Serbian power in particular had become too much for the weak federal apparatus in Belgrade to do anything about. Some were arguing that the only way to keep Yugoslavia from flying apart would be to forgive debt and authorize huge new loans to at least ease the economic situation. Yet, these pleas came at a time when national debts were high and public support for lending abroad was very low (especially in the United States). [23] Thus, it was evident by the end of the 1980s that Yugoslavia faced an uphill road in its effort to resist divisions within and pressures from without. Close observers were increasingly worried about the growing strength of the centrifugal forces that plagued Yugoslavian unity, but few realized how bad it had become.

THE END OF THE COLD WAR AND ELECTIONS IN YUGOSLAVIA

When Soviet domination of Eastern Europe ended in 1989 after 45 years of political repression and economic control, a sense of optimism spread through the region. National movements for democratic reform and market-oriented initiatives arose from the old communist regimes that had been part of the Soviet sphere of influence. Onlookers and participants alike were heartened by the new geopolitical circumstances in Eastern Europe, which were making it possible for the first time since World War II for national polities to choose for themselves the types of political and economic systems they wanted. Finally, the principle of self-determination, which the Allied leaders during the

Yalta accords in 1945 had promised (but failed) to defend for the countries rescued from Nazi control, would be put into practice.

Only in Yugoslavia was the prospect of self-determination a troubling one. This was particularly ironic, since Yugoslavia, unlike the rest of Eastern Europe,[24] had never suffered under the yoke of Soviet control. It had, in fact, pursued a "middle road" between the capitalist west and the Soviet model. It had participated extensively in the international economy, and for years it had been considered a "model" for worker participation in a state-planned economy.

In global geopolitics it held a special place. On the one hand, the Soviets worked to maintain relations even though Yugoslavia's leader after the war, Marshall Tito, had publicly broken ties with Stalin and had followed a path of communism that was distinct from that of Moscow. On the other hand, the United States and its allies in the West encouraged Tito's schism with the Soviet bloc through various aid packages and through the development of stronger ties with the capitalist institutions of the IMF and the General Agreement on Tariffs and Trade (GATT). Strategically, Yugoslavia was very important during the cold war because it could play both sides in the international competition, and its military potential was significant. Each side worried that Yugoslavia's political and economic (and therefore military) orientation and resources could be placed at the disposal of the other side in some possible future confrontation. Therefore, it was well positioned to advance its interests with either superpower while maintaining a fairly neutral course.

Thus, when the cold war ended, Yugoslavia was in a very different situation than that of its neighbors to the north and east. While the Soviet bloc nations had fairly clear objectives, which focused on moving away from Soviet-style economic and political practices and toward the establishment of democratic societies with free-market economies, Yugoslavia's direction was much less clear. It tended to be driven by the same problems that had plagued it since its creation—national divisions and an absence of common direction and commitment.

When the Berlin Wall collapsed, there were many in Yugoslavia who did see this pivotal event as an encouragement of democratic reform in their own country as well. However, even many of these people viewed democracy as secondary to the opportunity for self-determination for their respective nations. Elections took place throughout the six republics during 1990, but they had less to do with democratic choice than they did with expressing nationalistic sentiment. In the spring of 1990 the pro-separatists won in Slovenia, promising a referendum on independence from Yugoslavia by the end of the year. In Croatia, the anti-Communists won, but not so much because they were anti-Communist in ideology as because they were anti-Yugoslav and anti-Serb. By December a new Croatian constitution had been written that denied the Serbian minority the rights it had previously enjoyed. In Serbia Milosevic's authority was reaffirmed, buttressed by a popular campaign that played on Serbian fears about the fate of all Serb nationals if Yugoslavia were allowed to break apart. Meanwhile, Serbia again cracked down in Kosovo, suspending the government and parliament and imposing direct rule. Its goal was to "Serbize" the province—to claim for Serb benefit the region that was so symbolically important in the history of Serbian resistance against the Ottomans in the 14th century.[25] Throughout the country, in case after case, the interests of the national groups still took priority over nationwide democratic reform and respect for individual rights.

INTERNATIONAL REACTION AND THE UNRAVELING OF THE STATE OF YUGOSLAVIA

At the end of 1990 the Slovenian people voted in a referendum to declare their independence from Yugoslavia. In May 1991 the Croatian people followed suit, and in June both republics declared their separate sovereignty. In the meantime, however, events demonstrated that, besides Slovenian and Croatian interest in national self expression, other factors were at work to encourage the disintegration of Yugoslavia. First, Milosevic, who was proving to be a key factor in the rising nationalism among Serbs, made it clear that he was happy to see Slovenia go. Apparently "he couldn't tolerate their liberal, independent ways, nor their merciless criticism of Serbian policy in Kosovo."[26] With Slovenia out of the way it appeared that he could concentrate on his goal of a greater Serbia through the domination of what remained of Yugoslavia, opposing further separations because of the presence of significant Serb populations.

However, despite his public admonishments against Croatia for its separatist activities in violation of the Yugoslavian constitution, once he realized that the Croatian declaration was a *fait accompli* Milosevic sought a special arrangement with Croatian President Franjo Tudjman to divide Bosnia-Herzegovina between them. Their plan, discussed during the spring of 1991, was to eliminate Bosnia-Herzegovina as a separate republic, to divide its territory between them to maximize the incorporation of Serbs and Croats respectively, and to deny the Bosnian Muslims their separate status. Using highly charged rhetoric to denounce what they saw as an attempt by the Bosnian Muslims to establish an Islamic state at the expense of their two peoples, both Milosevic and Tudjman coveted the territory that had once been a constitutionally designated republic of Yugoslavia. As one of Milosevic's associates commented to the U.S. ambassador, "Bosnia will have to be divided between Serbia and Croatia. Of course, the Muslims can choose what part they want to live in."[27] In this environment, despite efforts by Bosnian president Alija Izetbegovic—himself a Muslim— to hold the republic together, fighting broke out.

Ironically, regardless of their common objective of gobbling up Bosnian territory, Milosevic and Tudjman continued to target each other in their public statements, inciting animosities between Serb and Croat and kindling fear whenever it served their respective political ends. In Krajina, the Serbian region in eastern Croatia, these fears were inflamed by Serbian politicians who spread "rumors that Croats and Muslims were plotting new massacres against them."[28] The war that broke out in Croatia following Tudjman's declaration of sovereignty and the Krajina Serb referendum on separation from Croatia was encouraged by Serbia, but also by the unwillingness of Tudjman to reassure the Serbian minority. In fact, Milosevic's propaganda seemed to them to be prophetic after Serbs "were purged from the police force, their guns retrieved from army arsenals in Krajina, and signs with Cyrillic Serbian words were replaced with Latin-lettered Croatian signs."[29] Faced with these blatant actions against them the Serbs rebelled, calling for unity within a greater Serbia, a creation that would fall nicely within Milosevic's plans. In July the Yugoslavian federal army intervened, purportedly to serve in an "even-handed mission of interposing itself between the combatants. As the summer wore on this profession of neutrality became increasingly specious. In the guise of pacifying villages, the JNA [Yugoslavian army] began to turn them over to Serbs."[30] Thus, as Tudjman talked openly about a greater Croatia that would include Bosnia-Herzegovina, Milosevic and his supporters claimed that they only wanted to protect their fellow Serbs, but increasingly utilized the remnants of the Yugoslavian army to strengthen their territorial control.

Slovenian independence had much different consequences. It benefited both from the fact that Slovenia had virtually no minorities (and so no groups that would draw outside intervention) and from the fact that its own republican militia, trained by the Yugoslavian army itself, was prepared to resist any military interference from Yugoslavia. Thus, when the Yugoslavian army arrived it was met with stubborn resistance and a united stand in favor of independence. After less than two weeks of fighting it withdrew from Slovenia.

Outside Yugoslavia, reactions to these events were mixed. On the one hand there were many, both in Europe and in the United States, who welcomed the declarations of independence of Slovenia and Croatia, which had, after all, resulted from public referenda. It seemed fitting that one of the last bastions of communism should give way to the self-determination of its people, especially after the end of the cold war had opened the way to freedom for the rest of Central and Eastern Europe. However, those who knew Yugoslavia well were much less supportive. The U.S. ambassador, Warren Zimmerman, was one of the more vocal voices against Slovenian independence, hoping instead that some kind of democratic confederal solution could avert the disintegration of Yugoslavia. German leadership, while having a good deal of sympathy for the Slovenian cause, seemed to think that the declarations of independence by Croatia and Slovenia and the reactions elsewhere in Yugoslavia were "mainly tactical exercise[s] designed to secure a position of strength in the inevitable negotiation on a new constitutional order [within Yugoslavia]" and therefore "underestimated the determination of such republics as Slovenia and Croatia to completely break free of the Yugoslav federation."[31]

Other key powers, such as France and Britain, who later criticized Germany for what they perceived to be premature acceptance of the Yugoslavian breakup, joined the United States in worrying about the consequences of Slovenian and Croatian actions, but did little themselves to assist the United States in its diplomatic efforts to help stabilize the Yugoslavian confederation until after the Slovenian and Croatian referenda.[32] Greece and Italy, each of whom shared borders with Yugoslavia, were less sanguine, but they too chose to refrain from unilateral action. Collectively, the European Community had for some time treated events in Yugoslavia as an internal matter, and despite concerns, was not prepared to intervene except in the most benign diplomatic way. This was also the position of the Conference for Security and Cooperation in Europe, which had met to discuss the matter in March, issuing a declaration that supported "unity and territorial integrity of Yugoslavia with emphasis on a continued dialogue and a peaceful solution, coupled with a warning against taking recourse to the use of force." Furthermore, the "ministers stressed that it is only for the peoples of Yugoslavia themselves to decide on the country's future."[33]

The declarations of independence by Slovenia and Croatia and the military actions against Slovenia changed the complexion of the situation, prompting the Western European states to consider the matter more energetically. Having only months before signed the Treaty on European Union, which embraced the principle of a unified foreign policy, the member states of the European Union (as it was now being called) looked at the Yugoslavian crisis as an opportunity to express its unity in foreign affairs. This was also welcomed by the United States, who viewed the matter as a frustrating but essentially European concern, but which also worried that matters were deteriorating rapidly.[34] The EU Council leadership met twice in Belgrade between June 28 and July 1, convincing the parties to the conflict to agree to "a cease-fire and retreat of the [Yugoslav army] to barracks, a three-month moratorium on the implementation of the Slovene and Croat declarations of independence, and the election of Stipe Mesic to the chairmanship of the federal presidency."[35] (Mesic was the Croatian president whose rotation to the chairmanship of the federal presidency had been blocked by the Serbs earlier.)

When the cease-fire was not respected, the EU began an arms embargo against all the parties in the conflict and sponsored a conference on the Yugoslavian situation. Serbian President Milosevic refused to participate in intra-Yugoslavian negotiations mediated by the European Union, seeing them as an "internationalization" of the situation that might favor the Croats. Tudjman, on the other hand, was willing to take part, apparently because his strategy all along had been to draw the international community into the conflict as a way of buttressing his position.[36]

European efforts were followed in the United Nations by its own arms embargo in September. However, the existence of a well-equipped military in Yugoslavia inherited from the Tito era meant that many arms—especially in the hands of the Serbs—were available, and the fighting escalated. By the end of October, war had ignited over one-third of Croatia, with atrocities and ethnic cleansing reported on both sides. Serbs had taken over the collective presidency of Yugoslavia, and the Bosnian parliament had voted for sovereignty.

In the meantime pressure was growing for the international recognition of Slovenia and Croatia. The German position by the fall of 1991 was that Serbian expansion at the expense of Croatia should not be rewarded by the international community by continuing to treat the matter as a purely internal affair. Foreign Minister Hans Dietrich Genscher was the strongest spokesman for this viewpoint. Meeting with the Yugoslavian ambassador to Bonn in August, he stated that "if the bloodshed continues and the policy of *faits accomplis* by force supported by the Yugoslav army is not halted immediately the Federal Government [of Germany] must seriously examine the recognition of Croatia and Slovenia in their given frontiers. It will also commit itself to a corresponding examination within the European Community."[37] Those opposed to recognition argued that it would not only bring about the end of Yugoslavia but would unleash an even worse and more widespread conflict. This was the worry expressed by Bosnian Prime Minister Izetbegovic, who was convinced that Bosnia would be torn apart by Serb-Croat competition for territory and control.[38] However, even as these concerns were being voiced, the situation within Yugoslavia was worsening.

By December the German government had decided that continuing to deal with the Yugoslavian crisis as an internal matter was fruitless. It recognized Slovenian and

Croatian independence and introduced the matter in the EU Council. In January, despite misgivings, especially on the part of France, Britain, and Greece, the EU decided to join Germany in its position and recognized the two republics as independent nations. Not wanting the EU's new common foreign policy to break down in a public display of contention over Yugoslavian policy, an agreement was reached. However, despite EU efforts to place monitors in the cease-fire zones and to try to contain the conflict with an arms embargo and ongoing diplomatic discussions, conflict continued to escalate. By March 1992 war had broken out in Bosnia, with the Bosnian Serbs allying with Belgrade to achieve a greater Serbia and Croatians sometimes in alliance with the Muslims against the Serbs and sometimes in collusion with the Serbs against the Muslims. Despite a series of UN-brokered peace accords, the fighting continued and intensified.

The world began to awaken to the situation as the "largest refugee crisis in Europe since World War II" spewed hundreds of thousands of former Yugoslavians into neighboring countries,[39] and as report after report of ethnic cleansing, atrocities, mass exterminations, and forced expulsions filtered to the outside world. What had been a single country characterized by inter-regional competition and nationalistic divisions had now become several countries locked in a major international conflict on the doorstep of Europe's most developed nations. Yet, even then the world community remained reluctant to intervene in any significant way. The people who perished, the refugees who lost their homes, the hatred and fear that became endemic to the region had changed it forever. The post-cold-war world had not proved to be so bright as some had thought it would be, and everyone who cared wondered what should have been done to have changed the course of events.

CONCLUSION

The disintegration of the sovereign state of Yugoslavia was a blow to the international community, as well as to those "Yugoslavs" who maintained a vision of a common federal structure for an otherwise diverse polity. The fact that disputes between regions within Yugoslavia and between different groups within the regions could escalate from civil disagreement to civil war (and then international war) in a country that had existed for 70 years was very troubling for anyone who had thought that such occurrences on the boundary of politically and economically developed Western Europe were too improbable to be contemplated. The wars that ensued demonstrated that civil co-existence does not necessarily lead to civic trust, and that peaceful relations among diverse groups cannot be ensured when resentments and mistrust are encouraged by constitutional structures that fail to make the common good as strong a force as separate interests.

In dismay, the international community observed events unfolding in Yugoslavia between 1989 and 1992, yet no other country's leadership proved willing to intervene to change the course of history. Many would argue that ultimately this was a Yugoslavian affair, and despite the horrendous bloodshed and human rights violations that occurred, the international community was "better off" keeping its distance. Others would counter that such a holocaust should never be allowed to happen, whether it is confined to a particular geographic area or not, and that the international community shares guilt for the horrors that occurred. Had a major intervention been organized by NATO or the United Nations, what would have been the outcome? Would international "occupation" of Yugoslavia been necessary? Would military intervention have saved lives? When do the events in other countries become the concern of those of us who might rather overlook them?

Discussion Questions

1. After World War I, how did the interests of a "Greater Serbia" differ from Croatian interests, and how did these differences fuel later conflicts?
2. How did the collaboration of the Croatian fascists with the Nazis during World War II affect relations between the Croatians and the other "nationalities" in Yugoslavia?
3. How did Tito attempt to accommodate national differences in the new constitutions created under his leadership, and, ironically, how did the Yugoslavian constitution contribute to deepening differences between nationalities?
4. Using this case as an example, how do national political and economic structures contribute to, or detract from, national unity?
5. When Slovenia decided to declare its independence from Yugoslavia, why did nations such as the United States find themselves ambivalent about this expression of self-determination?
6. What impact did the end of the cold war have on the emergence of conflict in Yugoslavia?
7. Can the international community prevent conflict if it is unwilling to intervene militarily to do so, and does this case remind you at all of the case on the futile attempt to prevent World War II?

Notes

1. The Ottoman Empire extended over the region during the 1300s. At the battle of Kosovo, still considered a great moment in Serbian history (despite Serbian defeat), the Ottoman Turks conquered Serbia in 1389. A number of Serbian revolts against the Ottoman Empire finally resulted in Serbia becoming an autonomous state within the Ottoman Empire and then in independence in 1878. During the same period Bosnia-Herzegovina was also conquered, and many Bosnians converted to Islam, but Serbs within Bosnia as well as in neighboring Croatia continued to agitate for a "Greater Serbia" that would include them as well. The region became the point of confrontation and competition between the Austrian Empire and the Ottoman Empire, as well as the focus of Serbian autonomy and expansion up through World War I.
2. All these figures were taken from Leo Tindemans, et al., *Unfinished Peace: Report of the International Commission on the Balkans* (Washington, D.C.: Carnegie Endowment for International Peace, 1996), p. 7.

3. The U.S. ambassador tried to convince the Bush administration and the American Congress to realize that without considerable outside help, Yugoslavia as a state would disintegrate, and conflict would follow. See Warren Zimmerman, *Origins of a Catastrophe: Yugoslavia and Its Destroyers—America's Last Ambassador Tells What Happened and Why* (New York: Random House, 1996).

4. Sabrina Petra Ramet, *Balkan Babel: The Disintegration of Yugoslavia from the Death of Tito to Ethnic War* (Boulder: Westview Press, 1996), p. xiv.

5. Ibid.

6. Robert D. Kaplan, *Balkan Ghosts: A Journey Through History* (New York: Vintage Books, 1994).

7. Ibid.

8. Vojislav Stanovcic, "History and Status of Ethnic Conflicts," in Dennison Rusinow, ed., *Yugoslavia, a Fractured Federalism* (Washington, D.C.: The Wilson Center Press, 1988), p. 26.

9. Ibid., p. 5.

10. Catherine Samary, *Yugoslavia Dismembered,* trans. Peter Drucker (New York: Monthly Review Press, 1995), p. 48.

11. Ibid., p. 49.

12. Ibid.

13. Stavovcic, "History and Status of Ethnic Conflicts," pp. 34–35.

14. Steven L. Berg, "Political Structures," in Dennison Rusinow, ed., *Yugoslavia, a Fractured Federalism,* p. 14.

15. Francine Friedman, *The Bosnian Muslims: Denial of a Nation* (Boulder: Westview, 1996), p. 158.

16. Gregor Tomc, "Classes, Party Elites, and Ethnic Groups," in Dennison Rusinow, ed. *Yugoslavia, a Fractured Federalism,* p. 70.

17. Ibid., p. 72.

18. Ibid., p. 73.

19. Friedman, *The Bosnian Muslims,* pp. 159–60.

20. Ibid., p. 162.

21. Ibid., pp. 160–161.

22. Stavovcic, "History and Status of Ethnic Conflicts," p. 36.

23. Zimmerman, *Origins of a Catastrophe,* p. 50.

24. Albania, although for different reasons, was also able to remain outside the Soviet bloc.

25. Samary, *Yugoslavia Dismembered,* p. 79.

26. Zimmerman, *Origins of a Catastrophe,* p. 145.

27. Ibid., p. 117.

28. Dusko Doder, "Yugoslavia: New War, Old Hatreds," *Foreign Policy* (Autumn 1993), p. 18.

29. Ibid.

30. Zimmerman, *Origins of a Catastrophe,* p. 153.

31. Michael Libal, *Limits of Persuasion: Germany and the Yugoslav Crisis, 1991–92* (Westport, Conn.: Praeger, 1997), p. 4.

32. Zimmerman, *Origins of a Catastrophe,* p. 147.

33. Ibid., pp. 8–9.

34. Ibid., p. 147.
35. Libal, *Limits of Persuasion*, p. 14.
36. Zimmerman, *Origins of a Catastrophe*, p. 146.
37. Libal, *Limits of Persuasion*, p. 39.
38. Zimmerman, *Origins of a Catastrophe*, p. 176.
39. Woodward, *Balkan Tragedy*, p. 1.

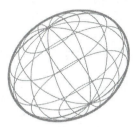

CHAPTER 11

CONCLUSION

....

HISTORICALLY SPEAKING

THE AFTERMATHS OF WORLD WAR I, WORLD WAR II, AND THE COLD WAR

As we look back upon the 20th century, it becomes apparent that much of what we know about our international environment today was shaped in the aftermath of the two world wars. Some of the world's most noteworthy international institutions were born from the lessons of the world wars and the interwar period. The failures of the first war settlement influenced policy makers to consider new directions in international relations after the second war. As we have seen, the rivalries and suspicions that caused World War I were never dispelled in the peace agreement at Versailles. In fact, a whole new set of resentments and grudges was created by the Versailles Treaty. Consequently, even though warfare ended (at least for the time being) in 1918, international economic and political conflict resumed immediately. Instead of viewing their world as a place of interdependence and mutual benefit, leaders in the 1920s and '30s saw the international environment as one to be exploited and jealously guarded. Imperial Japan and Nazi Germany both sought to create such formidable empires that in their respective spheres of influence their dominance over resources and trade, as well as their repression of dissenters, would never be challenged. While these dictatorships were by far the most ruthless in their pursuit of power and wealth, even other more liberal nations, such as the United States and Britain, sought to protect their economic interests at the expense of other nations and hoped to avoid war by allowing both Japan and Germany a degree of latitude in their respective expansionist policies.

However, unable and/or unwilling to prevent economic and political catastrophe in Germany, Nazi expansion in Europe, or Japanese aggression in Asia, and subsequently unable to avoid World War II, U.S. leaders began to plan early in their wartime struggle for a very different world from that which they had inherited. In particular, the United States sought a new world order that would be based more upon free-market competition and international diplomacy than upon military conquest and balance-of-power politics. Its plans for international monetary and trade regimes, as well as its hopes for a United Nations, promised to launch the developed countries into a new era of cooperative relations.

To a large extent the post–World War II American vision for the international economic and political system was realized. The International Monetary Fund and the General Agreement on Tariffs and Trade did facilitate multilateral cooperation in exchange-rate management and in the reduction of trade barriers. The countries that emerged from World War II entered into the most prosperous relationships in history, and although many disputes and changes in the regimes emerged by the early 1970s as more and more competitors entered the world market, it was clear that the global capitalist system was producing unprecedented wealth and incentives to cooperate, even if benefits remained unequally distributed. In particular, the industrialized countries, whose reconstruction from war the United States helped to achieve during the late 1940s and '50s, benefited from strong and relatively open trade relationships. Moreover, the security alliances created under U.S. leadership reinforced a generally cooperative approach to relations more generally defined. Even many of the developing countries, by the 1970s, '80s, and '90s were clearly reaping the benefits of the open trading system that visionary policy makers in the 1930s and '40s hoped would remove many of the motivations for nationalistic behavior and international conflict. Today, as we observe the character of global interdependence, including trade and investment, we are looking at a system of relationships whose beginnings are 50 years old and whose features and underlying principles remain fundamentally the same. The idea that if nations could trade freely, all would benefit, and, therefore, all would prefer peace and prosperity to war, is still the rationale for many international commercial arrangements. The World Trade Organization, the European Union, and numerous other contemporary regional trade associations exist to foster cooperation through stronger trade relations.

However, despite this success in creating far-reaching and influential regimes in economic affairs, the cold war rivalry that emerged following the end of the Second World War altered the role that the United States had originally intended in other areas. As a consequence of this, given the influence of the United States at the time, the shape that the postwar world took was much different from that which had been envisioned by the U.S. State Department in the late 1930s and early 1940s. Fear of Soviet power and the spread of Communist ideology preoccupied the United States to such an extent that U.S. leaders drastically revised policies that at the outset of World War II had seemed firmly set. Shifting its attention from the defeat of Germany and Japan to its concerns about how to contain Soviet influence, the United States moved away from several of its avowed wartime commitments. Self-determination for the subjects of imperialism, multilateral governance for settling international disputes, and the indefinite punishment of the former Axis powers for the peace of mind of the neighbors of Japan and Germany were all policies that generally fell by the wayside. For the United States, a new enemy loomed larger and more menacing than those which had just been defeated, and so a new set of policies and commitments was created.

The decision to reconstruct Germany was a major event in both European and international politics. For the Soviets it was the event that proved the hostile intentions of the United States and solidified the Soviet commitment to a divided Europe and to its own military machine. For Europe it marked the indefinite division of Germany, but with the historical twist that West Germany (with West Berlin) would thrive as a capitalist nation and key American military ally while East Germany would become the socialist client and armed camp for the Soviet Union. Interestingly, it also marked the beginnings of European integration in the West. The fact that the United States pressured its allies in Western Europe to accept German reconstruction motivated French leaders to take the initiative to shape the character of postwar economic cooperation in Europe rather than allow it to be shaped by the United States. The emergence of the European Coal and Steel Community in 1951, the first of the European Communities, marked the beginning of several deepening integration efforts that have led to the current European Union. A supranational organization whose member states have committed themselves to a single market, cooperative governance in commercial affairs, and cooperative diplomacy in foreign affairs, the European Union is testament to the fact that age-old rivalries can be eliminated through interdependence.

Still, one of the darker features of the World War II era and its consequences was the invention and use of nuclear weapons. Having demonstrated both the capability and the willingness to use atomic weaponry against Japan, U.S. policy makers paradoxically were both emboldened and frightened by the power they could wield—a power soon harnessed by the Soviet Union as well. While, on the one hand, nuclear weapons gave the United States a sense of authority and influence in world affairs, their existence in the hands of the Soviets created vulnerabilities that made U.S. leaders uncertain about their future use and yet committed to a seemingly never-ending and always escalating arms race with the Soviet Union. The existence of nuclear weapons heightened the fear felt in the United States about the Soviet threat and reinforced the prevalent view that the containment of communism—wherever it threatened to take control— was essential to the survival of the Western democratic world.

This view, which dominated U.S. policy making from 1947 until the United States ended its Vietnam intervention in 1975, caused American leaders to intervene militarily in a number of conflicts around the world. Covert operations aimed at assisting friendly (meaning capitalist and not necessarily democratic) governments against Marxist revolutionaries or assisting friendly opposition groups against Marxist governments became commonplace during the 1950s and '60s as the United States resisted the expansion of Communist influence, and the Soviet Union encouraged it. In addition, the United States involved itself in both small- and large-scale military operations in its effort to thwart what it perceived to be the rampant spread of Soviet power.

Nowhere was the U.S. preoccupation with—and accompanying belief system toward—the Soviet rivalry more evident, nor more tragically illustrated, than in Vietnam. Here, the United States took a 180 degree turn away from the policy it had intended toward Vietnam during World War II. Rather than embracing self-determination for the region as President Roosevelt had intended, the Truman, Eisenhower, Kennedy, and

Johnson administrations all placed the perceived struggle with Soviet surrogates in Vietnam, as well as allied relations with France, above self-government for Vietnam. Fearing Communist influence more than imperialism or dictatorship, U.S. policy makers sided first with the French and then with their own series of puppet regimes in a protracted and costly effort to defeat the Communists.

Only after 25 years of escalating involvement did the United States finally accept the fact that the defeat of the Communists in the region would require an indefinite and costly presence, which the American people and American allies would not support, and that the "fall" of Vietnam to communism would not constitute a fatal loss to U.S. security after all. On the contrary, many analysts realized that it was not the loss of Vietnam to Communist influence that hurt U.S. credibility and power so much as it was the fact that U.S. leaders could allow themselves to be sucked into such a quagmire at the expense of other priorities and at the expense of U.S. democratic ideas. In retrospect, the U.S. experience in Vietnam has been viewed as a great waste of human lives and effort, causing policy makers after 1975 to be very cautious about when and where to employ military force. Some have argued that the U.S. defeat in Vietnam was evidence of its lost position as hegemonic world leader since World War II, but perhaps a better interpretation is that the Vietnam intervention was a terrible mistake motivated by mistaken views about the situation at hand. Withdrawal was finally a recognition of the erroneous thinking that drove two and a half decades of policy in the region. It was also a "reality check" for U.S. policy makers about the limits of U.S. influence and about the unwillingness of the American public to indefinitely support protracted interventions.

In many respects the pattern of U.S. foreign policy that had dominated international affairs after World War II was altered after the Vietnam defeat. The United States became more cautious (and its public more critical) about getting involved in conflicts abroad. A concept known among analysts and the public as the "Vietnam Syndrome" soon seemed to guide (some would say plague) U.S. foreign-policy decisions. Skepticism about the ability of the United States to affect outcomes abroad through the use of military intervention, coupled with a profound unwillingness to put another generation of young men and women through a potentially futile struggle, affected the willingness of policy makers to embroil U.S. military forces in limited wars in foreign lands. Civil strife in particular raised public suspicions about the appropriateness—or at least the efficacy—of U.S. involvement. While U.S. military interventions were carried out after 1975, they have all been shadowed by lessons learned from the Vietnam fiasco. Thus, the reluctance to get involved in "another Vietnam" altered the character of U.S. competition with the Soviet Union. However, this certainly did not eliminate U.S.–Soviet Union conflict and competition.

Nowhere was this more evident than in the arms race, which sped on virtually unchecked through the early 1980s, despite a series of arms control agreements that had been aimed at at least managing the competition, if not truly limiting it. As the 1980s decade got under way, the fear of nuclear war between the United States and the Soviet Union was at new heights. New weapons systems, including the American proposal for a space-based defense system, were threatening to destabilize an already precarious and hostile relationship. Rhetoric on both sides was even more highly charged than it had been for some time, and many worried that a crisis might trigger overt military conflict. This renewed animosity and the military preparations that accompanied it were ominous reminders that the cold war, which had begun in the aftermath of World War II, was still raging after four and a half decades, still dictating U.S. foreign policy, and still shaping the character of the international system.

CURRENT FORCES IN INTERNATIONAL POLITICS: NEW DIRECTIONS AND CHALLENGES

Alongside this bipolar international security system was a more mixed international political economy. While the U.S.–Soviet rivalry was also part of a larger capitalist-communist rivalry, with each side cultivating economic allies and markets, the global economy could never be fully characterized as bipolar. A more apt description is that the world capitalist economy dominated global economic interactions, and although the Soviet bloc and other Communist-state economies (such as China's) were somewhat insulated from it, they still remained a part of it.

Thus, at the same time that international security politics were being dominated by the bipolar rivalry of the United States and the Soviet Union, the international political economy was largely dominated by U.S. leadership and capitalist-oriented interdependent relationships. As we have seen, the GATT system generally has governed trade in the post–World War II era, with the European Community providing regional trade governance in Western Europe. However, in recent decades other trade initiatives have also emerged, demonstrating the effort of some nations to better manage their specific regional trade relationships rather than rely solely on GATT procedures to do so. The Canada–U.S. Free Trade Agreement and its successor the North American Free Trade Agreement are such efforts. These initiatives marked a new direction in the international political economy, demonstrating that even though the GATT/WTO system remains functional at the end of the 20th century—and some would even argue robust—there is great potential for trade expansion and dispute settlement via more specific regional trade agreements.

At the same time, the 1980s and '90s also witnessed change in the position of the United States in the world economy. Still by far the single most economically powerful country in the world, the United States nonetheless had become a much more "normal" nation in comparison with its position after World War II. It discovered by the 1970s that its industries had to compete with the industries that were developing elsewhere, and by the end of the 1980s it was apparent that there was no such thing as guaranteed market shares either domestically or abroad.

Probably because of the historic relationship between the United States and Japan, as well as the energetic market prowess of Japanese producers, the rise of Japanese competition was particularly symbolic of the declining position of the United States in the global political economy. The trade conflicts that emerged between Japan and the United States, largely over U.S. fears of growing Japanese market share, but also over resentments about the failure of Japanese society to open its own market reciprocally, marked a new era in U.S.–Japan relations, and more importantly, a new era in U.S. commercial leadership. No longer capable of placing military security issues ahead of economic issues, U.S. policy makers engaged Japan in a series of negotiated arrangements to open the Japanese economy to U.S. goods and to preserve U.S. market share when possible. The ideals of GATT multilateral and nondiscriminatory governance over such issues were being sidestepped by U.S. unilateral and bilateral efforts to preserve its own position in a new era of fierce competition. The new role being played by the United States was also influenced, after 1990, by the fact that cold-war-era security arrangements no longer dictated economic relationships.

Prior to 1990 the bipolar competition for power had been taken for granted so much that it was nearly beyond imagination to consider a different international environment. However, during the 1980s the foreign policy initiatives taken by Mikhail Gorbachev to reduce the threat of nuclear war and the domestic reforms he introduced to liberalize the Soviet system suddenly changed everything. Within a few short and dramatic years, the superpower rivalry was gone, the vast military forces that had been amassed on both sides of the "iron curtain" had been removed, and a new world system was emerging. The reunification of Germany in 1990 became symbolic of the end of the cold war, and despite the difficulties it created for the German political economy, it ushered in a new era of relations with Central and Eastern Europe that meant the erasure of old East-West divisions. Immediately, the transition to market-oriented, democratic societies became the priority of former Soviet bloc nations. The attraction of the European Union and even the North Atlantic Treaty Organization, the defensive alliance created by the United States, Canada, and their Western European allies in 1949, quickly displaced Soviet economic and security structures in the region. During the final decade of the 20th century a very different world structure had emerged, as the nations formerly subjected to Soviet domination were finally allowed self-determination and access to the global market economy that had transformed so much of the world during the previous 45 years. A new era in security and economic relations had definitely begun.

As we have seen, however, in the midst of great expectations about this new era, the most deadly conflict to stain European soil since World War II erupted in Yugoslavia. This country, whose economic and political structures never overcame ethnic and regional divisions, ripped itself apart in the aftermath of the end of the cold war. Neither European nor American leaders were capable of preventing conflict, nor were they capable of preventing its escalation. The disintegration of Yugoslavia, and more importantly, the terrible warfare that ensued, demonstrated that even though cold war rivalries were over, sources for conflict among people still remain. Security, trust, economic welfare, and legitimacy of governance remain essential ingredients for peaceful coexistence. Moreover, the Yugoslavian situation has demonstrated that the major nations within the international community must decide if global commitments to humanitarian goals warrant significant military involvement in another country's affairs, and if so, what mechanisms should be created and/or utilized to achieve them.

SUMMARY

At the end of the 20th century it is clear that many institutions and patterns of interaction have been inherited from the post–World War II period, but it is equally clear that a number of changes have occurred that bring new challenges and possibilities for the 21st century. The global political economy is more multipolar than it was at the end of the war. The United States, although very significant, is not the only important and influential participant. The European Union, Japan, China, and others are also economic forces to be reckoned with, and regional trading arrangements are supplementing the GATT/WTO system of multilateral negotiation and trade. On the security front, the world may actually be more unipolar than anything else. The disappearance of the bipolar competition that characterized 45 years of 20th-century history has created a new world whose power and security structure is far less defined. While the Russians, French, British, and Chinese all have significant military capabilities, it is the United States that has both the force-projection capability (the ability to place forces around the globe in significant numbers) and the leadership experience to do so. Still, the fact that several nations possess nuclear weapons and that many have a significant regional military presence makes it difficult for the United States, despite its dominance, to fully influence outcomes elsewhere. Much can be learned from the "pivotal decisions" that we have studied, yet new circumstances also demand fresh ideas. The challenge for future decision makers (and for us as citizens) will be to discern when the lessons of the past are appropriate and when they are not.

THEORETICALLY SPEAKING

No conscious effort has been made to provide theoretical frameworks for the cases contained in this collection. Rather, it has been the intention of this author to provide narratives that allows the reader to apply theoretical and analytical concepts learned elsewhere. The purpose of international relations theory is to help us better understand the world environment through systematic explanations of cause and effect. Yet even the most ardent proponents of any given theory will admit that no single explanation fits all circumstances. The analytical challenge is to discern which causal factors play the most significant role in determining particular outcomes and then to decide how much these can be generalized to other, similar situations.

Moreover, it has been my intention to offer enough information in the historical reviews to allow the reader to apply different levels of analysis to the cases, and often the discussion questions focus attention on this. The purpose is to encourage students to think about the *sources* of influence in making key decisions. In reading these historical vignettes they should consider whether the international system seems most influential in affecting decisions, whether state-level structures and institutions play a role, or whether individual policy makers have a special place in determining why a nation implements one policy over another. Must we fully understand the interplay of all levels of analysis in a given case, or does it suffice for explanatory purposes to focus exclusively on one? If so, what generalizations can be drawn from one or more cases about the character of international political decisions? Can we generalize about some factors more than others?

Basically, it is my hope that students will not only gain a rudimentary understanding of the historical decisions highlighted in this book but that they will think creatively about how various theoretical and analytical approaches help us to better understand the way that these decisions get made. After all, it is the application of theory and analytical structure to historical information that improves and refines our understanding of the forces that move nations to take (or decline to take) action in international affairs.